FINANCIAL INDEPENDENCE
The Doctor's Guide

FINANCIAL INDEPENDENCE

The Doctor's Guide

Stuart Wesley Young, M.D.
and
Royal J. Bartrum, Jr., M.D.

Raven Press ■ New York

Raven Press, 1140 Avenue of the Americas, New York, New York 10036

Made in the United States of America

Library of Congress Cataloging in Publication Data

Young, Stuart W.
  Financial independence.

  Includes bibliographies and index.
  1. Physicians—Finance, Personal. I. Bartrum,
Royal J. II. Title.
R728.5.Y68   1984   332.024′616   83-43127
ISBN 0-89004-552-6

The material contained in this volume was submitted as previously unpublished material, except in the instances in which credit has been given to the source from which some of the illustrative material was derived.

Great care has been taken to maintain the accuracy of the information contained in the volume. However, Raven Press cannot be held responsible for errors or for any consequences arising from the use of the information contained herein.

To James W. and Dorothy J. Young
and to Jane

PREFACE

At first glance, the title of this book appears to be a contradiction. Aren't doctors by definition financially independent? Unfortunately, in many cases, no. Although most professional people—M.D.s, dentists, Ph.D.s—have a yearly income greater than that of the general population and enjoy an enviable position of having a good cash flow, a great many are *not* financially independent.

Financial independence involves far more than the ability to earn $50,000 or $100,000 in the upcoming calendar year. You are not financially independent until you have accumulated sufficient assets to guarantee an income that will provide financial security for yourself and your family in the future.

For example, when you retire, will you have enough money (buying power) to maintain the lifestyle you desire? Suppose you want to retire early, could you afford to do it? Suppose you became disabled next Tuesday, would there be the financial resources to provide for yourself and your family in the next year? Five years from now? At age 60? Approximately $250,000 is currently required to support a child through college. If you have school-age children, can you afford to give them the higher education you desire?

Suppose your income were to decline by 30%. This is a very real possibility in the not too distant future as the government comes to grips with escalating health care costs and prospective payment for health insurance becomes the standard. It is no secret that there is an oversupply of lawyers, Ph.D.s, and dentists, and the GMENAC study on medical manpower now suggests that there will be approximately a 130% excess of physicians by the end of the century.

The consequences of these demographic and economic changes are already being felt. Example: a company called Omnident advertised recently in a Washington suburb for a dentist to run a free-standing dental clinic in a shopping center. The salary was just over $20,000. This may not sound too bad but was, at the time, less that half the salary made by entry-level dentists a few years earlier in private practice. The real shock was that even though the salary offered was way below the expected market, there were over 30 applicants for the job. Example: a 300-bed hospital in Boulder, Colorado, in its first 5 months of the new prospective payment system for medical bills, experienced a drop of 1,000 routine chest X-rays, and general surgery suites that had been fully booked are now empty during many hours of the day. As a result, nearly all of the medical staff is expecting income cuts;

the hospital radiologists have taken a 15% salary cut; and the hospital posts a list of the medical staff who spend more than the money allotted on hospitalized patients. Such a list is no idle threat. A cardiac surgeon in Texas has been dropped from the medical staff of a large hospital for consistently spending over the fixed D.R.G. (disease-related group) allotment on hospital care.

For teachers, lawyers, Ph.D.s, and dentists, the current economic situation is already bad; for physicians, it may get worse. Have you heard of some lawyers and Ph.D.s driving taxis between jobs? Some dentists and M.D.s may soon have similar experiences. How would similar events in your practice alter your future financial security? True financial independence requires careful planning and the optimal use of today's income to insure tomorrow's needs.

Despite good incomes, most successful professionals have not made much progress on the road to financial independence. With little training in money management and investment, they tend either to do nothing or to delegate investment responsibilities to others (stockbrokers, accountants, bank trust officers, senior partners in the group, friends, etc.), often with disappointing results. After all, no one will care as much about your financial future and assets as you do. No one will do the job as well as you can.

The task of planning a personal investment program is not an easy job. There are thousands of ways to go wrong, and even the most prudent financial planning and investment decisions may not work out (as we know from personal experiences and the tales of countless colleagues). The job may not be easy, but it is doable. We have learned to successfully manage money, and so can you. It takes some study and considerable personal discipline, but you will be well rewarded for your efforts. If you are a physician or other professional and have established a successful practice, you can certainly travel the road to financial independence. This book will help you get started.

ACKNOWLEDGMENTS

We are indebted to our colleagues and clients who have supplied us over the years with much of the practical experience utilized in this book. We thank Barbara McNeil and Hanan Bell for a critical review of the book. We are also grateful to Margaret Mariscal, Terri Soule, and Marie Graham for assistance in manuscript preparation. Finally, we thank Holde Müller for her continued excellent support in data analysis and figure preparation.

CONTENTS

1

WHY WE FAIL

Everyone has an investment horror story. Doctors usually have more. Most of us do not have to look far from home to find some damage.

One of our fathers was a successful general practitioner in the Midwest with the standard prerequisites for the good life—a home that had been paid off early, a handsome yearly income, and two sons in medical school. However father's future financial planning amounted to owning vast amounts of whole-life life insurance (the investment that you have to die to win), which had been purchased, with the best of intentions and advice, from a long-time family friend of impeccable credentials—a member of the million dollar life insurance round table. Although the premiums were exorbitant, it seemed like a wise, safe investment. Unfortunately, following his untimely death, the whole-life insurance policies provided minimal income while tying up in annuities large amounts of capital that could have been much more productively used. The value of the insurance itself was, of course, decimated by the runaway inflation of the 1970s. A $170,000 life insurance estate, although not meager, fell far short of providing the financial security for the family that father had sought.

Of course, with family counsel, father was not completely conservative either. He was known to lend a sympathetic ear to an occasional smooth-talking salesman with high-risk "opportunities" such as Gyrocopter. The idea was that if the engine failed, the machine would float gently back to the ground. More than the engines failed; both the copter and the company sank like stones. A fling at wildcat oil wells was not a total disaster; one of the wells did find water. His bond portfolio yielded a whopping 4%, but at least it didn't contain any New York City or W.P.P.S. bonds. We have found this combination of extremes—conservative and wildly speculative investing—to be a characteristic of physician investors.

Without breaking the mold, our own initial efforts were scarcely better. Confronted with a modest amount of surplus funds and having no idea of what to do with them, we consulted a well-respected local stockbroker. With the utmost calm and confidence, he assured us that if we turned the money over to him, we could sit back and watch it grow and prosper. Our financial worries would be over because our money was now in the hands of an investment professional backed by millions of dollars worth of computers, investments research, and Wall Street knowledge. Our investment certainly did not remain static—within 18 months 40% of the money had been lost. ("Don't be upset, this is a wonderful tax loss," our broker advised. Somehow the value of this eluded us!) Unfortunately, such experience is all too common.

There are two married academic physicians in St. Paul, both in their 60s, who came to us having accumulated only their homes and a $50,000 pension fund annuity to provide for their retirement.

There is a doctor in San Francisco with a friend on the periphery of the Hunt family who had inside information on silver trading and was going to make—and nearly did—a fortune. The Hunts survived the terrible silver debacle, but then they started with several billion dollars.

There is a Ph.D. from Austin who, while on sabbatical in California, drove 200 miles to a condo sales promotion at which he had a chance to win an ocean cruise, a television set, or a calculator but ended up buying some land and a condominium in Lake Tahoe. As Will Rogers said, "After all, they aren't making any more land." (Will can be forgiven for a little overstatement since no one knew about plate tectonics back then.) But this Ph.D. should have leaned a little more on P. T. ("a sucker born every minute") Barnum than on Will Rogers for investment advice. Five years later, although his condominium was said to be worth 80% of what he paid for it, he could not sell it. It rents only 20 weeks of the year, and the monthly payments are a serious drain on his cash flow.

There is a dentist in Charlotte, North Carolina who thought time-sharing a condominium at Myrtle Beach (which could be exchanged for a week at any other condominium virtually anywhere) was a good idea. But one of his two weeks turned out to be during the hurricane season, and the company that sold him the time share will buy it back for only half of what he paid for it.

There is a savvy colleague in Boston who, while in the 70% income tax bracket, bought railroad cars. The cars were professionally managed, gave him tax write-offs, and generated good income to boot. At least they did at first. In the past 2 years, the cars have sat rusting on the sidings, the tax write-offs are diminishing, and he must write out a $1,100 check every month to cover his payments.

The list could go on and on. There is a joke we used to hear at Stanford Business School: "A doctor making a bad investment is redundant."

Investment disasters do not just happen to doctors. A March 4, 1982 article in the (San Francisco Bay area) Peninsula Times-Tribune reported that a well-respected investment advisor associated with a well-known investment firm had set up a $2 million limited partnership to invest in commodities and stock options. The partnership had lost nearly a million dollars for its investors, who included a Stanford University department chairman, two internationally known athletes, several physicians, and a Nobel laureate in economics!

Similarly, investment disasters do not happen just to individuals. We like to think that our pension funds are secure and competently managed by knowledgeable investment professionals. Many of us are wrong. There is a large, multispecialty group practice in New England that contributed over a million dollars a year to its pension program. From 1976 to 1982, the value of the funds in the pension program appreciated by only 6%, far below the prevailing inflation rate and less than was needed to fund the pension liabilities created.

We know a group of doctors in Chicago who discovered recently that $1.5 million from their pension fund had gone to Mexico with one of the fund's managers, a senior partner who had taken some unexpected leave!

As chronicled in the March 5, 1984 issue of *Barron's*, from an article titled "How Do You Spell Prudent?":

> The California State Teachers Retirement Fund is taught a costly lesson in investing. How a slick operator wormed his way into a key role on the fund's board and maneuvered a $50 million loan for a highly speculative oil venture run by an exconvict....

You could undoubtedly add some stories to this list (not too many, we hope, from personal experience). There is a common thread to all investment horror stories: The victims were all delegating too many important financial decisions to others. No one cares as much about your money and financial future as you do; no one can manage your money as attentively as you can. Of course, you must use advisors and outside information along the way, but to have a high likelihood of success, you must make the important decisions yourself. In this book we shall discuss the basic aspects of financial planning and investing so that you can develop a basis for making these decisions. Let's begin by looking at the three most common reasons for failure: no goal, no plan, and no discipline.

NO GOAL

One of the reasons that investors fail to achieve financial independence is that they never establish a financial goal. If you aim at nothing, your chances of hitting nothing are pretty good. This situation is particularly ironic for doctors; as a group they have been aiming at goals for most of their lives and are among the most motivated of individuals. When it comes to financial planning, however, they seem to get fuzzy. Their concept of a financial goal is often as vague as "making a million dollars" or "having a net worth of $300,000" or "earning $100,000 a year" or "retiring at 40." These are not very satisfactory goals because they are not specific. They basically express only a general desire to do well. When setting a financial independence goal, you must get down to hard numbers and specific requirements. It is important to have a well-defined estimate of what you want to obtain and when you wish to have it done because without a clear idea of where you are going, it is hard to know whether you are getting there.

For example, are you satisfied with your present lifestyle? If so, you might have as one part of your goal having enough financial resources to provide your current lifestyle when you retire. Perhaps you think you would be able to live on less at retirement than you do now. If so, then you would have a different financial goal. You will have to take different actions and make different sacrifices along the way to reach these differing goals, and if you do not plan appropriately today, it is quite likely that you will never arrive at the right target tomorrow.

Another very important consideration is to specify the time at which you desire to achieve your goal. Continuing our simple example, in addition to deciding the income you need to be financially independent, you must also decide at what age you wish to achieve this goal. Your financial strategy will have to be different if your target is age 60 than if you want to wait until age 65.

We have used retirement as a specific example of one type of goal, but actually a goal should be much more comprehensive. Adequate retirement income is only one portion of financial independence. Other areas include providing resources for family needs such as children's education, providing security for unforeseen changes in your earning ability, providing a lifestyle that satisfies both today and in the future (perhaps you will want a second vacation home in 10 years), and providing enough flexibility to permit work and lifestyle changes in the future. Suppose you become fed up with medicine at age 50 and decide to become an artist. Since most professional groups practice LIFO—last in first out—accounting, what if friction develops in your practice group and your partners fire you?

Everyone's goal will be different, and everyone's goal will change as life progresses. It is important to start somewhere, however. Even though you do not know for certain today what assets you will want to have 10 years from now, you should sit down and make your best guess. Goals can always be reviewed and modified as desires and situations change.

A goal should not be overly conservative but should represent what you hope to achieve at certain points in the future. You may not be completely successful, but you certainly won't get there if you do not try. On the other side of the coin, the goal must be realistic. You will be forced to take unnecessary risks and tend to make bad investment decisions if you strive for a pie in the sky. Regardless of the final form of your goal, the most important aspect is to start today. The longer you wait to establish a goal, the more difficult it will become to obtain it. We shall take a closer look at how to formulate a goal in Chapter 2.

NO PLAN

Establishing a financial independence goal is only the first step; you must also have a plan for achieving the goal. Some doctors do have a fairly specific goal such as being able to retire at age 62 with a certain yearly income, a paid-off retirement home in some warm location, and three children sent to graduate school. Yet they have not established a plan that will help them achieve these objectives in terms of the buying power they will require. They somehow assume that because they have a good yearly income, the money for tuition payments or the vacation home will just be there when they want it. They fail to take account of the effects of inflation (or deflation) on financial assets and have not appreciated how many dollars they must commit today to achieve a particular situation in the future.

A common problem is failure to appreciate what money must do over time to achieve the financial goal. If your disposable income is relatively low and your aspirations are high, you will have to assume considerably more risk in investing than someone with a higher disposable income and more modest goals. The older you are, or the shorter the period of time you have to achieve your goal, the more dollars you must commit and the more conservative your plan must be, since you will not have enough time to correct for investment errors.

It is important to identify how much you can realistically commit to your program; the more you commit now, the less risk you will need to assume to achieve your goal. Most individuals seriously underestimate the number of dollars they have available for investing. They have considerable idle money and unknown equity that could be mobilized into their overall investment plan. We shall discuss ways to maximize the dollars available for investment in later chapters, but it is important to realize that the more resources you have working for you, the more options you will have in your plan, and the more likely you are to achieve your goal on time. In this sense, investing is a little like chess. The more you have your pieces working together, the more synergistic will be their overall force. Sending an isolated queen into enemy territory often results in a forced retreat, but this move, when backed by a rook, a knight, and a well-placed phalanx of pawns, will result in a powerful position for you. Much of this book is devoted to synergistic strategies you can use in obtaining your financial goal.

NO DISCIPLINE

The third and most insidious reason why doctors fail to achieve financial independence is a lack of discipline. The carefully designed financial goal and well-thought-out financial plan are worthless if they are never implemented. Procrastination is probably the greatest single hazard in trying to establish financial independence.

It is not clear why lack of investment discipline is such a severe problem for doctors. It may relate to the fact that prior to their earning years, most doctors live lives of deferred gratification. They give up most of their free time and material comforts during a training period that can extend past age 30. Marriage and children are postponed and debts acquired. Finally, at age 35, the debts are paid off and the practice set up; the first investment is more likely to be a sports car than a mutual fund.

The generally high income of doctors also inhibits the development of financial discipline. They spend on impulse. They do not plan in advance how next year's or the next 5 years' income will be utilized. First it is an expensive vacation and new clothes, then a home, then children, a new office, cars for everybody, a $6,000 skiing vacation, and so on. Somehow, spending money on an investment the return from which will not be seen until some time in the future is foreign to many doctors. The only future problem most of them see is retirement, and, after all, retirement has negative connotations for everyone and is so far away that there will always be time to take care of it.

You can take a major step in improving your financial discipline if you stop thinking only in terms of retirement and start thinking in terms of financial independence. Financial independence is a goal that has many different facets and can be much more real.

Regardless of the cause, most individuals who do not develop the discipline to commit some of today's funds for financial independence in the future will end up with considerable disappointment. The investor who is always waiting for the "right time" to start an investment program will never get anywhere. The "right time" was yesterday. You will never have extra unallocated funds. Your expenditures will always rise to consume available dollars. If you do not pay for future financial independence now, you will never be able to afford it.

SOME INVESTMENT LIABILITIES OF DOCTORS

The three major causes of financial independence failure—no goal, no plan, and no discipline—are not unique to doctors but apply to many types of investors. However, there are some specific liabilities that are relatively unique to doctors. We have already talked about the long period of training and deferred gratification that contribute to a lack of investment discipline. Before finishing this chapter, we need to consider some of the other liabilities.

In working with doctors and their financial plans, we have discovered a very common investment profile. Doctors tend to be overly conservative investors. Their money is tied up in low-yielding, "safe" (a misnomer as we shall see) investment vehicles, such as bonds, certificates of deposit, and life insurance. Certainly there is an appropriate place for each of these in many financial plans, but doctors tend to overdo it.

A much smaller group takes the opposite tack, throwing handfuls of money after wild speculative gambles with little chance of success. These individuals make enormously risky investments with the idea of potentially enormous returns. They get their advice from old roommates, colleagues they meet at conventions, or high-pressure salesmen. The vast majority of these investments end in failure, but so what? There is always that good yearly income to fall back on. We can start over and try again. Some day we'll hit the jackpot.

The most common stance is to blend the above extremes, committing the bulk of funds to "safe" investments (the *primum non nocerum* philosophy) and using the remainder for speculation ("it's a long shot, but the only chance the patient has"). This schizoid investment attitude makes it very difficult to formulate a workable financial plan.

Doctors seem to get more than their share of poor investment advice. Much of this is an extension of the delegation of financial decisions to others ("it seems like straightforward congestive failure to me and I would probably just give some digitalis, but the consultant thinks she needs zinc, and who am I to question his judgment"). Another source of difficulty is the vast variety of potential investment vehicles, each promoted by an aggressive salesman. The salesman with the best pitch often wins the day, even if his product is not appropriate for the individual's financial plan.

Most doctors fail to appreciate the subtle difference between an advisor and a salesman. A true financial advisor has nothing to sell but advice. He can evaluate potential investments for use in a financial plan and even make specific recommendations. However, when he also sells an investment product, he ceases to be an advisor and changes into a salesman. A salesman is not necessarily dishonest or even a bad source of advice. The problem is that a salesman has an inherent conflict of interest; he wants to sell a product regardless of whether it is the most appropriate one for that individual's financial goal and plan.

Sometimes the distinction between a salesman and an advisor is difficult to perceive. We all know that the life insurance man is a salesman even though he may speak of ordinary or whole-life insurance as a wonderful investment vehicle. Similarly the high-pressure condo salesman who promises to double your money while providing you with a vacation paradise is easy to spot. It is not so obvious that your stockbroker is also a salesman. He has a wider variety of products but is a salesman nevertheless. He, and his firm, make money on commissions, and they are interested in convincing you to make a transaction. Most of the time they will not deliberately steer you toward a bad transaction, but their prime goal is completing the sale. Problems arise because what is a good investment for one person's financial plan may be poor for another. The company computer is not programmed for your individual investment plan. We do not mean to imply that your stockbroker is devious or evil; just remember that he is only one source of advice and that, in the end, he is a salesman.

The bank trust officer who pushes certificates of deposit and the federally insured IRA program is also a salesman. Your accountant who sees only your tax liability and stresses tax shelters is also a salesman of sorts, since he emphasizes the need for tax shelters without regard to the overall investment plan. Failure to distinguish between an advisor and a salesman can lead you into many poor investments.

Doctors are particularly susceptible to the lure of the "tax-advantaged investment" (a.k.a. tax shelter). There certainly is a role for a well-planned and executed tax shelter, but the most important attribute must be its value as an investment. Blinded by the lure of a tax advantage, the doctor frequently ends up with the ultimate tax shelter—a big loss. A man never went broke taking profits, but he certainly can go broke losing $1 to save 50¢ in taxes. Many doctors who have just emerged from a world of 70% income taxes and 12% inflation have not realized that the world is now a 50% income tax rate and an inflation rate somewhere south of 6%. Failure to make this adjustment has been and continues to be very costly.

Doctors have a terrible sense of investment timing. This is a problem common to most small investors but is particularly acute with doctors. Contrary to the established principle of successful investing, they tend to buy high and sell low. This is directly traceable to a lack of investment discipline and too much reliance on outsiders for advice. Lacking a satisfactory investment plan and the resolve to utilize it, they are unduly swayed by this morning's investment news and tips. They are often fighting the last war. When the Dow Jones average is down, they wait until it has risen 200 points, finally conclude that a bull market is on, and buy right at the top. As the market starts down, their mistake is driven home with a moral thrust ("see, you really don't know anything about investing and shouldn't be in this business"). They quickly try to rectify their mistake by selling out before their investments get any lower. As we shall see in later chapters, good investment timing is vital to any successful program. The successful investor learns to anticipate movements and commits his funds before the move has run its course or makes regular fixed investments regardless of market action. He does not wait for newspapers and *Wall Street Week* to certify that the bull market is on.

Doctors tend to lack investment flexibility. In the financial and economic world, all values cycle: stocks, bonds, real estate, interest rates, inflation, the economy, DeLoreans, and the weather (wheat futures). What is a good investment at one time may prove a terrible investment 2 years later. Single-family housing was a great investment in the early 1970s but a poor investment in 1980. Bonds were a poor buy between 1966 and 1979 but a great opportunity in 1981. The financially successful investor is flexible and adjusts his game plan according to the prevailing cycles and trends. It is possible to go north on a southbound train, but it is a lot easier if you and the train are going in the same direction.

Another problem confronting doctors is the potential for a decreased annual income in the future. Most doctors assume that their yearly income will continue to increase throughout their lifetime and thus insulate them from the consequences of failed financial planning. There are many reasons to believe that not only will incomes fail to increase, but they may actually decrease in the future. In the medical field, the major reason is the developing oversupply of MDs. The Graduate Medical Educational National Advisory Committee has estimated that in the year 2000 there will be an excess of 144,000 doctors, with 13,000 new graduates being turned out each year. Since the estimated need for doctors at that time is only 498,000, this represents a 30% oversupply. In some specialties there will be two doctors for every available job.

The government is beginning to take effective measures to combat rising health care costs. Recent Medicare and Medicaid regulations prospectively limiting payments per patient and setting limits on fee reimbursements do not augur well for continued expansion of physician incomes.

As we shall see in ensuing chapters, of all the variables that are important to establishing financial independence, time is the most important. The time factor has two components: you must provide a sufficient amount of time for your financial independence program to work out, and you must devote enough of your personal time to be informed about changing economic trends. In this regard, doctors have an additional liability in that their effective working years are somewhat shorter than those of the population at large.

Most are in their mid-30s by the time they begin practice and are at least 40 by the time they begin an investment career. This considerably decreases the time they have available to achieve their financial independence goals.

That's the bad news. But doctors also have some important things going for them. They are, are as a group, intelligent and have demonstrated their ability to learn and practice new techniques. They have a higher income and live a few years longer than the average.

Finally, they have this book. It will show how to formulate a goal and develop a financial plan that can succeed. All that is needed is some diligence in attacking the problem and the discipline to begin immediately.

2

DEFINING YOUR GOAL

One of the major problems with the financial structure of professional people is the lack of a clearly defined goal and objective. When asked to define their financial goal, they usually reply with generalities such as "I'd like to be a millionaire," "I'd like to retire at 40," "I'd like to be independently wealthy," and so on. All of us would like to control the cosmos. This is clearly not possible, but it is possible to realistically establish what you need to become financially independent. Then, if you achieve two, five, or 10 times your goal, so much the better. However, in starting to formulate a well-defined financial goal, you should begin with the minimum requirements.

There are hundreds of ways to be financially independent. Tramping, for example, is a very independent lifestyle based primarily on a minimum of needs. At the other extreme, if you could hold the solitary patent on the computer, that would provide a financially independent lifestyle based on having more assets than you could possibly spend. For most of us the answer lies somewhere in the middle. However, each individual will have a unique answer based on the circumstances in his life and his own desires. If you want to live in the fast lane, take that into account in your goal. If your investment metabolism is such that you can't sleep comfortably at night unless there are minimum risks, then you will have a different goal. The saying that one man's food is another man's poison is absolutely true in financial planning.

In beginning to define their goals, most people recognize two obligations. One is to provide for a comfortably adequate income to live on when they stop working (not necessarily synonymous with retirement at age 65). The other is to provide for family and loved ones in the event of an untimely death. These provisions should be included in almost anyone's goal for financial independence. However, your goal will probably go beyond these two basic needs. It may include money for the children's education and discretionary funds to spend on "lifestyle" (such as expensive vacations, a second home, a fur coat, a hot tub), philanthropy, or early "retirement."

An indispensable component of your goal must be a firm concept of time to target. In other words, at what point in the future do you hope to achieve financial independence? Most of us would answer "yesterday," but a touch of realism must also be factored in. If you wish to achieve your financial independence goal in 10 years, you will have to utilize a different plan than if you have 20 years in which to work. In general, the less time you allow, the more risk you must assume.

Clearly, you cannot sit down for an hour and structure the rest of your life. Defining a goal is an ongoing process. There is an informal division of courses at Stanford Business School into two groups: hard courses (number oriented) and soft courses (people or "concept" oriented). Unfortunately, defining your goal means a short brush with the "hard courses," so let's begin with simple basics, and then you can make adjustments to tailor the goal to your personal situation.

THE BASIC GOAL

The place to start is with your current income. Is it enough? Do you believe that the income you will need in the future is the same as, less than, or more than your current income? Are you happy with your present lifestyle? If so, how does your current income provide for this lifestyle? Would you be happy in the future if you could stay exactly where you are today in financial terms? If so, the basis of your goal is relatively simple: you simply have to provide your present income (in inflation-adjusted dollars) at the time you wish to be financially independent. If you feel you will need more or less income in the future, you can adjust the figures accordingly. Now that we have a starting point for a financial goal, we need to calculate the types of resources that are necessary to meet the goal. In order to go through this process, we shall work on a simple financial goal for a hypothetical physician. Let's call him Sam B.

Sam is 45 years old and is earning $50,000 per year from his medical practice. Sarah, his wife, is 42 and was formerly a nurse but is now a housewife. They have two children aged 6 and 8. Sam has no long-term indebtedness other than his home mortgage, and the family has decided that they are happy with their present lifestyle and current family income. Sam and Sarah have made the first decision in their financial goal—that they would like to insure their present yearly income.

Next, they must decide when they would like to reach this goal, that is, at what time can Sam stop working and be certain that the family can still maintain their $50,000 per year income. Sam decides that he does not want to have to work forever and that he would like to retire in 20 years when he is 65. ("After all, I want to have time to enjoy myself before I'm too old.") Sam and Sarah have now made a second key decision—that they want to reach their financial independence goal in 20 years. In other words, they now know that within the next 20 years they must accumulate enough financial assets to provide $50,000 per year independent of their need to work. How much money will it take to do that? How much capital will Sam and Sarah have to accumulate in the next 20 years to provide a yield of $50,000 per year?

We shall have to make some assumptions from now on. There are many different ways to accumulate capital and many different ways to deploy it to provide a steady stream of income. Let's assume that Sam and Sarah have a very nervous investment metabolism and want safety and security above all. There is nothing safer than U.S. Treasury bills, so we will assume that 20 years from now they will put all of their resources into treasury bills. Let's also assume that at that time an average treasury bill yield will be 8%. We now have an equation:

$$P \times 8\% = \$50,000 \tag{2.1}$$

where P is the amount of capital required at a yield of 8% to provide $50,000. Solving this equation for P yields $625,000. If Sam and Sarah can accumulate $625,000 in the next 20 years and invest it in treasury bills with an average yield of 8%, they will reach their goal of $50,000 income per year.

But $625,000 is a lot of money! To reach that figure in 20 years, they would have to save $31,250 per year. That's going to be difficult considering that the family income is only $50,000 per year. There is also another problem Sam and Sarah must consider—the effects of inflation. Remember that they have decided that they would like to maintain their lifestyle, which means they want to have an income of $50,000 a year in today's dollars. In other words, they need buying power, not nominal dollars. Since it's likely there will be some inflation in the intervening time, they need to adjust their estimates to take this into account.

It is difficult to know exactly what the inflation rate will be over the next 20 years. Since 1930, the average annual inflation rate has been between 3 and 4%, but all of us are aware of recent times when it has been much, much higher. However, the fiscally conservative political trends in this country suggest that double-digit inflation may be, at least for a while, a thing of the past. A realistic estimate of the average inflation rate over the next 20 years might be on the order of 7%. (You will have to make your own inflation estimate based on your perception of the way the country's economy is going; be conservative, overestimate.) Appendix A, *Future Value of $1.00 Factor*, illustrates the effect of various inflation rates over a given period of years. From the table, the factor for a 7% inflation rate for 20 years is 3.87; that is, we must multiply $50,000 in today's money by 3.87 to determine the number of dollars needed in 20 years to have the same purchasing power. Using these new figures, Sam and Sarah recompute the amount of principal they will need for their goal. First, they multiply $50,000 by 3.87 (the inflation factor) and arrive at $193,500 as the yearly income they will need. Plugging this figure into equation 2.1

$$P \times 8\% = \$193,500$$

they arrive at the answer: P is $2,418,750. The amount of money they need is enormous!

If you have never gone through an exercise like this before, you are probably as shocked as Sam and Sarah were. We hope that this will focus your attention on the need for financial planning and bring home the realization that to have a financially independent future, you must start work today. The situation is not hopeless. So far, Sam and Sarah have been working with very simple assumptions and have disregarded some factors that will make their job much easier.

FINE TUNING THE GOAL

The initial formulation of the goal that Sam and Sarah designed is clearly not attainable. Even if they saved all their $50,000 income for 20 years, they could only contribute $1 million and would only have $1 million plus some interest, not $2.4 million. They now need to think more closely about their needs and take into account other resources and ways of generating an income stream.

First, they have probably overestimated their income needs. It will probably not take as much money to maintain their current lifestyle 20 years from now as it does today. Their housing cost should decrease since they will have paid off their mortgage and perhaps moved into smaller quarters; the children will be grown and will no longer need to be provided for; and it is not likely that they will consume on the same level as they did when they were younger.

There is also the possibility of other sources of income besides a big hunk of money invested in treasury bills. Sam and Sarah may have inherited equity from parents; there will likely be social security income; there may be other retirement benefits for which they qualify. Obviously, it is impossible to make accurate calculations of a financial position 20 years in the future, but it is still important to make the best estimation possible. Using this estimation, Sam and Sarah will be able to adjust their financial plan in the intervening years to reflect any important changes.

How about social security? We believe that Sam and Sarah should be very conservative in estimating social security benefits. Everyone is familiar with the financial difficulties that plague the social security system and threaten to make it totally inoperative in 20 years' time. Changes will be instituted, and it is unlikely that the government will allow the system to fail totally. Nevertheless, it is an unalterable fact that in 20 years' time the financial demands on the system will probably surpass the ability of the working population to support it at today's levels. There will probably be some type of basic social security protection, but it is unlikely that it will provide any money to maintain more than the basic life essentials. It is also likely that individuals with independent sources of retirement income will be discriminated against in the system. Again, each individual will have to make his own decision on where the system is going in the future. For the purposes of our example, let's conservatively assume that the benefits will remain the same as they are in 1982 but that there will have been no cost of living adjustment in the intervening years. This means that Sam and Sarah would receive $7,500 per year in social security benefits.

Sam and Sarah won't need their nest egg forever. In addition to the interest they will be receiving from their treasury bills, they could sell some of the treasury bills every year to help provide income. Sam and Sarah are now really getting into "hard courses," since this problem requires consideration of an annuity. Estimating the amount of money needed to be financially independent utilizing retirement of principal as well as accumulated earnings is a problem of annuity.

Annuities have gotten a bad name during the inflationary days of the 1970s and 1980s, but as a technique in solving our current problem they can be very useful, and there is nothing intrinsically bad (or good) about them. We are all more familiar with annuities than we might have realized. The payment of a fixed-rate mortgage is an example of an annuity. You agree to make monthly payments for a fixed period of time, and at the end of that time the loan is retired and you owe nothing. An annuity is the payment (or receipt) of a series of periodic payments, each equal in amount and paid at regular time intervals. We shall encounter the use of an annuity payment into an investment fund a little later; for the moment, we are interested in the present value of an annuity or, in other words, the amount of money we shall need to last a certain number of years if a fixed dollar amount is withdrawn at regular intervals.

The formula for calculating the time-related value of annuities is derived as follows: the number of dollars or present value of an annuity (PV_a) needed to provide financial independence is obtained by knowing the amount of regular withdrawal (P_{out}) and the withdrawal annuity factor (A_m) associated with various rates of return and time intervals:

$$PV_a = P_{out} \times A_m \tag{2.2}$$

Appendix B gives a more detailed explanation of this formula and its use. For now let's return to Sam and Sarah and their problem of how long a sum of money will last.

They get out the pocket calculator. In their first estimation, they anticipated needing $193,500 per year. They decide to reduce this amount by 25% in anticipation of decreased expenses at that time (the grown children, etc.). In addition, they subtract $7,500 for anticipated social security benefits and $2,000 for the estimated retirement benefits that Sarah earned during her working years. They find that these adjustments have decreased their yearly income requirement to $135,625. They also decide to retire their principal over 30 years and assume an effective annual yield of 8%.

Solving the annuity equation using the annuity factor 11.26 for 30 years and 8% (from Appendix B)

$$PV_a = \$135,625 \times 11.26$$

they arrive at $1,527,138 as their latest estimate of capital they will require.

Sam and Sarah are beginning to feel a little better, and some color is returning to their faces. This project may not be impossible after all! Still, $1.5 million is a lot of money to raise in 20 years' time. Is it possible to do this on a $50,000 a year income? We believe that the answer is yes. They can realistically expect to earn between 8 and 10% per year on their investments with only a moderate degree of risk (and they should be able to earn 20% assuming greater risk). With a 15% annual return and the principle of compounding return over time, Sam and Sarah should be able to reach their goal.

Appendix C gives a table for calculating the total value of an investment of $100 per month compounded at different rates for differing periods of time. Sam and Sarah feel that they should be able to earn a return of 15% on their investments over the 20 years. Using the table in Appendix C, they find that for every $100 per month they invest at a compound rate of 15%

a year, they will have $122,932 at the end of the 20-year period. They then divide the $1,527,138 of total assets they will need by $122,932 and get 12.42. This is the multiple of $100 per month they will have to invest to reach their goal. $1,242 a month is not a small amount, but it is possible with an income of $50,000 per year.

Sam and Sarah have probably been overly conservative in their estimates. They have, for example, assumed the most conservative investment vehicle for generating income during retirement. Chances are they will have discovered that they can earn 15% on their money during their working years and will, therefore, be inclined to put at least some of their retirement capital into higher-yielding investments than 8% treasury bills. Doing so would reduce either the total amount of capital needed or the total time required to reach the goal.

They have also made no allowance for an increase in disposable income in the intervening years. In the past, doctors have been able to increase their incomes at a rate in excess of general inflation. However, as we have already seen, this may not be possible in the future. Nevertheless, Sarah may be able to return to work when the children are grown, there may be potential inheritances, and so on.

Sam and Sarah have not taken into account equity they currently own. For example, they may already have some savings, which can be profitably reinvested to help them reach their goal. They probably have several other sources of idle money and equity such as cash value in whole-life insurance, unnecessary tax payments, and prepaid obligations. (We shall discuss the problem of idle money further in later chapters.)

Finally, as we shall see in later chapters, it is quite likely in this current economic climate that they can have an investment return in the neighborhood of 17 to 20% rather than the 15% figure they have been using.

YOUR PERSONAL FINANCIAL GOAL

Sam and Sarah are hypothetical. We have introduced you to them to illustrate the basic processes involved in defining a personal financial goal. Sam and Sarah's goal is not complete at this point. They have not considered items such as children's education or major lifestyle changes, and they have not yet worked on their plan. It might turn out that some of the investments they would have to make to achieve a 15% return would be too risky for them to accept; in this case, they might want to modify their goal so that the financial demands are less stringent. We can see that defining a financial goal is a highly personal process. No one but you and your family members can define your personal goal and objectives. We have illustrated the thought processes you need to go through, and now it is time for you, your spouse, and family to work out the details of a goal for your family. It is important for all family members to actively support this project. Even one person left out of this process will limit the success of the financial independence plan.

You must not only define what you want and at what time in the future you want it, but you must also ask difficult questions of yourselves. How skillful are you in managing investments? Realistically, how much money can you afford to divert to your investments? Are you actually willing to commit that much, or does it just seem like a good idea? How risk averse are you? Your feeling about financial risk may be different from that of your spouse or your children. The answers to these types of questions may not be totally clear in your mind at this time, but they will come into sharper focus as you read and assimilate the chapters that follow. Above all, do not make the mistake that so many doctors do and merely coast and remain unfocused, living from day to day with no financial plan or objectives. You may not feel that you need to accumulate $1.5 million, but regardless of how modest your goal, it will be far easier to attain if you start immediately.

Do not let your strategy be totally directed by those who sell financial products and services. Remember that they are only one source of investment information and that they have a strong vested interest in selling you a certain product; although that product may be a good general investment, it may be inappropriate to your goal and financial plan. Straddling pork bellies may be an ideal investment for your neighbor, the airline pilot, but living with such uncertainty in your financial future might take years from your own life expectancy (and be hazardous to your wealth). Unless you have clearly thought about your personal financial goal and plan, you will be unable to evaluate the financial advice you receive from experts.

3

THE FINANCIAL
INDEPENDENCE FORMULA

> Nothing in the world can take the place of persist-
> ence. Talent will not; nothing is more common than
> unsuccessful men with talent. Genius will not; unre-
> warded genius is almost a proverb. Education will
> not; the world is full of educated derelicts. Persistence
> and determination alone are omnipotent. The slogan
> "Press On" has solved and always will solve the
> problems of the human race—*Calvin Coolidge*

Once you have set up your personal financial goal, you must then design a plan to get yourself to the goal on time. The rest of this book will deal with strategies that can be used in financial plans. Some will be appropriate for you, and others will not. However, it is important that you have a thorough understanding of all of the available options so that you can select the most appropriate tools for your task. The basis of any successful financial plan is the financial independence formula:

Time × (Money + Judicious investments) = Financial independence

Financial independence is a combination of three factors. The first is money. You must have money to invest; there are no magic genies or John Beresford Tiptons around. You can't raise a crop without planting the seeds. It is unlikely that you will achieve financial independence by pur-chasing a $1 state lottery ticket or hitting the million-to-one shot at Las

Vegas. You must be willing to commit a fair portion of your income to the cause of financial independence. As we shall see, it is quite likely that you can make your money grow by a compound 15 to 20% a year. Even at this rate, however, if you only invest $1,000 a year, you will not have much to show for it in the long run.

The need for a judicious investment seems obvious. After all, who could speak for an injudicious investment? Nevertheless, injudicious investments abound, and you should know that a disproportionate number of them are owned by doctors. For example, unless your financial position is so desperate that you must take excessive risks, there is no reason to invest in any type of commodities. Tax shelters are fine as long as they are also a good investment, but there is nothing good about a tax shelter that achieves its results by losing money. Perhaps the least appreciated injudicious investment is the low-yielding, "safe," federally insured account. If you have your money sitting in a 5¼% passbook savings account and the inflation rate is 6%, that is an injudicious investment! If you are making large annual payments on a whole-life insurance policy that is yielding 3%, that is an injudicious investment! If you bought a condominium 8 years ago, you're probably all right. If you bought it in 1979, you're in trouble. If you buy a triple-A–rated bond when interest rates are low, you will find the value of the bond drastically reduced as interest rates rise—another injudicious investment. (Of course, when interest rates are high, the reverse situation holds, and bonds can be a very judicious investment.)

Judicious investments are closely related to the inflation rate. Because the 1970s and early 1980s were periods of accelerating inflation, many people believe that continuing inflation is inevitable. This is probably not so. In the past there have been periods of high inflation that have been followed by price stability and deflation, such as occurred in Germany during and after World War I and in the United States in the 1920s and 1930s boom and bust (the Depression). There is reason to expect that this type of pattern will occur in the United States again. More often than not, the difference between judicious and injudicious is simply a matter of timing and being on the right side of the next change in the inflation rate.

The final component of the equation is time. This is probably the least appreciated factor of all and, in many ways, is the most important, since it has a multiplier effect on the other two. You can always make up for past errors in committing money to a program and in picking a poor investment, but there is no way to make up for a month's lost time. In fact, time is such an important component of the equation that we shall consider it first in discussing the strategies for a successful financial plan.

4

TIME AND RISK

Time is the most important and least appreciated factor in the financial independence equation, and it is the keystone of any financial plan. Money takes time to grow, and there is very little any of us can do to hurry it along. A year, a month, or even a day that is wasted can never be regained. If you have $100 in a money market fund that yields 10%, it will earn 3¢ a day in interest. On the other hand, if you carry that same $100 around in your billfold, you have nothing at the end of the day; regardless of what you do with the money tomorrow, the 3¢ it could have earned today is lost forever. Now 3¢ a day here and there doesn't sound like much, but over the course of several days, a year, or 5 years, these wasted resources can be very significant. This is particularly true because of the compounding principle.

THE COMPOUNDING PRINCIPLE

The legendary investor Bernard Baruch has described compound interest as "the eighth wonder of the world." It may well be. Although the basic concept of compounding is easily understood, most people do not truly grasp the significant multiplier effect it has on yields. Compounding means that not only are you able to earn interest on the principal, but you also earn interest on the interest. The next day you earn interest on the principal plus the first day's interest and the second day's interest. On the third day, in addition to all of these, you earn interest on the interest that was earned on the second day on the first day's interest! It's easy to see how compounding can be beneficial for your wealth and why it is such a potent force in making investments successful.

INVESTMENT RISKS

Although we all have a general idea of what constitutes risk, risk is an *a priori* phenomenon introduced by elements of uncertainty. There is a risk involved in driving a car, in smoking cigarettes, and in a sedentary lifestyle. As an example, look at the performance of three investments charted in Figure 4.1 and in your own judgment determine which of the three is the riskiest. Do you think it is the bottom graph? As a matter of fact, the risk is about the same for the three investments. An investment's risk is simply the probability that its return will be different from what is expected.

As an example, a U.S. Treasury bill is a very low-risk investment. The bill promises to pay $10,000 in 90 days, and an investor can be virtually certain that he will get his $10,000 at the end of that time. On the other hand, an investor who places $1,000 with the Lebanese Development Corp., which is planning to build a luxury hotel and golf course in West Beirut, is unlikely to see a penny of his promised $10,000 return. This is a high-risk investment. There are several different factors that can alter the risk of an investment.

It is important for all investors to have some idea of the amount of risk they are willing to assume. One way of assessing risk is to establish the investor's utility function. Essentially, the utility function is established by determining the potential benefit needed to induce any given individual or population to assume a certain risk. For example, in flipping a silver dollar, Sam B. knows that the probability of the coin coming up heads or tails is 50–50. We begin establishing Sam's utility function by offering to pay him 50¢ if he calls the coin correctly but taking the coin if he calls it incorrectly. If Sam accepts this offer, he would be considered to be risk seeking. In other words, for Sam, the chance to gain 50¢ is more attractive than the chance of losing the entire dollar. If we next offer Sam an even bet (in other words, if he calls the coin correctly, he wins a dollar but loses the coin if he is incorrect) and if Sam accepts this set of uncertainties, he would be considered to be risk neutral. In other words, he perceives the chance of gaining one additional dollar sufficient inducement to accept the risk of losing the dollar. If, however, we must offer Sam $2 in order to induce him to risk the loss of the silver dollar, Sam would be considered risk averse. In other words, it is necessary to offer him 100% more in potential gains than he would risk by entering into this type of uncertainty.

It is important to recognize that the circumstances which make an individual risk seeking at one time and risk avoiding at another can change

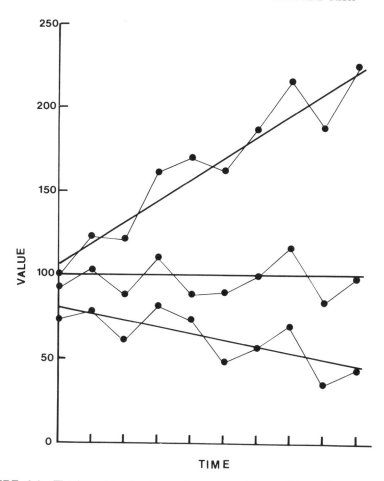

FIGURE 4.1 The investment price performance of three different investment vehicles is graphed over time with their individual values and mean values depicted. In assessing the risk involved with each of these individual investments, there is a tendency to believe that the lower graph represents the most risky investment because it is losing value. In financial analysis, however, risk simply is an estimate of the uncertainty or probability that a return on a given investment will be different—not specifically higher or lower, just different—than the investor expects. Technically, this is calculated as the standard deviation around the mean value of the investment, and in the above example the uncertainty involved is approximately the same for all three. That is not to say that they are equally good investments; it is obvious that the top graph significantly outperforms the other two.

quite dramatically depending on the circumstances of the individual and probabilities of gain and loss.

The method of evaluating the overall outcome of any given decision made up of probabilities and outcomes is established by calculating the expected value of the decision. For any given situation with a probability

(P) and outcome (outcome 1) and also a second outcome (outcome 2) with an associated probability $(1 - P)$, the expected value (EV) is calculated as follows:

$$EV = P \text{ (outcome 1)} + (1 - P) \text{ (outcome 2)}$$

Investors must be aware of not only their own abilities to seek or avoid risk but also the methods of evaluating uncertainty in an investment. For example, Sam is trying to decide whether or not to invest $100 in one of three investment alternatives: treasury bills, investment X, or leveraged investment X. His first step is to determine the expected value of each of the investment alternatives outcomes and associated probabilities as follows:

Investments	Probability	Possible outcome ($)
T Bills	P	105
	$1 - P$	103
Investment X	P	200
	$1 - P$	0
Leveraged	P	2×10^6
investment X	$1 - P$	-2×10^4

This is a standard investment dilemma in which the treasury bills have a very high certainty of returning an expected amount. The investment X might be comparable to an investment in a growth stock with a high potential return, but also some potential of a total loss. Finally, the third example might be illustrated by buying a stock on margin in which the expected returns are much higher, but there is also a potential of losing more than the amount of money actually placed at risk in the investment due to the borrowed funds. The expected values of these three investments are as follows:

$$
\begin{aligned}
\text{T Bills (EV)} &= P(105) + (1 - P)(103) \\
\text{Investment X (EV)} &= P(200) + (1 - P)(0) \\
\text{Leveraged investment X (EV)} &= P(2 \times 10^6) \\
&\quad + (1 - P)(-2 \times 10^4)
\end{aligned}
$$

Of course, the exact expected value depends greatly on the assumptions made about the probabilities of the outcomes and these are often unknowable.

To illustrate this technique, suppose Sam B is evaluating the investment in treasury bills and assesses the chances that he will be able to hold the treasury bill to maturation and receive $105.00 for his $100.00 investment at 99 in 100. (He thereby assumes that there is one chance in one hundred that he will have to sell the treasury bill before its maturation and thus receive the lower amount of $103.00.) Sam calculates the expected value as follows:

$$EV = 0.99 \times \$105 + 0.01 \times \$103$$
$$EV = \$104.98$$

Establishing the expected value of all the alternative investment vehicles is an effective way of determining their relative investment merits. Many investment outcomes, of course, are not binary, as in the case of the treasury bill illustrated in this example, but rather are most accurately depicted by a family of outcomes with their associated probabilities. Establishing the expected value under these conditions can be somewhat complex and you may need some expert assistance.

However, it is important in analyzing alternative investment decisions to rank them by your best estimate of their relative expected values. Two important implications of this type of analysis in an overall program of financial independence deserve some additional emphasis. First and most important is illustrated by the Wall Street aphorism, "If at first you succeed, stop and don't take any more chances." Once you have enough nominal dollars to attain financial independence, by all means decrease your uncertainty and risk as much as possible and use very risk-averse investments, such as treasury bills. Second, you can actually set limits on the worst case. In other words, you can assure that your investment program will not be in debt at the time when you are supposed to be financially independent by never making leveraged investments in your financial independence program.

All of the uncertainty associated with investing is not included in this type of analysis however. It may, for example, be unacceptable for you to have a certain 6% rate of return over a 20-year period if the inflation over that period is averaging 12%. In other words, although there is a certain return in nominal dollars, the program has actually lost buying power over the time interval. In the following sections we shall deal with some forms of investment risk; although we shall continue to refer to these as risk factors, it is perhaps better to think of them as investment "uncertainties."

INFLATION

Everyone is familiar with the effects of runaway inflation. We have already seen how you must take inflation into account in formulating a financial goal and plan. It is important to realize that inflation can increase or decrease the performance of some types of investments. In times of increasing inflation, the value of "hard" assets (that is, real things such as real estate, gold, physical property) will increase dramatically. Anyone who bought a home in the early 1970s was the beneficiary of a rapid inflationary increase in home values during the latter half of the decade. On the other hand, in times of deflation or a stable economy, hard assets may not perform well. Anyone who bought a house in 1980 and tried to sell it during the following 3 years will attest to this fact.

In analyzing the risk of an investment, the sensitivity of that investment to changing rates of inflation must always be considered. Inflation also has a strong effect on interest rates, and this gives rise to another type of risk.

INTEREST RATES

Interest rates have a major bearing on the value of certain types of assets. Short-term interest rates tend to respond to the supply of and demand for money, whereas long-term interest rates tend to be governed by the prevailing inflation rate. A change in interest rates can have a dramatic effect on the value of investments that are designed primarily to yield income. The prototype of such an investment would be a bond.

Most people tend to think of bonds as a conservative, "safe," risk-free investment that is immune to the forces that cause change in the value of investment vehicles. Nothing is further from the truth. In times of changing interest rates, bonds can be a very risky investment. Suppose in 1964 you had purchased a bond yielding 8% for $1,000. This bond will pay you $80.00 per year throughout its life. However, in the 1970s, in response to a high inflation rate, the long-term interest rate on bonds being brought to market was approximately 16%; any bond that yielded less than this could not be sold to the public. Therefore, in order for your bond to yield 16% interest, the price of your bond would have fallen to one-half of its original value or only $500.00. In other words, if you were to sell your bond in the 1970s, you would only receive $500.00 for it despite the fact that you had paid $1,000. Of course, you could always hold the bond until it matured in 1999. But in doing so, you would have $1,000 tied up in a relatively low-yielding investment.

The situation can work in reverse, of course. Suppose you sold your bond in the 1970s for $500. The person who bought the bond would be receiving $80.00 a year in interest for a 16% yield. And, when interest rates declined, the market value of the bond would increase as well. We can see that when interest rates are high, long-term bonds can represent an excellent investment. However, when interest rates are low, there is considerable risk involved in purchasing a long-term bond.

Changing interest rates often have a strong impact on the value of real estate investments. In times of increasing interest rates (almost always accompanied by inflation), real estate values appreciate rapidly; when interest rates begin to decline, the value of real estate may fall. The reason for this relationship at first may be somewhat obscure, but the explanation is similar to the reason why long-term bonds rise and fall with interest rates. Prior to 1980 most housing was financed with conventional, fixed-rate 30-year mortgages. Fixed-rate mortgages perform just like bonds during the times of rapidly increasing inflation. In other words, if you had purchased a home with a conventional mortgage at 7%, and, subsequently, interest rates and mortgage rates rose to 14%, the low interest mortgage would become an asset of the property. This would enable the owner/seller to negotiate a higher price for the property since a buyer's alternative would be to finance the same amount of money at 14% instead of 7%.

The shorter the term of an investment, the less susceptible it is to interest rate risk. There are two reasons for this: first, interest rates do not tend to change rapidly over short periods of time, and second, if the value of an asset were to decline because of an adverse interest rate move, the asset could be held to maturity without losing too much of the time value of the investment.

BUSINESS RISK

Business risk results from the changes in production and sales activity within a firm or industry. These fluctuations may be caused by strikes, foreign competition, shortages in raw materials or skilled personnel, or changes in the general economic level of the country. In traditional (fundamental) stock analysis, business activity is measured by the net earnings of a company and when these begin to have a negative trend the dividend on the company's stock as well as the stock value may decrease.

MARKET RISK

The price of any investment vehicle is determined by supply and demand. Supply and demand are affected by investor preferences, and changes in these preferences can drastically alter an asset's price giving rise to market risk. Investor preferences are often influenced by crowd psychology and the news media; this can result in an over- or undervaluation of investments for considerable periods of time.

A good example of this occurred with the commemorative medallions and statues sold by the Franklin Mint. These medallions, made of gold and silver, were issued throughout the time of increasing inflation, devaluation of the dollar, and rising gold prices. The value of the Franklin Mint stock as well as the resale value of many of these commemoratives did very well during this period. However, when the price of gold began to decline, the value of the medallions collapsed. A medallion that had sold for more than its intrinsic gold value suddenly could not command even the price of the gold it contained. Many of the medallions could not be sold at any price whatsoever. The effect of this rapid decline carried over to the stock in the Franklin Mint as well and resulted in a rapid decline in its value despite there being very little change in the Mint's actual business.

POLITICAL ECONOMIC RISK

A business or any other investment can be adversely affected by a sudden change in the economy or politics of a country. We are all aware of the increased number of bankruptcies in the early 1980s that were brought on by a general economic recession rather than a specific inadequacy of the company. A change in political fortunes can wipe out an investment overnight. In the late 1970s, Mexico was a land of promise; massive oil reserves had been discovered, new economic progress seemed imminent, and investors flocked to the Mexican Stock Exchange. This country's largest brokerage firm set up a mutual fund to trade exclusively in Mexican securities. Less than a year after the creation of this fund, the situation had reversed. The price of oil had collapsed, and the value of the peso was trading at a fraction of its earlier value. The country was insolvent, and an investment in the Mexico Fund had lost 75%.

LIQUIDITY

Liquidity is not a measure of the success of last year's Christmas party but rather relates to how quickly a given investment can be converted into cash. In general, the greater the liquidity of an investment, the less the risk. United States Treasury bills and bonds, corporate bonds, and stocks that are traded on major United States exchanges have a high degree of liquidity and proportionately less risk than illiquid investments in real estate, oil and gas drilling programs, or limited partnerships. The longer it takes you to get your money out of an investment, the less likely you will be able to take advantage of an increase in its value or to avoid being caught in a decline.

LEVERAGE

Leverage refers to the percentage of borrowed funds used in making an investment; the less of your own money you have to put down, the more you are leveraged. (We shall talk more about the uses and abuses of leverage in later chapters.) Leverage increases the yield that can be obtained from an investment, but it also increases the risk substantially.

For example, suppose you purchased a single-family house as an investment for $200,000 in 1980. You could have made a down payment of $60,000, in which case you would have 30% equity and 70% leverage. Alternatively, you could have made a $10,000 down payment, which would have given you 95% leverage. If things went well and you were able to sell the house 2 years later for $220,000, you would have realized a $20,000 gain. If you had used 70% leverage, you would have earned 33% on your money ($20,000 on a $60,000 investment). On the other hand, if you had used the higher leverage, you would have earned 200% on your money ($20,000 on a $10,000 investment)!

Sounds great. But suppose things went against you. In actuality, in 1982 you would have been lucky to have received $180,000 for the house. In this case you would have lost $20,000. On your 70% leverage, this would represent a loss of 33%. However, on the highly leveraged investment, you would have lost 200%! Not only would you have lost all of your initial investment, but you would have had to come up with another $10,000 to satisfy your obligations. And you would have been paying out more interest while you held the investment. The greater the leverage, the greater the risk.

TERM

The longer the time or term of an investment, the greater the risk. This should be fairly obvious. The longer your investment is exposed to the risks described above, the more likely it is that one of them will get you. This is why, in general, long-term bonds yield a higher rate of return than short-term bonds. There is a greater chance of an adverse event occurring in 25 years than there is in the next 6 months. In the past couple of years, there have been some exceptions to this relationship, but, as a general rule, the longer the term of the investment, the greater the risk.

THE RISK–RETURN RELATIONSHIP

The risk–return relationship is a fundamental principle of investing. Simply stated: *risk is directly related to return*. In other words, a larger rate of return can only be obtained by increasing the exposure to higher risk. The principle works in both directions. If you assume a more risky investment, you will also be entitled to a higher rate of return. The risk–return relationship is not difficult to grasp and is a logical extension of a free market economy.

Many investment advisors subscribe to the "random walk" or "efficient market theory," which states that everything known about a stock is immediately reflected in the market price of the stock. In other words, new information is very quickly reflected in the price the investment will command on the free market, and thus all issues are at all times fairly valued. Although we don't believe that the market is 100% efficient, it is efficient enough that the risk–return relationship is always operative. It is easy to understand why this is so.

There are literally thousands of investment alternatives available, all of which are competing for a share of the investment dollars. There are also thousands of professional research analysts who spend all of their time searching for the best combination of return and risk among the whole spectrum of available investments. Most of these analysts are reasonably bright, well intentioned, and experienced. If these analysts collectively became aware of a 4-to-1 return on a "sure thing," risk-free investment, the demand for that investment would rise precipitously. The rising demand would also cause the price of the investment to increase. As the price of the investment increased, its return would decrease. Suppose the initial investment could return $400 for every unit invested, and an individual unit was priced at $100. This would be a 4-to-1 return. However, if demand forces the price of a unit up to $200, the return will be only 2 to 1.

Of course the system does not work perfectly efficiently, and everyone knows a story about someone who bought Krugerrands at $100 and sold them at $800 or made a killing on the condo in Palm Springs. At any one time there are some investments with an unusually low risk–return ratio, and you may be lucky enough to stumble into one on occasion. Even a broken clock is right twice a day. Although on the scale of life it has been better to be lucky than smart, you can't bank on luck, and the chances of any individual consistently outperforming the vast majority of investment analysts is quite small—especially if that individual is a doctor trying to manage a busy practice and family on the side. In general, it is the best policy to assume that there are no free lunches and that the return on an investment will bear a direct relationship to its risk.

Just because the market in general places a fair balance between risk and return does not mean that someone will not try to sell you shoddy goods. It is important that before undertaking any investment, you make some assessment of the risk involved and decide if the investment's potential return justifies that risk.

THE TIME VALUE OF MONEY

We believe that investors should always make the final investment decisions. Advisors are necessary. But among all of the alternatives offered by advisors, which do you choose? There are two principles to keep in mind: (1) Time and money are interchangeable and (2) the value of any investment must be adjusted for risk. The most important concept in ranking the relative merits of investments is the *time value of money*.

Time and money are interrelated and evaluating the time value of money is one of the most important concepts you must learn in establishing your financial plan. It is also one of the most powerful tools for evaluating the advice you are getting from professional investment advisors. The time value of money is simply a way of comparing two sums of money with respect to the time interval between them. In other words, if we presently have a certain amount of money, which we will designate as P, and at some point in the future we'll have another amount of money, designated as AF, then we can pictorially represent this relationship as follows:

$$P \qquad\qquad \ldots \quad AF$$
$$| \qquad\qquad\qquad\qquad |$$
$$0 \quad 1 \quad 2 \quad 3 \quad \ldots \quad N$$

where P equals nominal dollars held presently; AF equals nominal dollars at some point in the future; and N equals the number of time units elapsed between the two sums.

In order to begin exploring the time value of money, let us first begin with a very simple problem. If you have a dollar and place it in a CD (certificate of deposit at a bank) for 1 year at 10%, how much money will you have at the end of one year? Simple, right? $1.10. That's our original dollar plus 10% interest on the dollar: $AF_1 = \$1.00 + (\$1.00 \times 0.1) = \$1.10$. If $1.10 is the value at the end of the first year, then what is the value of this program at the end of the second year? The second year is a slightly more sophisticated version of the first problem. The value of a dollar placed at 10% interest for 2 years is given by solving the problem for the second year starting with $1.10. In other words, $AF_2 = \$1.10 + (\$1.10 \times 0.1) = \$1.21$.

We could proceed to any number of time units and solve the problem accordingly. However, there is a much simpler way to do this. If we return to the original equation

$$AF_1 \;=\; \$1.00 + (\$1.00 \times 0.1)$$

then instead of using $1.00 in the calculations, we could actually let P represent any amount deposited at 10% as follows:

$$AF_1 \;=\; P \text{ dollars} + (P \text{ dollars} \times 0.1)$$

and, factoring,

$$AF_1 = P[1 + (1 \times 0.1)]$$

If we now want to calculate the value of this equation for the second year, AF_2, we get the following equation:

$$AF_2 = P(1.1 \times 1.1)$$

$$AF_2 = P(1.1)^2$$

and for the third year, similarly,

$$AF_3 = P(1.1)^3$$

and for any number of time units, AF_N,

$$AF_N = P(1.1)^N \tag{4.1}$$

The values we have computed for $1.00 placed in an account yielding 10% per year are shown on a time scale similar to the one we used above:

Year	0	1	2	3	. . .	10
	|	|	|	|		|
$	1	1.10	1.21	1.331	. . .	2.594

Instead of viewing this from the point of view of the amount of money available in the future, we can also consider the values shown as time-related equivalent amounts. In other words, if the expected return is 10% then $1.00 now is equal to $1.10 in 1 year, $1.21 in 2 years, or $2.549 10 years hence. If you turn your dollar over to someone now, their giving you $1.10 in 1 year or $2.594 in 10 years would be equivalent and would make no difference to you; your investment would be compounding at a rate of 10%.

Similarly, but perhaps more importantly, if someone with another investment scheme offers to take your dollar from you now and in 10 years pay you $2.00, although that is a 100% profit, it falls short of your objective (assuming your objective is to make 10% compounded on your money per year).

Of course, we don't always invest exactly at 10%, and to allow for other interest rates or rates of return we can completely generalize our basic equation to:

$$AF_N = P(1 + i)^N \tag{4.2}$$

where N is the number of years; i is the interest rate; P is the present amount of money; and AF is the future value.

Let us emphasize again that the concepts we are discussing are more important than the actual mathematics at this point. In order to assist you in getting started, we have computed the $(1 + i)^N$ terms in equation 4.2 for several interest rates and numbers of years. This factor, as it happens, is exactly the same factor we used in Chapter 2 to calculate the effect of inflation on buying power and is included in Appendix A.

Equation 4.2 is versatile. Given any two of the variables, we can solve for the third. There may be times in which we have to make assumptions regarding the number of time units involved or the interest rate or return on a given investment, but at least we have a way of solving not only for the future value of amounts available now but also the present value of a sum of money at a given point in the future. The latter can easily be performed by solving for P in equation 4.2 as follows:

$$P = AF/(1 + i)^N \qquad (4.3)$$

In this latter form, the equation is probably more powerful because there are many more cases in which it is desirable to know what a future return is worth in terms of today's dollars. For example, suppose you have just been offered an investment in real estate that promises to return $1.25 in 3 years for every dollar invested now. In contemplating the purchase of this investment, you decide you would like to make at least a 10% rate of return, which is what you can get in a time deposit account. With these three pieces of information (future return, timing of that return, and your desired return on your investment), you can compute the value to you, in today's dollars, of the $1.25 you will receive 3 years from now. Substituting the information into equation 4.3 $[P = \$1.25/(1 + 0.1)^3]$ yields $P = 0.939$ dollars. You would kindly reject this opportunity because the amount you are being asked to invest now, i.e., $1.00, exceeds the present value of the investment, which is only 94¢.

Although as potential investors we should reject the opportunity to pay $1.00 we would have invested in this program for $0.90 because we would be getting an investment value that would meet our required 10% return.

To restate this important principle: after you have calculated the present value of some investment in the future, if a broker expects you to pay more than that amount, you should reject the offer. The offered price, in other words, exceeds the economic value of the investment to you and your rate of return will be less than you desire. If, however, you can obtain an investment for less than its present value, you should buy it.

An alternative method of evaluating the return of an investment is to solve equation 4.2 for i:

$$i = (AF/P)^{1/N} - 1 \qquad (4.4)$$

Although equation 4.4 looks formidable, it is actually quite easy to solve on any small pocket calculator and it provides a direct measure of the compound rate of return.

Using the formulas just presented and a pocket calculator, try solving the two problems that follow in order to test your understanding of the concepts discussed as well as the computational processes involved.

EXAMPLE 1   THE BLUE MAX DIAMOND DEAL

One day you receive a phone call from your stockbroker announcing the fact that his brokerage firm is handling a limited partnership in Blue Max diamonds. To induce you to participate, he cites the record of 15 previous offerings in which the average limited partner investor received a 100% profit at the end of the 7-year life of the partnership. Assuming that this offering will do as well as the previous ones, this means that in 7 years you would receive $20,000 for your $10,000 investment. What is the compound annual rate of return of this investment? To calculate the rate of return we should use our handy pocket calculator and solve equation 4.4 for i:

$$i = \left(\frac{20,000}{10,000} \right)^{1/7} - 1 = 0.104$$

The compound rate of return for this investment is 10.4% annually. To get an idea of the relative value of the investment, you call up the local Federal Reserve Bank and find that current 7-year treasury notes are paying 16% interest. Therefore, you politely reject your stockbroker's kind offer for this spectacular investment.

We could also have assessed the rate of return using the present value of a future return concept. To do this we would use equation 4.3: $P = AF/(1 - i)^N$. In order to use the equation, we must select a rate of return against which we wish to compare this investment. The current rate of the treasury bill is a good standard, and, therefore, we will use the formula and set $N = 7$, $i = 0.16$ (the current return on the treasury note), and $AF =$ the $20,000 promised future amount. Solving the equation shows that the present value of the investment is only $7,077. That is, we could invest $7,077 in a risk-free treasury bill and have the same $20,000 at the end of the term. The Blue Max people would like you to invest $10,000 in a much more risky investment for the same final yield.

EXAMPLE 2   GEOSCARCE

On another day you receive a phone call from a different stockbroker announcing the fact that his brokerage firm is handling a new oil and gas drilling program, which is sponsored by Geoscarce, one of the most reputable and successful drillers in the business. He tells you that in the long history of Geoscarce no investor has received less than a 5:1 return after tax in the limited partnerships available and that, luckily for you, the driller has a policy of capping successful wells and waiting for the price to go up before sales operations begin. The partnerships last 12 years, and at that time Geoscarce offers to buy all partners out slightly above the market value of the reserves. The minimum investment is $10,000, and the broker has quickly calculated for you that at 5:1 you will get $50,000 back in 12 years. He pauses expectantly, hoping you will reach for your checkbook. Instead you reach for *this book* and the telephone number of the nearest Federal Reserve Bank. They inform you that 12-year treasury bonds are currently yielding 14%. Next, you turn to equation 4.4 to calculate the annualized rate of return on the 5:1 investment for 12 years.

$$i = (5/1)^{1/12} - 1 = 0.144$$

In this case, the annualized rate of return is 14.4%, which is slightly better than the 14% the treasury bond is paying. However, the extra 4/10 of a percentage point does not justify the increased risk of the oil drilling venture.

If you wish to evaluate this using the present value of a future return concept, we would solve equation 4.3 using $N = 12$ years, $i = 14\%$, and $AF = \$50,000$. Solving this equation gives a present value of the investment of $10,378.

Well, Geoscarce certainly beats the Blue Max and, at $10,000, represents a slightly better yield than the completely safe treasury bond (for which you have to pay $10,378 to get the same yield). However, you would still do yourself a favor by refusing the Geoscarce offer. Geoscarce represents only a very slight increase in yield over the treasury bond and is a far, far riskier investment. In order to justify assuming this risk, the present value of the investment would have to be considerably greater than that of the treasury bond.

ASSESSING RISK

Since risk is relative, you must analyze the return on any prospective investment. This can be done in two ways: either by calculating the present value of a future return (equation 4.3) or by calculating the compound rate of return (equation 4.4). Once you have analyzed the value of the investment's return, you need a yardstick against which to compare its risk. The place to start is with the truly risk-free investment.

In this country, the closest you can get to a risk-free investment is the 90-day United States Treasury bill. The United States Treasury has never defaulted and, unless the country completely collapses, will never default on paying the interest on its obligations. (If and when the government defaults, it won't make much difference which investment vehicle you own.) The reason for this, of course, is that the government can always print money to pay its bills and must maintain public confidence by paying debts at all costs. You can consider the risk on a 90-day United States Treasury bill as essentially zero, and everything else will have some greater degree of risk associated with it. Consequently, any other investment you undertake should give you a higher rate of return than the current United States Treasury bill. Figure 4.2 shows the relative rates of return among typical investments plotted against that investment's risk. In general, the further out investments are on the risk–return line, the higher the rate of average return as well as the increased level of risk.

Thus, if you are offered a limited partnership in cattle breeding that is intended to return to you 20% per year for a 5-year period, and at the same time you can get a 15% return on treasury bills virtually risk-free, you should reject the limited partnership because the enormous risk involved in cattle breeding does not warrant the meager 5% difference in return.

This concept can be generalized into two principles. (1) *If two investments have the same rate of return, select the less risky one.* For example, if you are offered two limited partnerships in apartment buildings, both of which yield 22% after taxes for a 7-year period, and one of them is in Durham, North Carolina and the other is in Villahermosa, Mexico, you should take the investment in Durham. (2) *If two investments have equal risk, select the investment with the higher return.* For example, if you are scanning the back pages of *Barron's* trying to select a bond and notice that two triple-A bonds with the same maturity and the same coupon rate are available but that one is selling to yield a quarter of a percentage more than the other, by all means take the one with the higher yield.

THE ULTIMATE RISK

We have discussed many types of risks that may be involved in investments, but we have left the ultimate and ever-present risk for the end. The ultimate risk in any investment and any financial plan is wasted time. Every day that an investment dollar is wasted is a day lost irrevocably. Any time that is wasted means there is that much less time available to achieve a financial goal and this means that any subsequent investments will have to provide a higher rate of return and, consequently, will have to assume more risk. *The biggest single thing you can do to minimize risk in your investments is to make maximum utilization of the time value of your money.*

This bears directly on the third common investment error—lack of investment discipline. The best financial goal and most well-thought-out financial plan cannot work if you do not have the discipline to implement

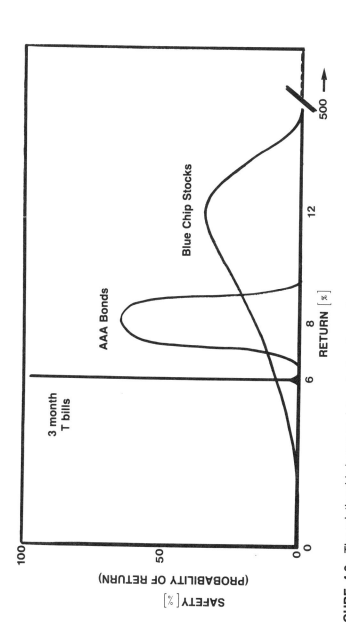

FIGURE 4.2 The relationship between risk and return is very important to bear in mind when considering alternative investments. The 3-month treasury bill can be considered an essentially risk-free investment. In other words, you are virtually certain of getting both your principal and the return on your principal back in the time frame designated. Since investors in general are compensated for assuming greater risk and uncertainty, the more risky an investment the greater should be your expected return before making that investment. This schematic representation depicts three relatively conservative investment comparisons between 91-day treasury bills and a slightly more risky AAA corporate bond and a slightly more risky still blue chip stock portfolio. Moving to the right increases uncertainty and risk, but, as noted, so do the historical returns on these investments increase. In other words, higher rates of return are gained with increasing uncertainty.

it. We bring Will Rogers back to illustrate this one: "Even if you are on the right track, you'll get run over if you just sit there." Most doctors procrastinate because of fear of the uncertainties and risk in an investment, little realizing that their procrastination is simply increasing their risk of failure.

Because of the extreme importance of the time factor, the ultimate value of any investment is measured by the amount of cash that flows immediately into your pocket. Money that you earn today or in the near future can immediately be put back to work, making maximum use of time. This is an extremely important principle to remember. Many investments—especially those that are sold primarily as tax shelters—rely on large initial expenses, which are written off income tax, in exchange for a promised capital gain at some time in the future. We have discussed enough about the time value of money to recognize the possible fallacy in this arrangement. The potential capital gain must be enormous to justify forgoing immediate income and what it could earn for you when reinvested for several years.

In summary, never underestimate the value of time and current income. The only value an investment has is the income it produces. (Paper income and fictional losses can indeed save some tax money, but they cannot be reinvested and cannot take advantage of the time factor.) The only satisfactory substitute for current income is very large capital gains in the future, so large that they themselves will enable you to reach your financial goal. Recall that Bernard Baruch said, "The eighth wonder of the world is compound interest." He did not say that the eighth wonder of the world is capital gains. Investor preference and crowd psychology may bid prices up and down, but the underlying value of any investment is related to its income stream. Those who invest in something that is priced above its value must realize that they are doing a foolish thing and that they are relying on the hope that they can ultimately find a bigger fool than they to bail them out. Speculation is exciting, but Mark Twain was right: "There are two times in a man's life when he should not speculate: when he can't afford it and when he can."

5

MONEY
(WHERE TO FIND IT)

Money is the second component of the financial independence equation. Even with all the time in the world, it will be difficult to reach your financial goal without having some money working for you. This concept is difficult for many people to accept, since they assume it necessitates downgrading lifestyle: long periods without vacations, meager meals of beans on toast, and a tattered sport coat. For most doctors such hardships are not necessary. With relatively modest adjustments in spending patterns, you should be able to generate enough extra dollars to completely satisfy your investment objectives. In the next three chapters we shall discuss some ways to generate the money for your financial independence equation.

The first thing we must do is realize that dollars can be more than slips of green paper we use to settle transactions or a tally sheet of ins and outs in the family bankbook. Instead, we must think of them as our allies or partners, out there working 24 hours a day to earn more money for our financial goal. Dollars can be more effective at this than any individual. Sam B. may be the most skillful doctor in the world, a canny diagnostician and brilliant therapist who works around the clock doing good for multitudes of grateful patients who are happy to pay his fees. This may give him tremendous personal satisfaction and will certainly provide a steady source of income for his family, but it is unlikely that it will provide him financial independence. The wages of a single individual, no matter how creative and successful, rarely generate enough income to provide for that individual should he choose to change his working pattern.

The efforts of one person simply are not enough, he must have partners or allies working with him. Ray Kroc was a hard worker with a brilliant, innovative idea and a taste for hamburger. But he did not make his fortune by cooking and selling McDonald's hamburgers himself. He made it by having 2,500 other McDonald's restaurants cooking and selling the hamburgers and giving him a fraction of a penny on each one sold.

The Vanderbilts did not acquire the means to build a mansion in Newport by loading and driving the family trains. Rather, they had others do this work and pass back to them a small percentage of each transaction.

Not all financial independence partners need be human. Dollars placed in judicious investments can be just as effective workers for you as a teenager cooking hamburgers at McDonald's or a train engineer. You must start thinking of every dollar as a potential partner, a dedicated ally working around the clock to help you toward your financial goal. Once you have accepted this concept, it will be much easier to keep track of your money and make certain that every dollar you own is busy earning its keep rather than getting a free ride in your wallet or lounging in your bank account.

THE THREE TYPES OF MONEY

Money falls into one of three categories: active, lazy, and dead.

"Active" money is invested and produces an after-tax rate of return greater than the current inflation rate. Active dollars are out there pulling their share, bringing home the bacon, earning their keep. Because the after-tax return of active dollars is greater than the inflation rate, they are producing yet more dollars, which can also be put to work to help you achieve financial independence. Active money makes full use of the compounding principle and is absolutely essential in a successful investment program.

"Dead" money is the opposite extreme. Dead dollars just sit around, not invested in anything, and not producing any return. Whether they are found in checking accounts or in wallets, they might just as well be stuffed in a mattress or burned in the fireplace; they are of absolutely no help to you in obtaining financial independence. Not all dead dollars are deadbeats, of course. Some of them are providing real services by paying the grocer bill and the house mortgage or providing that new tennis racket, ski outfit, or Mercedes. To the extent that these provide for the necessities and comfort in our lives and give us pleasure, they are certainly in service and doing useful "work" for us. The problem is that most people have lots of deadbeat dead dollars—money that is not being used to enrich lifestyle and is also not out working for financial independence.

The most obvious example of dead money is the dollars you pay in taxes. Every dollar you send to Washington is dead; it is doing no work on your financial independence project. This was the cause of much of the initial resistance in the 1980s to President Reagan's proposed withholding tax on interest and dividends. Had this withholding bill passed, the government would have converted 20% of interest and dividend earnings into dead money. A less obvious example of dead money is those traveler's checks you have been saving for an emergency as Karl Malden recommends. If you paid cash for your $2,000 plane tickets to Hawaii rather than charging them on your Visa card and paying for them 30 days from now, you have converted $2,000 to dead money for a month. (In a money market fund at 9% interest, that $2,000 would have earned $15 for you during those 30 days.)

"Lazy" money is working and earning some return, but the after-tax gains are not keeping pace with inflation. Money in a conventional 5¼% savings account or a demand checking account is a prime example of lazy money. Lazy money is pervasive and insidious. Most of us have far more of it than we realize, and it is a main reason why most people never achieve financial independence. Lazy dollars just aren't pulling their weight; they are counting on your daily work efforts to replenish their gradually diminishing buying powers. They are devious rascals because they masquerade (or are sold) as hard-working dollars producing some income. The problem, of course, is that they do not produce enough income; they lose ground to taxes and inflation. For them, the time factor is working in reverse, inexorably eating them away and diminishing their numbers.

The first step in successful money management is learning to recognize and classify money into one of the three categories. You must automatically scrutinize every dollar that is under your control and decide whether it is active, lazy, or dead. To a large extent, the category into which your money falls is under your control, and you must strive to have as much of it in the active category as possible. As we have said before, most professionals have enough total dollars available to them to achieve their financial independence goal. Problems arise because too many of these dollars are lazy or dead rather than active. Therefore, a basic principle of any successful financial independence program is to purge lazy and dead money and convert it to active money.

WHERE THE MONEY GOES

To begin a realignment of dollars, we need to look at how the average doctor disposes of his yearly earnings. Figure 5.1 shows how a "typical" professional allocates his income. Notice that Figure 5.1 *does not* include any "fringe benefits" or "perks" (which can be very important, as we shall see later).

Taxes take about 25%. As we have seen, tax dollars are dead dollars, the worst type of all. Any dollars that can be rescued from this category will certainly help our goal. This is hardly news. Unfortunately, in trying to rescue dollars from the tax man, many doctors have sustained big losses and created more dead dollars than they started out to save. We shall go into more detail on ways to minimize the tax bite in Chapter 7.

The 10% or so of income that is spent on insurance contains dollars in all three categories. Although insurance dollars never generate income that exceeds the inflation rate (unless you die prematurely, which is not part of most people's investment plan), many of them can be thought of as essential or active money. This is because they are protecting the rest of the financial independence program from a devastating or terminal loss. Like the offensive linemen on a football team who get little recognition for their efforts, the dollars working in an insurance policy are providing the security that permits the remainder of the assets to be actively invested. Problems arise when money is inappropriately placed in insurance, purchasing protection that is not necessary or is being used as a low-return investment program. These dollars are either lazy or dead and need to be eliminated. In Chapter 6 we discuss methods of minimizing lazy and dead insurance dollars.

The 3 to 5% of income in the savings category represents the average commitment to a financial security program and encompasses not only savings accounts but other investment vehicles. Unfortunately, this is simply not enough money for most doctors to achieve financial independence. To make matters worse, much of this money is usually lazy, working in injudicious investments that are not producing a rate of return greater than inflation and taxes.

Perhaps we should take a moment and see how much you need to raise. Just how much money should you plan on committing to your financial independence program? This, of course, depends on what type of goal you set, how long you have to reach it, and how much risk you are willing to accept. Our experience in working with doctors suggests that most plans require the contribution of 25 to 30% of annual gross income. As a first target, we think we should aim for 30%.

Thirty percent of gross income, you say, impossible! Where is this going to come from?

Don't panic! Things are not as bad as they might seem.

First, the data in Figure 5.1 do not take fringe benefits such as monies paid into corporate or practice retirement plans into account. For most

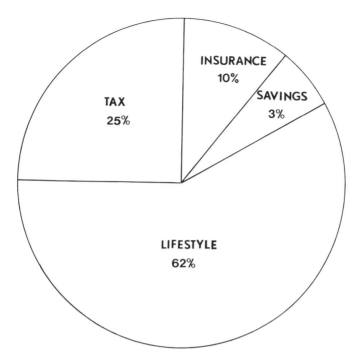

FIGURE 5.1 The pie chart of expenditures is meant to indicate the general categories of expense experienced by most individuals. Not only are there wide variations among individuals in any given population, but the patterns of spending change substantially from time to time.

doctors, this already represents a fair percentage of take-home income and goes a long way toward the 30% goal. Moreover, since the retirement plans are tax deferred, any money in them can be considered very active, almost twice as active as money in taxable programs. Viewed in this light, many professionals are already contributing 15 to 25% to a financial independence program. Second, most doctors can whack a few percentage points off the tax dollars and convert this to active investment money. Third, it should be possible to convert some of the lazy dollars in insurance into active dollars in an investment program.

Any shortfall that remains will have to come out of lifestyle, but for most of us, the alterations should be minor and not unduly traumatic. It is really more a matter of philosophy and discipline than of self-denial. If you can develop a habit of scrutinizing your expenses, you will find many dead and lazy dollars that can be recruited for the financial program with a minimum of disruption to the quality of your life. Let's see how this can be done.

A PENNY SAVED IS TWO PENNIES EARNED

Sadly, because of the progressive, suppressive income tax, you are usually better off if you can cut your expenses rather than generate new income. The well-known "bracket creep" caused by inflation has moved most working Americans into progressively higher tax brackets, and you do not have to creep very far before you are at the 50% ceiling. When state and local income taxes are added in, most doctors find that they are near the 50% tax bracket—or higher. (We shall assume, as do most financial writers, that you are in only the 50% tax bracket, since this makes it easier to understand the calculations and comparisons.)

Now, being in the 50% tax bracket means that you will have to earn an additional $2 in income to provide $1 for investment purposes. However, if you save $2 in expenses, it can all be directly channeled into your program for financial independence. Thus, a penny saved is two pennies earned. You will have to decide if perhaps it is easier to defer an expense or two rather than earning more, since you will only get to keep half of what you earn. Another way of conceptualizing this is to realize that you need only save half as much in expenses as you would have to earn in income to get the same net return. Suppose you are contemplating a little moonlighting to generate an extra $5,000 a year in income. You could realize the same net income by decreasing your expenses by only $2,500, which, for most of us, represents a better return on the use of our time and results in a more pleasing quality of life.

The first place to look for extra money then is in the daily budget. Scrutinize it carefully, particularly the little nickel and dime items. These expenses often arise from carelessness rather than any real need. They frequently occur because we have no other plans for the money at the time and a "what the hell, I've paid my dues, hang the expense" attitude. Little savings of $25 here and $50 there can quickly add up to a significant amount, which could be painlessly redirected into a financial independence program.

If your will starts to falter, remember the principle that the dollar you save is the equivalent of $2 you would have to earn. Just double the cost of everything as marked—it will slow you down. The next time you are perusing a wine list and are tempted to buy a $25 vintage wine ($50 in earnings) rather than the $10 house bottle ($20 in earnings), remember that the pricey wine will actually have to taste $30 better than the house wine.

When a family member protests that "the ultra model" tennis racket is *only* $35 more than the "deluxe model," remember to multiply the figure by 2. Is it really worth your having to earn $70 extra to keep up with the Joneses?

You will probably feel better on your ski holiday if you buy that flashy new $400 outfit. But remember that you are only going to ski in it for 6 days, that you actually had to earn $800 to buy it, that it won't make you ski one bit better, and that when you do fall down, you will generate more snickers from the chair lift.

It is also important to carefully scrutinize your future expenses and commitments. Because of the ready availability of credit, it is very easy to tie oneself into excessive future expenses. A recent example of this was the widespread use of "balloon" mortgages in the late 1970s and early 1980s. In order to encourage home buyers to purchase overpriced houses they really couldn't afford, financing was arranged so that the mortgage payments in the early years were small and seemingly within the family budget. Four or five years out, however, the mortgage and principal payments increased significantly (the euphemistic "balloon"). At the time of closing, these future payments may not seem too important—"we will figure something out," "we are sure to be earning more money," and so on. When the actual day of reckoning comes however, the expense burden can be crushing.

One of the most commonly overlooked future expenses is the cost of raising children. Everyone grossly underestimates the amount of money they will spend on their children during their dependent years. Although virtually all of us would agree that it is money well spent, it is important to realize how much it actually takes. In the early 1980s, it cost the average professional family over $250,000 to raise a child through college. And that figure represents a no-frills passage without piano lessons, summer camp, or winter ski vacations. God forbid graduate school!

GETTING DOLLARS OFF THE DOLE

Most of us have many lazy and dead dollars in our ordinary monthly cash flow. Remember that there is no place for lazy or dead money in a good financial independence plan, and this applies even to those dollars that you have already committed for other expenses. The principle here is to keep money working for you as long as possible. If you pay your bills at the end of the month rather than at the first of the month, you, rather than your creditors, will receive an extra 30 days of interest. Never pay for anything in advance if possible; remember that you want your money working for you as long as possible. If you defer $1,000 each month for a year, you will earn $45 in interest.

One area where doctors are frequently remiss is in leaving money with the Internal Revenue Service. Most doctors overpay their taxes in advance. It may be psychologically less stressful to receive a hefty refund check from the government rather than having to ante up some extra money on April 15, but this is poor money management. In effect, you have been making the government an interest-free loan. It is far better to have the minimum amount of tax withheld, take the difference, and put it to work for you during the year. Do not think of this money as yours; just think of it as dollars on loan from the government doing a little work for you. When April comes and you finally have to write the check to pay the taxes, remember that you aren't really parting with your own money; you are just repaying a no-interest loan to the government. Over time, who gets the no-interest loan—you or the government—makes a difference.

This same principle applies to all expenses, of course. Unless you receive a discount for paying in advance or paying early, do not pay your bills until the last minute. When possible, charge large expenses on a credit card rather than paying cash, and if you buy on the billing day of the credit card billing cycle, you will have 60 days before you actually have to pay the bill. (Be sure to pay the credit card balance before interest charges accrue, however.) Always be on the lookout for the opportunity to procure these small "interest-free" loans. Be just as wary of taking out "high-interest" loans by maintaining a balance on your credit card or with the local department store.

Try not to lend your money interest-free. Any time you pay for a service or product in advance, you are making an interest-free loan. When you hold onto a traveler's check, you are making an interest-free loan to American Express. Whenever you put down a deposit, you are making an interest-free loan. Remember that money is going to be working for some-one—make certain that someone is you.

The foregoing may sound like nit-picking. After all, what's $10 worth of interest here and $40 there really worth? Actually quite a bit. You won't get rich overnight on these amounts, but the nickel and dime savings do add up over the years, particularly when the effects of compounding are considered. Perhaps even more important is the awareness of the principle of getting the most for your money. After all, it requires no great effort or sacrifice to pay for things at the last minute rather than in advance, and, in doing so, you are receiving a slight discount on the expense.

Another common source of lazy or dead dollars is "rainy day cash." Many investment advisors and texts on financial planning suggest that everyone have at least 3 months' living expenses in readily available cash deposits. Although we agree that everyone needs enough funds available to feel comfortable and not to suffer from temporary cash flow problems, we also believe it is unwise to have this security in the form of uninvested, lazy dollars.

A better way of handling this problem is by the effective use of credit. In reality, it is the availability of funds rather than the actual cash on hand that is the issue. We believe it is more prudent to have a large line of credit rather than a large stack of rainy-day dollars. For most doctors there should be no problem in obtaining a personal credit line of $10,000 to $20,000. The new "gold" versions of the major credit cards generally have very high credit limits, and nearly any bank will be happy to establish a personal credit line to cover three months' living expenses for a professional family. Although the cost of using the credit is relatively high (between 18 and 25%), remember that it is free until actually used. Most of us will never need to tap it, but having it available will free up a considerable amount of money, which can be put to active use in our investment program.

BORROWING

Borrowing is a way to obtain money for use in an investment program. During the high rates of inflation experienced in the late 1970s, many investment advisors encouraged their clients to mobilize equity by borrowing. This most often took the form of refinancing the family home or taking out a second mortgage. During the 1970s this was indeed an effective strategy, since the money generated could usually be invested at a higher rate of return than the cost of the mortgage.

However, borrowing is a tricky business and requires careful analysis. It boils down to the inflation-adjusted cost of the loan versus the risk–reward relationship in the investment. Taking out a 12% second mortgage on your home can be good business when the inflation rate is 16%. The 12% loan really only costs you 6% since it is deductible on your income tax. When the inflation rate is 16%, and you can borrow money for 6%, you are making 10% right off the top. However, when the inflation rate is 4%, you are losing 2%. Also remember that taxes will take half of what you earn from reinvesting the money, so the benefits shrink even further.

There is also risk associated with this strategy. It is possible that the borrowed funds will not produce the income return you anticipate and might even suffer a loss. There is also the very real risk that the value of your home could decline, and you would be unable to sell the house should you wish to move since you could not get enough money to pay off the mortgages.

Borrowing money for the sake of investing is only practical when the loan can be obtained at a much lower rate than the prevailing inflation rate. Such loans are hard to come by. As we shall discuss in later chapters, we believe that the 1980s will be a decade of relatively low inflation, which will make it even more difficult to make a profit on borrowed funds, and that it is unwise for most doctors to engage in this type of transaction.

EARNING MORE

As we pointed out earlier, because of their high marginal tax bracket, most doctors will find that earning more is an inefficient way of generating extra investment dollars. The cost in time and decreased quality of life outweighs the benefit of the extra income. Most professional people can generate enough money for their financial program by merely rearranging expenses. But earning more is certainly an effective way to finance an investment program. If you and your family decide that additional income is needed to get you to the point of financial independence, then the first place to look is in the area of your hobbies and avocations. Are you a gourmet cook? Do you give lectures for which you receive an honorarium, or are you paid to write articles or edit a journal? Turning this enterprise into a business helps in two ways. First, since you are making expenditures to support the hobby or avocation anyway, turning it into a business will enable you to take some of your ongoing expenses as a business deduction. And, by actively pursuing clients, you are likely to generate more income than just dabbling has brought in. These activities often can be very satisfying and lead to new careers as well as aiding in getting tax breaks for your current expenses and bringing in extra funds to apply to your financial independence program.

PAY YOURSELF FIRST

Now that we have taken a hard look at our spending patterns and mobilized the lazy and dead money, it is very important to make certain that these funds are applied to the financial independence program rather than to a new pair of Guccis. This is the hardest part. Because the returns from an investment program are never immediately apparent, it can be difficult to write out a check. It is much easier to spend the money on a vacation or new car and promise to start the investment program next month. The road to financial independence is not paved with good intentions; it requires the commitment of cold cash. In fact, if you do nothing else but develop the discipline to make a small investment every month, you will do far better than the average professional.

The golden rule for financial independence is *pay yourself first*. Although easy to say, it is as hard to implement as stopping smoking or losing weight. Our experience in counseling investors has shown that it is almost essential to have an automated and mechanical technique for the regular commitment of funds to an investment program. We are all used to this concept. We routinely accept the fact that every month there are certain bills that must be paid. There is the mortgage, the utilities, the car payment, school tuition, the credit cards, and so on. All we need do is add another item to the list:

The Monthly Financial Independence Payment (MyFIP)

The MyFIP represents a payment to yourself for financial security in the future, and, as such, it should have priority over all of your other monthly bills. When you sit down to pay the monthly bills, always write the MyFIP check first; that way, if you are short on funds that month, it will be one of your other creditors that must wait, but not your investment program. We are not advocating that you welch on your debts, but in our experience, it is very easy to roll over at night and promise yourself that next month, when you have more money, you will put some money in the investment program. Somehow that month never comes. On the other hand, unpaid creditors generally manage to get their money, either by making you feel guilty or by turning off your lights.

If you have trouble getting started, one technique that has worked in the past is to make out a series of 12 envelopes addressed to the MyFIP program each year, file them with your bills, and write this check first. An even more effective way to assure that you make the MyFIP is to arrange for a direct bank transfer of funds from your savings or checking account into some investment vehicle at regular monthly intervals. Just as with income withholding tax, you never see the money, so you never really miss it and never have the opportunity to spend it on something else. In later chapters, we discuss various investment vehicles, and virtually all of them have provisions for accepting direct transfers of money from bank accounts. Although this approach may seem Draconian, it is actually the most effective and least painful way of ensuring an adequate flow of money into your financial independence program.

Regardless of whether you write the check yourself every month or have the money transferred by your bank, it is essential that the MyFIP be made. If you do not do this, you will have difficulty achieving financial independence.

6

INSURANCE

You probably spend a lot of money on insurance; 10% is the average. Insurance is a necessary and good investment, and no one starting out on the road to financial independence should be without it. However, many investors do not obtain proper value for their insurance dollars. They either waste money through excessive payments for the wrong types of insurance or, even worse, risk financial bankruptcy by being underinsured. Many do both. Before instituting any plan for financial independence, you should carefully scrutinize the family insurance policies. You will likely find some lazy and dead dollars that can be mobilized toward your goal, and, even more important, you may discover some glaring holes in your insurance protection, which could leave you open to financial disaster. In this chapter, we shall look at the types of insurance most doctors carry with an eye to maximizing the value received for the dollars invested.

First we must be certain that we understand the reason for having any insurance at all. The only reason to own insurance is protection from severe financial loss; insurance simply is a pooling of risk among a group of individuals. It is a bet, just like putting some money on the outcome of the Super Bowl. You are betting that you will suffer some misfortune or financial loss, while the insurance company is betting that you will not. The odds on this bet are in the favor of the insurance company, and therefore the amount you wager—your premium—is less than the amount the company must pay if they lose. Of course, insurance companies never lose in the long run. Although their policy holders occasionally win—junior may smash up the family car, or you may be hit by lightning—the total return from all of their bets will be positive. Have you ever wondered why many of the largest and fanciest buildings in our cities are owned by the insurance companies, whereas the policy holders hold forth in more humble digs? It is the same reason there are fancy hotels in Atlantic City and Las Vegas. Insurance is a form of gambling in which, on average, the odds are in the favor of the insurance companies.

Why, then, should anyone buy insurance? For protection. Although it is unlikely you will ever suffer a significant financial loss, the consequences of being one of the unlucky few could be so dire as to not only torpedo a financial independence program but force a major alteration in lifestyle as well. Insurance is a hedge against unacceptable risk. The less financial independence and security you have, the more insurance you need. When you have achieved financial independence, you will need very little insurance, since you will be able to cover the risks yourself. However, in the beginning, all of us need adequate insurance protection.

Since insurance is generally good business for the insurance companies, there is a lot of competition for your insurance dollar, and aggressive salesmen are everywhere. The general effect of this competition is good since it promotes a variety of different insurance plans and tends to keep costs to a minimum. However, it also creates an atmosphere in which insurance salesmen may be more interested in closing the deal than in getting you the appropriate coverage for your needs. We do not mean to imply that most insurance salesmen are dishonest. Rather, we mean that you need to carefully decide what type of and how much insurance coverage you need and how much risk you can assume yourself. Once you have an idea of what you really need, you are ready to talk to the salesmen to cut the best deal you can. Among insurance companies that are financially solvent, reputable, and provide good service, there is little basis for choice except cost.

LIFE INSURANCE

Life insurance is the most important type of insurance to own since it covers the greatest risk your family will take—the possibility that your earning power will be lost. Most young doctors have too little life insurance and pay too much for what they have. Most older doctors have too much life insurance for which they paid too many dollars in the past. Life insurance is a major source of lazy money.

Let us begin by looking at five basic principles of life insurance.

1. Life insurance is misnamed; it should be called "death" insurance. What you are really buying is insurance against your untimely death

and a resultant loss of your income-earning ability. Although insurance companies gain a certain euphemistic edge in using the term *life* insurance (and we shall continue to use this commonly accepted term), always remember that what you are really buying is protection against the risk of your death.

2. You only need life insurance if you have dependents. You do not need life insurance if you are unmarried, if you are married with a working spouse, or are otherwise without dependents. If you are young, have small children, impoverished aging parents, few assets, and an unemployable spouse, you need a very large amount of life insurance.

3. As your assets increase and your dependents become self-sufficient, your life insurance needs drop drastically.

4. Dependent children and unmarried college students do not need any life insurance. So do not let anyone sell you life insurance for your children. They do not need it, and no matter what the salesman tells you, taking out insurance on your child does not "freeze" the rates on the policy.

5. Do not buy insurance vehicles that combine insurance and some form of investment plan or savings policy. These types of policies go by various names, such as "ordinary" life, "whole" life, "20-pay" life. Remember that the reason to buy insurance is to protect against risk. The "investment" or "savings" portions of life insurance policies are always poor investments with extremely lazy dollars. You should only buy term life insurance.

The hardest thing about life insurance is deciding how much you need. Most young doctors are underinsured. They are under the misconception that life insurance, like a fancy car or a bigger house, is a luxury and that they should start small and add to it as their fortunes progress. This is just backwards. When you have no money and your family has little financial security, you need as much life insurance as you can afford. When you have generated $50,000 in assets, you can drop $50,000 worth of life insurance. The chances are that if you are under 50 and have children still in secondary school, you have too little life insurance! If you are under 35 and have preschool children, you probably cannot afford as much life insurance as you should have!

There are many different ways of estimating your life insurance needs, and any life insurance salesman will be more than happy to explain them to you. We will only look at the basic concepts here.

The simplest approach for a young family with dependent children and few financial assets is to take the annual family income and add a zero to it. If this seems like a lot, remember that it takes about $250,000 to sponsor a no-frills (such as music lessons, summer camp, graduate school) trip for your child from conception through college. This amount of life insurance should adequately cover the family's needs in its present lifestyle (probably more than adequately).

Most of us can get by with less than this amount of insurance because we will be willing to take some risk on ourselves and because life insurance proceeds represent an instant "endowment," the proceeds of which can be put to active work generating considerable income.

A better way to estimate your needs is the so-called income stream analysis, which is based on the amount of yearly income your family will need. First, decide how much income your family needs presently to live a minimally acceptable lifestyle. (This should probably be something less than your current earnings, since most doctors could downgrade their lifestyle without serious adverse consequences.) Next, subtract approximately one-third of this amount, since, without you, the family will not require so much income. Now you have an estimate of your family's current annual income needs. Subtract from this amount the estimated social security benefits you have accrued (this is constantly changing and increasing; check with your regional social security center for the latest figures). This leaves the net amount of annual income that will have to be provided by your life insurance.

You should probably do some fine tuning at this point. We believe that it is risky to count on much of a social security benefit. It is well known that the social security system is not financially sound and will eventually be bankrupt (depending on whom you read, this will occur sometime between the next 3 and 30 years). Although it is unlikely that benefits will be totally eliminated, it is almost certain that they will not be maintained much above a subsistence level and might well be eliminated for those with other means of support.

You should also anticipate large, nonrecurring expenses such as a college education for your children. A satisfactory estimate can be obtained by taking the present cost of a year of college, multiplying by 4, and adding the amount to your final life insurance package. Although the cost of a college education will undoubtedly rise by the time your children are entering freshmen, the life insurance proceeds will presumably have grown at the same rate. Also, your children may be eligible for scholarships that would be unavailable if you were alive. If you do not die, you will not be receiving the earnings on this insurance, but you will presumably be acquiring your own financial assets during this period, which will cover the increase in educational costs.

If your spouse has the potential for working and earning more income than at present, this figure should be taken into account in determining the income that must be provided from your insurance policies.

If there are other anticipated sources of income (such as stock options, wealthy grandparents, or a favorable estate settlement), your life insurance needs can be further adjusted downward.

Eventually you should arrive at a figure for the estimated annual income that must be provided by your life insurance policy. Next, you need to decide how long this income will be necessary. In 20 years or less, your children will be grown, and only your spouse's needs will remain. This should be continued out to normal life expectancy.

Now that you know the amount of money you need and the number of years you will need it, all that is necessary is to look up the amount of capital required to produce this income stream in an annuity table (Appendix B). An annuity is an endowment, effectively, a mortgage in reverse. It represents a fixed amount of capital that, given a certain investment rate of return, will produce a guaranteed annual income for a specified number of years. For example, to provide $10,000 of annual income for 20 years would require $150,000 of capital assuming that it was invested at a 3% return. To provide $10,000 annual income for 30 years would require $200,000 of initial capital at 3% interest. On the other hand, if the capital could earn at an 8% interest rate, the required amounts would be only $100,000 for 20 years and $112,000 for 30 years.

The insurance requirements drop considerably if a higher rate of return is assumed, and it is therefore tempting to anticipate that your life insurance proceeds could be safely invested at 15%. Chances are this will only happen if the rate of inflation is also high. It is most prudent to assume that life insurance proceeds will only outperform inflation by 3 to 4% and to use these conservative figures in estimating the required amount of insurance.

Now that you have worked through all this, you have probably arrived at a life insurance figure that is horrifying, on the order of $500,000. Compare this figure with how much insurance you now own. This may cause you to go back and reestimate your income needs downward. It is unlikely that you will be able to get it below four or five times your present annual salary, however. It is important to go carefully through these calculations, because they represent the "facts of life." If you wish to provide this much income for your family in your absence, you are going to have to provide them with a hefty estate. Of course, as you use the principles in this book, you will begin to build your own financial security and provide rapidly increasing amounts of this estate from your own investments. But, if you are just starting out, the only way to do it is with life insurance, and the only way to afford this much life insurance is to get the best buy for your money: term insurance.

WHAT KIND OF INSURANCE?

As we mentioned earlier, there are two basic types of life insurance protection: (1) policies that provide coverage only—commonly called "term" insurance, and (2) policies that provide some form of saving or investment program in addition to insurance. The latter policies go by a variety of names such as "ordinary" life, "whole" life, "cash value" life, or "universal" life.

Whole-life insurance or cash-value life insurance is a very poor investment. Much has been written about the disadvantages of these policies, in particular, an excellent book by Andrew Tobias, *The Invisible Bankers* (enjoyable and required reading). The premium paid for a cash value policy is divided into two portions. One portion is applied to life insurance, and the remainder is invested by the insurance company and represents a "savings account" for the insured. (There is actually a third, frequently large, portion of the premium, which goes for the salesman's commission.) Life insurance salesmen would have you believe that the "savings account" is a good deal, an enforced method of investment that will provide security in your old age. There are several fallacies in their reasoning.

First, historically, the return to the insured on the cash value (savings) portion of these policies has been in the range of 3 to 5%, well under that available for other forms of relatively risk-free investments. In other words, dollars invested in an insurance policy are lazy dollars. More recently, some universal life insurance policies have increased the rate of return, but they still lag behind other forms of investment and still represent lazy money. The reason these investment accounts are not great investments for you rests in the fact that after paying you for the use of your money, the insurance companies reinvest the funds. They must pay you less than they are making, or they are going to go out of business. Thus, whatever the insurance companies decide to pay you for the use of your funds, it's going to be less than your money is actually earning!

Second, this "savings account" is only useful if you live. If you die, all that your estate receives is the face value of the insurance policy, and all the money you paid into the cash value portion of the policy is forfeited. For example, suppose you purchased $10,000 worth of whole-life insurance and that, after 9 years, the policy had accumulated $5,000 in "cash value." Now this $5,000 "cash value" represents your savings account; it is money you have paid in premiums plus a 3 to 5% return. So far so good. But suppose you die the next year. Your estate would receive only the face value of the insurance policy or $10,000. The $5,000 cash value would be gone with the wind, helping to build a luxury office building for the insurance company.

But suppose you do not die. How valuable is the $5,000 of cash value? Well, the company will allow you to borrow that cash value out of the policy, and it does represent $5,000 you can tap. There is a catch, however. In order to borrow this money, you must pay the insurance company interest. The interest you pay will usually be less than the going interest rate, but considering that this is *your money anyway*, the rationale for your having to pay interest is difficult to understand.

Third, insurance companies cover the possibility of a bad year (more deaths and liabilities than they had anticipated) by charging more in premiums than they actually anticipate using. At the end of the year, they refund this overcharge to the insured and call it a "dividend." If you have received such "dividends," you may have wondered why you do not have to report them on your income tax. The reason is that they are not really "dividends" but rather are a return to you of your overpayment of the premium. Actually, these "dividends" are not paid out but are used to reduce the cost of the next year's premium. Salesmen often point this out and claim that "your" cost of life insurance is actually decreasing. To the extent that the premium decreases, it simply represents an increase in the previous year's overcharging. Your real cost of insurance always increases with your age group. There is no "freezing" of your premium, and don't let any denizen of the million dollar round table tell you differently!

Finally, the salesman receives a very hefty commission from whole-life insurance policies. For you, the investor, this commission represents dead money.

To summarize, cash-value life insurance policies are a combination of pure insurance plus savings. Generally, commissions and handling expenses are taken out of your payments before any premium dollars go into the cash value account. Since the face value of the insurance policy is fixed, no matter how much cash value is in the account, only the face value will be paid should you die. If you want to use the cash value in the policy, the insurance company will charge you interest on your own savings, and many companies will cancel the policy if you withdraw the cash value completely.

The worst thing about cash value insurance policies is their cost. Because of the inefficient savings portion, they are very expensive, and most young doctors cannot afford to buy the amount of insurance protection they need. For these reasons, we do not think that cash-value or whole-life insurance has any place in a financial plan.

The other general category is the pure life (death) insurance, called term insurance. There are several different kinds of term insurance, two of which are most useful.

The first is "renewable" term insurance. A term insurance policy is simply a contract with an insurance company to pay a specified death benefit should the insured die during a specified period of time, usually 5 or 10 years. In return, the insured will pay a fixed premium during the term of the policy. Renewable means that the company agrees to renew the policy for another term at its expiration. Of course, just as with all insurance policies, the risk of dying will increase as the insured gets older, and, therefore, the premiums will increase each time the policy is renewed. These premium increases simply reflect the actuarial certainty that the older you are, the more likely it is that you will die.

Term insurance is the cheapest form of insurance and is very economical for younger people. It represents the only realistic way of providing the amount of life insurance coverage that is needed for the young family. Suppose Sam B., at age 35, has determined that he needs $400,000 of life insurance. He finds that he can buy eight $50,000 10-year renewable term policies for $250 a year each. Therefore, he will have to spend $2,000 a year (8 × $250) to obtain $400,000 worth of insurance. Ten years later, at age 45, Sam wants to renew some of his policies. Since he is 10 years older, the premium on a $50,000 policy is now $350 rather than $250. However, Sam's financial investment program has been going well, and he has managed to acquire $150,000 in other assets during that time. He can therefore partially self-insure himself, drop three of the policies, and renew only five of them for a yearly cost of $1,750. Three years later, one of the children has grown, and Sam's net worth is $200,000. He therefore drops two more of the policies, and his yearly expense is only three times $350 or $1,050 per year. By age 50, his other child has grown, and his assets are worth $300,000, which would provide enough of an estate for his wife. He is now self-insured and drops the remaining three policies. This example illustrates an important objective in insurance planning—to get rid of it, or, rather, the need for it. The goal is to convert "death" insurance to financial independence and self-insurance.

Another type of insurance with much the same effect is "decreasing" term insurance. In decreasing term insurance, the premiums remain constant, but the amount of insurance purchased decreases as the years go by. This is simply a different way of accounting for the increased risk to the company; instead of increasing the premiums, they decrease the benefit. The advantage of decreasing term insurance is that it generally has the lowest cost of any of the types of term policies. Its disadvantage is that it has less flexibility than the renewable term policies and cannot be as easily adjusted to changing financial need. Suppose Sam B. had no will power and, instead of making monthly MyFIP payments into his financial independence program, made monthly payments on a Mercedes 500 and a condo at Aspen. He might find that, after 10 years, he had only accumulated $50,000 in his estate, but his term insurance had decreased $150,000. He would then have a $100,000 shortfall in his insurance coverage. If he were still healthy, he could buy two new term policies, of course. But if he had developed heart trouble during this period, he might find himself uninsurable and would have no way of covering this deficit. (Of course, this will not happen to you because you are going to have the discipline to pay yourself first and make those monthly financial security payments.)

To summarize about life insurance: the best insurance policy is a working spouse. You do not need death insurance if you do not have dependents. The hardest part is figuring out how much you need and accepting that, if you are young and have dependents, it is going to be a whopping amount of insurance. The easy part is deciding what type of insurance to buy. If you are confident of your financial plan, buy decreasing term; if you are more conservative, buy renewable term. Never buy cash-value life insurance.

THE REST

As we mentioned earlier, our experience indicates that most doctors have too little life insurance in the form of high-cost cash-value policies. However, with almost all other types of insurance the reverse seems to be the case. They seem to operate under the principle of "protect me against any risk." In reality, we never use most of the insurance that we own. Your chances of needing any of the various insurance policies are actually quite small. But it is important to keep in mind the basic reason for owning insurance—to be sure that a catastrophic event does not bankrupt your entire financial structure. You should only insure those risks that you could not easily pay for out of salary and savings. Insurance should not be used to eliminate all financial discomfort, only severe pain. You will generate a lot of dead money if you attempt to insure against first-dollar losses for every conceivable risk, and you will be ahead in the long run if you take these dollars and convert them into active money that will, in turn, help you eliminate the need for any insurance.

AUTOMOBILE INSURANCE

The two most important types of auto insurance coverage are public liability and collision. There is also a large selection of options or riders, which can cover everything from cat scratches to towing fees and rental car reimbursements. Public liability insurance is required in nearly every state and is the most important coverage. This is one area in which professionals should be heavily covered, since they are targets for high liability claims. Since the cost of liability insurance is relatively low, we recommend a minimum of $250,000, and a million dollars is probably better.

Collision insurance is a more costly business. Collision covers damage to your own car (damage to the other guy's car is covered by the liability insurance). It is by far the costliest of automobile insurance because of the high cost of auto body work and the large number of claims that are made. It is particularly expensive to obtain first-dollar coverage, and taking a collision policy with a $500 or $1,000 deductible will dramatically decrease its cost. Admittedly, no one likes to take a $500 hit when junior smacks up the family car, but paying a $500 deductible once every 3 years will be cheaper than paying the premiums for first-dollar coverage during that period.

It is also important to remember that collision coverage will never pay for more than the "book value" of your car. If you wipe out the side of your 4-year-old car sustaining $2,600 worth of damage, you will find that the insurance company will declare your car a "total loss" and pay you only the $2,100, which is the current "book value" of the car. It is difficult to get your money's worth out of insurance premiums on older vehicles, and you should consider dropping collision coverage on any car over three years of age.

It is possible to insure your car against practically anything, and the cost appears to be rather low. But consider how often you have needed to rent a car while yours was in the body shop. If you have only had your car towed once in 5 years, you would be better off dropping the towing coverage and buying a pair of jumper cables. Remember that when you buy unneeded insurance coverage, you are converting active dollars into dead dollars.

PROPERTY (HOMEOWNER'S) INSURANCE

Home, office, and personal effects property insurance is another area in which a wide range of perils can be covered. One can insure against anything from a loss by fire to a loss by nuclear war with a corresponding decrease in policy premiums as the likelihood of the event decreases. Again, you must make a personal decision on how much coverage you need. The fact is that most of us have never had a fire, never had vandals in the house, and do not live near a nuclear power plant. Here is an area where it makes sense to have a large deductible so as to have a small premium.

We do not really mind paying for the singed curtains above the kitchen stove ourselves; what we need to insure against is the whole house burning down.

As with car insurance, it is important to carry high levels of personal liability insurance so that when Fido bites the mailman you won't be bankrupt. Fortunately, the liability insurance is cheap.

MALPRACTICE INSURANCE

The malpractice problem is too complicated to discuss in depth here. Although high premiums have caused many doctors to "go bare," we believe this is foolish. It is not pleasant to pay those high premiums, but it will be far less pleasant to see 15 years of financial planning go down the drain with one malpractice suit.

MEDICAL INSURANCE

Medical insurance is usually not a problem for doctors. As with other types of insurance, you can get a lot more for your money if you take as large a deductible as possible. Group insurance is usually cheaper than individual policies, but it is often wise to check this. A group policy may include coverages that you do not need, e.g., maternity benefits.

DISABILITY INSURANCE

It is much more likely that you will need disability insurance than life insurance. Nevertheless, fewer people have disability insurance than life insurance. The principles are the same. Self-insure as much as possible. You certainly do not need to replace your income from the first day you are sick; you will have sick leave, vacation time, and other benefits to tide you over this period. Actuarial experience indicates that most people are back on the job within 6 months, and therefore a policy with a 6-month waiting period can decrease your premiums by as much as 50%. It is also not necessary to completely replace your salary with disability insurance. Try to estimate the absolute minimum benefit level that your family could get by on. Remember that in the event of total disability, you will be eligible for other forms of support such as social security, distributions from retirement and pension plans, and so on. Also, it is unlikely you will be so disabled that you cannot be gainfully employed, even though you might require a change in profession.

SUMMARY

All insurance policies should be designed to insure that a catastrophic event does not bankrupt your family. They should not be used to cover every out-of-pocket expense. The higher the deductible and the more risk you are able to cover yourself, the lower your premium payments will be. Any dead dollars you can rescue from insurance premiums can be applied to investment programs, which, in turn, will hurry you along the road to financial independence and lessen the need for insurance. This will free up even more dollars, and the cycle will accelerate until you are totally self-insured and no longer require insurance policies in any form.

7

TAXES

> There is nothing sinister in arranging one's affairs so as to keep taxes as low as possible
> *—Judge Learned Hand*

Justice Hand's statement still stands as the legal opinion on taxes. An individual is under no obligation to pay more than his minimum taxes. However, there are worse things than paying taxes. Bad investments are a common example. Although it is true that one never goes broke taking profits, it is equally true that paying a dollar in expenses to save 50¢ in taxes is a sure-fire way to avoid capital gains.

In this chapter we shall develop a general strategy for approaching your annual tax bill. The goal is to follow Justice Hand's advice and keep taxes as low as possible, thereby rescuing potential dead dollars from the fatal trip to Washington and converting them into active money in your financial plan. This is a subject most of us take to with a religious fervor. Though the annual tax bill is certainly a good place to look for dead dollars, it is also an easy place to get trapped. In their eagerness to avoid taxes, many doctors make ill-advised "tax-advantaged" investments, which end up losing them more money than they saved in taxes. Sheltering income from taxes is a worthwhile idea, but not if you have to take a loss to do it.

THE NATURE OF THE INCOME TAX

Few things are more condemned in this country than the "tax shelter" or tax "loophole." Every politician, from the most conservative to the most

62

liberal, never passes up an opportunity to speak out against these villainous devices. We are told that they seem to be everywhere and are single-handedly responsible for most of the economic woes in the country. We are told that they are the reason for the federal deficit and why honest citizens (like their constituents) must pay so much in taxes. Of course, these same politicians do not mention that they are the ones who created the "shelters" and "loopholes" in the first place. Every time a new tax law is written, more are created. We need to pause for a moment and consider just what constitutes a tax shelter or tax loophole and why they exist.

If tax laws were written simply to raise revenue for the government to pay its bills, there would be no such thing as a tax shelter. Complications arise when the tax laws are used to modify economic policy or social conditions rather than simply to raise revenue. By altering the way in which individuals and items are taxed, large sums of money can be shifted and large government subsidies provided without their being readily apparent to the public. Many programs that would be politically unpalatable with no chance of passing into law can be effected by (largely ignored) changes in tax laws.

Consider the interest expense deduction, for example. By permitting individuals to deduct interest payments from their income tax, the government is actually subsidizing borrowing. The main beneficiary of this subsidy is the mortgage and housing industry. If you were not permitted to deduct the interest on your mortgage payments from your income tax, you would not be able to carry as large a mortgage, which in turn would mean that you could not buy as expensive a house, which in turn would decrease the overall demand for housing. The government has decided that it wishes to promote home ownership and housing construction in this country; to do so it subsidizes the cost by making interest payments deductible. Exactly the same effect could be obtained by not allowing interest payment deductions but by providing a government grant to each person who takes out a mortgage, the size of the grant dependent on the size of the mortgage. The effect would be the same as permitting interest deductions, but it would probably be extremely difficult for such a massive government subsidy bill ever to be enacted. However, it is a relatively simple matter to effect this policy by creating a tax deduction.

Or consider the tax credit for child care. In the mid-1970s, Congress wished to make it easier for mothers with children to work. They could have passed an appropriations bill giving a grant to each family in which both parents worked. However, this would probably have been politically unpopular. It was much easier to allow the family to take an income tax credit for their child care expenses.

Or consider the individual retirement account (IRA). Part of President Reagan's economic program was based on stimulating savings and investment. In order to reward individuals for doing this, the government could appropriate money to be given as grants or rewards for their investment. This would have been an unpopular appropriation. However, there was little opposition to permitting individuals to establish tax-deferred retirement investment accounts and rewarding them by deferring taxes on the proceeds.

The list could go on and on. Virtually every tax shelter or tax loophole was conceived by thoughtful folk and politicians alike and was created with a definite, usually quite laudatory, economic or social goal in mind. Therefore, tax shelters and tax loopholes, although they do represent governmental meddling in the free market, are not really the devious perversions or careless oversights that election year political rhetoric would like us to believe. Rather, they are well-intentioned (and frequently very effective) methods of managing the country.

Problems arise when clever individuals attempt to use the tax benefits for purposes for which they were not originally intended or when the economic situations that generated the tax shelter no longer hold. For example, consider the oil depletion allowance. This is a form of accelerated depreciation on oil-producing land that, in effect, meant that an individual did not have to pay as high a tax on his oil well as on other types of income. An oil well is a depleting asset; some day it will run dry and be worthless. In an attempt to compensate the owner for this future loss, he is granted a break on his current taxes. This is done to make it more attractive to go out and discover oil, which is considered a vital national resource. However, when OPEC dramatically raised the price of oil, the profit in American oil wells soared and made the old break seem unnecessary and unfair. The windfall profits tax was enacted to try to correct some of the imbalance.

The point to keep in mind is that tax shelters, or "tax-advantaged investments" as they are now being called, do not result from some bureaucratic oversight but represent a conscious, planned government policy. They were all designed to stimulate some part of the economy or promote some seemingly useful but otherwise unprofitable activity. You should feel no compunction against using any and all that you can. However, it is just as important to realize that they are not lucky breaks or found money. Just because they exist does not mean that they are good for you as an individual. Some may be appropriate in your financial plan, and others may be a disaster. Do not use a tax shelter simply because it is available; use it only if it ultimately increases your financial independence.

THE CHANGING TAX ENVIRONMENT

Since 1974, there have been three major pieces of tax legislation (ERISA, ERTA, and TEFRA, to use the government's penchant for acronyms) that have made many significant changes in the tax structure. Although some of the effects of this legislation are uncertain, one thing that is certain is that they have created a very bullish environment for accountants and tax lawyers. We shall outline some of the important changes and how they affect financial planning and the investment process. It is important to be aware of these changes because many salesmen and even some financial advisors are still trying to tailor today's investments to yesterday's tax environment. Investors are often fighting the last war.

Perhaps the most significant change has been the reduction of the top marginal income tax bracket from 70 to 50% for all sources of income (the previous 50% ceiling applied only to personal earned income). This, coupled with the significant drop in the inflation rate in the early 1980s, has created a climate that provides considerable incentive for savings and investment. It has also decreased the value of many tax shelters.

Let's consider the net after-tax return on a hypothetical investment in the late 1970s and in 1983. Suppose that Sam B. earned $1,500 on a $10,000 investment for a 15% rate of return. Let's see what happened to his $1,500 after taxes and inflation:

	1979	*1983*
Gross income	$1,500	$1,500
Less marginal income tax	− 1,050	− 750
Net income	450	750
Plus original capital ($10,000)	10,450	10,750
Less inflation decrease in value	− 1,254	− 535
Net assets	$9,196	$10,215
Net rate of return	− 8%	+ 2%

Thus, in 1979, the combination of high inflation and high marginal tax bracket made a conventional investment with a 15% return a losing proposition, whereas in 1983, the same investment has a positive net return. In 1979, this would have been a lazy money investment, and in 1983, it had become an active money investment. In 1979, it might have made sense to consider a risky but potentially high rate of return tax shelter that would make much less sense in 1983. In 1979, tax-sheltered returns were highly desirable even if the merits of the underlying investment were questionable. In 1983, the underlying success of the investment is considerably more important because less of the profit is taxed away by the IRS and inflation.

Another important change is the overall decrease in tax rates. In 1981, a married couple filing jointly reached the maximum 50% tax bracket when their income was $60,000 per year, but by 1984 they will not reach the 50% bracket until their income is $162,400. In an additional attempt to stimulate investment, the maximum tax on long-term capital gains has been reduced to 20% (that is, 40% of the investor's tax bracket—thus, a maximum tax of 20%: $0.40 \times 50\% = 20\%$). The holding period to qualify as a long-term capital gain was also reduced from 1 year to 6 months.

Not all taxes have been reduced however. Many of the previous tax shelters have been eliminated. Particularly important was the initiation of the "at-risk" rule, which effectively gutted many of the more lucrative shelters. Before this rule went into effect, it was possible for limited partnerships to produce large "paper" losses that resulted in considerable tax savings. But these "tax losses" were fictional; the individual investor did not actually lose this money. Now, an investor can only deduct losses for which he is actually "at risk"—money that he theoretically can (and very likely will) lose. (We shall take a detailed look at how a limited partnership works in a moment.)

The real sleeper in the recent tax legislation has been the increase in the alternative minimum tax. In effect, this tax means that everyone, regardless of any tax deductions or breaks for which he qualifies, must pay at least 20% of his adjusted gross income in taxes. Since the average doctor only pays between 25 and 30% of his income in taxes, this means that there is not a tremendous amount of money to be wrung out of the Form 1040.

The net effect of all of these changes has been to increase the importance of more traditional and less risky investments and to decrease the value of the high-risk tax shelter.

THE BEST TAX SHELTER

There continues to be one very important tax shelter, which should be the basis of your tax-saving strategy. This is the tax-deferred retirement plan. Because of extensive publicity we all are familiar with the individual retirement account (IRA) and the fact that you can place up to $2,000 a year in such an account and write it off your taxes. This means that if you put $2,000 into an investment in an IRA, you will actually pay only $1,000, and the government will pay the other $1,000 (a sort of government matching program). It does not take any great insight to see that this is a bargain. Every eligible person in the United States should put $2,000 in an IRA every year—preferably on January 1st.

But an even greater advantage is the fact that the government does not tax the income earned by an IRA investment. Suppose your $2,000 investment earns $300 on a 15% rate of return. If you made the investment outside of your IRA, you would have to pay $150 tax on these earnings, so you would only be left with $150, and your real rate of return would have been only 7.5%. However, if the investment was made in the IRA, while it remains in the IRA it will not be taxed, and you will get to reinvest the entire $300 (the matching plan applies to earnings as well as contributions). This is a real, hidden value in the IRA (and other tax-deferred investment programs). The fact that the earnings are not taxed effectively doubles the number of active investment dollars available. Using an IRA is like taking $1,000 out of your pocket, retrieving another $1,000 from the revenuers, and placing $2,000 in your own investment program earning tax-deferred income. If you invest in a mutual fund (more on this later), your money hits the ground running and begins earning additional compounding dollars from the moment you open the account. This is an advantage over many tax shelters, which often lose money for years until the hoped-for "big payoff" at some time in the future.

The term *retirement* in IRAs is really inappropriate and deters many people. "I will probably be dead before I retire. Why should I throw away money on a retirement plan when there is that nice new sports coat in the window?" You must stop thinking of these tax-deferred programs as "retirement plans" and start thinking of them as "tax-sheltered investment plans." Because both the income and contributions to these investment programs are tax deferred, they produce geometrically more (because of compounding) income than the same unsheltered investment. IRA funds can actually be borrowed for short periods with no penalty or taxes as long as the funds are replaced. There is no reason that the assets in retirement plans must be held until retirement. You can withdraw them and spend them whenever you like. True, the government will make you pay a 10% tax penalty if you do this before age 59½, but this is really peanuts compared to the extra return you receive from the tax deferment. Table 7.1 illustrates how this works by comparing the value of a $2,000 investment in an IRA and the same investment made outside of the IRA shelter. Both figures have been corrected for all taxes; that is, the figures in the IRA column show the net return you would have after having paid both the income tax and the 10% penalty for withdrawing the money from the retirement account.

We can see from this example that for the first 5 years the tax penalty for early withdrawal from the IRA eats up more than the gains from the tax shelter. However, in the fifth year the IRA return pulls ahead, and after that it steadily outdistances the other investment. In 20 years the same investment will have produced more than twice as much disposable income

TABLE 7.1 Net (after all taxes) return
on a $2,000 investment
at 10%

Year	Outside IRA	In IRA
1	$1,050	$ 880
2	1,102	968
3	1,158	1,065
4	1,215	1,171
5	1,276	1,288
15	2,079	3,334
20	2,653	5,382

in the IRA as it would have outside it! Of course, if funds are withdrawn after the age of 59½, there is no 10% penalty, which further improves the relative IRA versus non-IRA return. This example used a relatively modest 10% rate of return. If the rate of return is higher, the break-even point occurs earlier, the difference in the figures becomes more marked, and the IRA has an even greater advantage.

You may be wondering why the returns in this example are way below the $2,000 investment. Remember that these are after-tax returns, and it illustrates what a big bite taxes take out of all our earnings. But also remember that even though you invest $2,000 in the IRA, you get $1,000 of this back on your taxes, so that your actual investment was only $1,000 out of your own pocket, and you will actually be experiencing a positive rate of return by the third year.

This example should make it clear how valuable the "retirement" tax deferred investment is in any financial independence program. Do not consider it retirement money; consider it investment money in your financial plan. More than likely you will withdraw some of the money prematurely and have to pay the 10% tax penalty, but if you wait only 5 years, you will still be ahead of the game.

The problem with the IRA is that you can't put much money into it. At $2,000 a year, you are not going to make much overall progress toward your financial goal. Fortunately an individual IRA is only the tip of the retirement tax-deferred iceberg. First, your spouse is also eligible for a $2,000 IRA if he or she works. It does not have to be full-time work, just some occupation. Bake some cookies. Sell some ties. Write a feature article for the local paper. Or hire your spouse to do some filing for you. Just find some type of minimal employment for your spouse so that you can put another $2,000 into an IRA. Now you are up to $4,000 per year. And,

$4,000 tax deferred per year compounding at 12% tax deferred for 20 years is *lots* of money. Look it up in the tables! You are on your way!

If you are self-employed, as most doctors are, you can also set up a Keogh Plan, which has the same tax advantages as an IRA but has the additional advantage that you can put up to $30,000 into it yearly. This can be a significant amount of money for most doctors and can constitute the major portion of their financial investment program. (There is a catch with Keogh Plans, however. You must make the same percentage contribution for all of your employees as you do for yourself. This should prove no great problem, since it constitutes a very valuable fringe benefit for the employees.)

Doctors who are incorporated or who practice in incorporated groups can set up corporate retirement plans, which are similar to IRAs and Keoghs, into which contributions up to 25% of the employee's income can be placed. If your practice situation permits it, you should definitely set up such a plan in consultation with your tax attorney. Make the maximum legal contribution of 25% of your income, and you will have funded most of your financial independence program all tax deferred! If you add to this your IRA and your spouse's IRA, you will probably have nearly fully funded the target investment amount of 25 to 30% of your income and will not have to take money from elsewhere for your financial program. And the beauty of it is that while you are contributing nearly 30% of your income toward your future financial security, you are doing it tax deferred and receiving over twice the return of ordinary investments.

OTHER TAX SAVINGS

Compared to the benefits of the tax-deferred retirement plans, most other tax savings are peanuts. Nevertheless, a peanut here and there can still amount to a hearty meal, and you should not overlook any reasonable opportunities to save taxes. The best way to go about this is to make sure you maximize your legitimate deductions. Most of us have far more legitimate deductions than we realize simply because we are careless and don't think about them. Of course everyone knows about the interest deduction and the deduction for other taxes paid and the fact that you can claim $500 to $1,000 of charity deductions with little documentation. What you are likely to overlook, however, is the potential for business-related deductions.

The government allows you to legitimately deduct any expenses that are useful for you in your business, either to improve the quality of the service you provide or to generate new business. In the tax sense, your "business" is anything you do that earns income or is intended to earn income on which you pay taxes. Thus, in addition to your business of being a doctor and generating fees for your services, you may also be in the "business" of giving lectures, consulting, or being an investor. Anything you read or buy to help you in your investments (such as this book) is tax deductible. If you are thinking about buying a condominium in Florida to generate rental income and want to go down and have a look at it first, that is a legitimate deduction. If you speak to the local medical society about your latest medical technique and receive an honorarium, you are in the lecturing "business." Costs related to producing these lectures (such as a camera to make slides) are deductions. Do you make educational video tapes on your VCR? If so, then the VCR, camera, and TV used to produce these tapes are a business expense.

By now you probably get the idea. It is really very simple and something of a game. Every time you spend money on something, take a moment and think to yourself: "Could this be tax deductible? Is it somehow related to some income I am producing and, therefore, a legitimate deduction?" Be creative and liberal in your interpretations. As long as you are not too far out in left field, the IRS will likely go along with you. (You probably cannot deduct the cost of your new TV set as a business expense because you watch Wall Street Week.)

A most important factor in selling these deductions to the IRS is to have adequate documentation. You must keep extensive and accurate records of your expenses at the time they occur. A carefully maintained log will usually head off any IRS inquiry into the validity of the expense. One of the easiest ways to implement this is to obtain a charge card that you use only for expenses that are of a "business" nature. When you pay for these expenses, simply write the date and purpose of the expenses on the back of your copy of the charge slip and keep it in your records. When it comes time to fill out your tax return, you will have all the slips ready so that you do not forget about any of the deductions, and they will also be there to document the deduction should you be audited. Of course, the IRS may disallow the deduction, but nothing ventured is nothing gained.

Another important principle to bear in mind is that small is beautiful. You can probably get away with a four-person luncheon to solicit patient referrals from other doctors, but if you invite 300 people to a New Year's Eve party and try to write it off, you probably won't get away with it.

It is also important not to get carried away with the deduction business and start spending money simply because you can deduct it on your taxes. Remember that the tax deduction only means that the government is paying half the bill; you are still paying the other half, and a person can quickly go broke spending a dollar to save 50¢ in taxes. It is easy to get lulled by the magic of the deduction and think that the whole trip is free. The best advice is to make your expenditure decisions independent of their tax consequences. If you would have spent the money regardless of taxes, go ahead and do it. After the money has been spent, just be certain that you deduct it if possible.

Although most people shudder at the idea, we think playing the tax game is actually fun. We look at Form 1040 as a game board in which we are locked in a struggle with the Internal Revenue Service, seeing who can lay the most creative and clever claim for tax dollars. The unique aspect of this game is that it is for real. If you can arrange it so that you get an extra $300 deduction, you have made yourself $150! Viewed in that light, the importance of doing a careful and thorough job on your tax return takes on new meaning. Don't think of it as onerous drudgery but rather as an opportunity to pick up some easy money that would otherwise go, by default, to Washington.

We believe that everyone should fill out his own tax forms rather than having a tax service or your friend, the tax accountant, do it. There are a couple of reasons for this. First, it is not really that hard. Despite their formidable appearance, the tax forms are written in fairly straightforward language, and anyone who can get through medical school certainly has the capability of understanding them. You cannot do it overnight, of course, and you should start in January and devote a few hours a week to the process with a goal of having the return completed by April. Using a spread sheet or data base management program on your personal computer to keep track of deductions as you go through the year can be an invaluable time saver as well as an efficient record-keeping system. In doing this you will find that it is not a great problem, and you will discover all kinds of interesting and creative ways to save tax dollars.

For example, are you familiar with Schedule C? Schedule C is for reporting income from a private business or profession and is much better than Schedule B (personal itemized deductions only). Its main advantage is that it has many lines for deductions. If you are used to itemizing your deductions on Schedule B, you find that there are only three or four lines labeled "miscellaneous deductions" into which you must squeeze most of your new creative write-offs. Schedule C has a whole page of lines, many labeled and just begging for deduction entries. A deduction taken on one of these lines is potentially far less likely to be audited than one squeezed into the miscellaneous deduction portion of Schedule B. Report as much income as possible on Schedule C, and you will find taking deductions much easier.

The second reason for preparing your taxes yourself is that the tax return can be no better than the raw data that goes into it. You will not be able to sustain a deduction unless you can adequately document it, and if you have to go to all the trouble of collecting the raw data and documentation for your tax preparer, you might as well go ahead and put the numbers on the blank yourself. You must remember that your tax preparer does not really know all the ways you earn income and all the things you do that might be tax deductible, and it is unlikely that he will be able to think of as many deductions as you can.

Finally, it costs a lot of money to have taxes prepared. Unless you are hopelessly awed by the tax forms, you will get better value for your money if you do them yourself. This is simply an extension of the basic philosophy of this entire book. When it comes to your personal financial matters, no one is going to be as interested in your affairs or do as good a job for you as you will do for yourself. (Being creative, you might be aware that your colleagues have as much trouble with taxes as you do, so you could set this whole system up, buy a personal computer, some software, hire your teenage daughter to solicit clients and run the tax-prep programs, call it "Tax-Docs" in Subchapter S, and write the whole expense off!)

WHATEVER HAPPENED TO THE GOOD OLD LOOPHOLE?

As we said earlier in this chapter, there is very little "found money" left to be made in tax shelters. The excessive write-offs of yesteryear have mostly been eliminated by the "at-risk" rule and the alternative minimum tax. All that remains of many of the previous tax shelters is their high investment risk. But, just because most tax shelters are no longer a good investment does not mean that they are not being aggressively sold, particularly to doctors. If you are like most doctors, you probably receive several solicitations a year to participate in "tax-advantaged investments." Most of these are in the form of limited partnerships, and most of them are bad investments. Not only will you not get the tax breaks promised, you will likely lose most or all of your money. Even if you do get some positive return, you will lose considerable liquidity, and the compound rate of return of the investment will probably be lower than you could have obtained in other, less risky vehicles.

Some tax shelters will be valuable, but you must pick and choose very carefully among the offerings. To demonstrate the problems you can get into, we will show an example from an actual solicitation that was mailed to a large group of doctors in New England in mid-1983.

This offering was for the purchase and subsequent lease back of new condominium units being built at "The Hermitage" (not its real name), a cluster condominium project in a wealthy and tourist-oriented New England town. Eight condominium units were available. Most were two-bedroom townhouses with a study and either a garage or a parking space. The offering price of $180,000 was about 20% higher than the price that similar units in the same general area had been selling for, but several condominiums had been built in the region, and they had all generally sold well. In addition, there was a good market for expensive housing in this particular town, and housing and condominium prices had shown a slow but steady increase in the 1980s at a time when housing prices in general were decreasing. Therefore, although the units were more expensive than the general market conditions, their price did not seem to be grossly excessive.

Moreover, there was very liberal financing: only 10% down payment was necessary, and the balance could be financed for 30 years at 10% interest. To increase the attractiveness of the investment, the developer was offering a lease-back arrangement whereby he would guarantee monthly rentals for 5 years' time. The offering was packaged with a financial analysis showing what appeared to be an irresistible investment opportunity. This first-year financial analysis is shown in Table 7.2.

On the basis of the bottom line of Table 7.2, it appears that an investment in one of these condominium units would produce a $5,000 positive cash flow and represent a 30% return on the investment. However, there are some dangerous pitfalls in this offering. First look at the actual cash flow as outlined in item III, *Operating information*. We can see that the developer guarantees $13,200 of income from the property. However, the investor has considerably more than this in out-of-pocket expenses. There are $3,000 of taxes, $1,000 condominium fee, $700 in insurance, and a whopping $17,000 in debt service. The actual net cash flow for the first year in operation is − $8,391. This means that the investor will have to come up with $8,391 a year or $700 a month out of his own pocket to meet the cash flow of the unit. This is in addition to the $17,750 he already has invested as down payment.

So where is the advantage? It is outlined in item IV, *Taxable income*. There is no taxable income. It is all tax losses. First, there is the $8,391 actual out-of-pocket expense. Next, there is the accelerated depreciation on the building, which is $19,020, and the accelerated depreciation on the equipment, which is $600. This is reduced slightly by the equity that is built up in the first year, but the net tax losses are $27,123. This is then interpreted as a tax saving of $13,561. How does this work? Well, if the investor is indeed able to deduct the entire $27,000 from his taxable income, he will be able to save $13,000 in tax payments. Without these deductions, he would have to write out a $13,000 check and send it off to Washington; with them, he can keep the $13,000 in the bank (to help him meet his $700 a month expenses). The final analysis implies that the investor will actually

TABLE 7.2 "The Hermitage," first full year of ownership

I.	Purchase information	
	Price	$177,500
	Cash invested	17,750
	Mortgage (90%)	159,750
	Debt service payments, 10%, 30 years	16,823
II.	Cost and depreciation	
	Land	15,000
	Building	158,500
	Equipment	4,000
	Total	177,500
	Depreciation method	
	Building, ACRS 15 years	
	Equipment, ACRS 5 years	
III.	Operating information	
	Guaranteed minimum revenues	13,200
	Operating expense	
	Taxes (estimated)	3,000
	Condominium association fee	1,068
	Insurance	700
	Operating cash flow	8,432
	Interest payments	15,935
	Principal payments	888
	Net cash flow (pretax)	<8,391>
IV.	Taxable income	
	Net cash flow (pretax)	<8,391>
	Depreciation, building (full year)	<19,020>
	Depreciation, equipment (full year)	<600>
	Principal payment (add back)	888
	Taxable income	<27,123>
	Tax savings @50%	13,561
V.	After-tax cash flow	
	Net pretax cash flow	<8,391>
	Tax benefits	13,561
	After-tax cash flow	5,170
	Cash invested	17,750
	After-tax return current basis on after-tax cash flow	29.12%

Brackets indicate a loss.

be ahead $5,000 at the end of the year because he will have saved $13,000 in taxes while only having to pay $8,000 in operating expenses. Where does the extra money come from? It arises because the investor is taking "paper losses" on his taxes in the form of building depreciation. He does not actually have to make these payments out of his pocket, and, therefore, he is getting a tax break for an expense he has not actually experienced.

So where are the problems? There are several.

The first problem is the alternative minimum tax. The developer's analysis implies that a $27,000 tax write-off will be converted into $13,000 of tax savings. Because of the alternative minimum tax, this is probably not so. Let's see how it would actually effect the income taxes of Sam B., our typical doctor. If we assume that his tax return looks like that of the average physician or dentist, he will have approximately $100,000 in total income and $96,000 in adjusted gross income. After subtracting $15,000 for item-ized deductions and exemptions, he is left with a taxable income of $81,000, on which he will owe $27,000 of taxes. He is in the 49% marginal tax bracket.

Now, what would be the effect of adding another $27,000 to his current $15,000 of deductions. It would drop his taxable income to $54,000, on which he would owe $15,000 of taxes. Thus, it would appear that he has saved $12,000 in taxes ($15,000 versus the $27,000 he owed without the new deduction). The $12,000 savings is somewhat less than the $13,000 calculated by the developer because, with the new deduction, Sam is no longer in the 50% tax bracket but only in the 44% bracket.

However, because of the large deductions, Sam can no longer use the regular tax tables but is liable for the new alternative minimum tax. The alternative minimum tax is calculated by taking the adjusted gross income, subtracting the ordinary deductions, and adding back any tax-shelter-type items. This amount is then subject to a 20% tax. In Sam's case, the adjusted gross income of $96,000 is reduced by the $15,000 of ordinary deductions for a first total of $81,000. Now Sam must add back to this figure that portion of his new $27,000 deduction that is considered tax advantaged. All of the depreciation expenses and some of the operating loss will fall into this category, and Sam will probably have to add back about $24,000, giving him a minimum taxable income of $105,000. His income tax will be 20% of this amount or $21,000!

In actual practice Sam has not converted his $27,000 of deduction into $13,000 of tax savings. He has only saved $6,000 in taxes ($27,000 before versus $21,000 with the tax shelter). Therefore, the analysis in item V, *After-tax cash flow*, should be changed; instead of $13,000 of tax benefits, there are only $6,000 of tax benefits, and the net after-tax cash flow is a $2,000 loss rather than a $5,000 gain! Instead of making 29% on his $17,000 investment, Sam will actually have lost 11%! And that is only the first year. Each year that he keeps his new investment, he loses another 11%.

The alternative minimum tax is not the only problem. Some day Sam will want to sell his condominium. He is assuming that the price will go up, but this is not necessarily so. Remember that he has already paid a price greater than the market value at a time when general real estate prices are stable and the condominium market in this town is becoming saturated. It is possible that Sam may have difficulty in selling his condominium for even what he paid for it. (If his purchase price were really a good deal, the developer would not have to offer the lease-back agreement to attract buyers.) In addition to his negative cash flow, Sam has assumed a considerable risk of capital loss in his investment.

But suppose things do not go too badly, and after five years Sam is able to sell the condominium for $200,000. It would appear that he has made a $22,500 profit over his purchase price. But wait a minute! Sam will still have to pay taxes on his capital gain. Now the accelerated depreciation that was creating the tax losses in the earlier years will come back to haunt him. After five years he has depreciated the building $100,000, so that his purchase price or cost basis for tax purposes is not $177,500, but only $77,500. Thus, he has a taxable gain of not just $22,500 but $122,500! Admittedly, this is a long-term capital gain, which is only subject to 20% tax, but the 20% tax bill on $122,000 is $24,000. Therefore, instead of a $22,500 profit, Sam actually has a $1,500 loss on the total investment. Actually, his tax bill will probably be higher since long-term capital gains are considered a tax preference item and, as he has a large amount of long-term capital gains in this tax year, he may find that he once again is subject to the alternative minimum tax.

There are still more problems with tax shelters—time value and risk. The salesman will say something like this: "You invest $10,000 in this condo. It loses money for 10 years, and then we sell it for $50,000." A 5:1 (translated, 500%) return, right? Probably not. *You* must adjust this for the time value of the investment; do not forget that if all you do is put the $10,000 in a CD at 12% it would be worth—certainly—$31,058 in 10 years, whereas the promised $50,000 sale price of the condominium may be more in the mind of the salesman than in the bank! You should be paid for taking risks. The compensation on this risky investment should be an order of magnitude greater than the return on a riskless treasury bill investment.

The old-style tax shelters of the 1960s and 1970s are not appropriate for the 1980s. Although there may still be a few bargains around, the percentages are definitely against you, and we think you should steer clear. Bleak as the picture we have painted is, it is getting worse. You may find a really good investment that is also a tax shelter only to have the Federal Government change the rules before the shelter has gone full cycle. Many have had this experience already, and we need look no further than the March 12, 1984 issue of *Barron's* and read about "Exposed Shelters, Washington Takes Dead Aim at Wall Street's Tax Schemes" to know that there is political risk aplenty still present in the shelter business.

The reason for this is pretty easy to understand. There are many voters worried about $200 billion budget deficits, but there are only a few stockbrokers worried about the closing of another tax shelter loophole; and even a politician can tell the difference between a stockbroker and a voter. You are already receiving an excellent tax break in your retirement plans. Do not neutralize the gains you make in this area with losses in risky tax shelters.

ESTATE PLANNING

The government has compressed the old saw, "nothing is certain but death and taxes," into a single document, Form 706, the Federal Estate Tax Return. With apologies to Jacques Brel, death and taxes are alive and well and living in Form 706. Before leaving the topic of taxes, we should be aware of some of the basic principles of dealing with this unsavory document in order to minimize (and, we hope, eliminate) its ravages.

Most people view estate taxes at any level as being unfair. After all, taxes have already been paid on all of the assets in an individual's estate, so why tax them again at the time of death? Estate taxes were not created to raise revenues but rather to break up and recirculate large concentrations of wealth. Estate taxes help channel the wealth concentrated in certain families back into the economy. Some proponents of estate taxes have contended that without such levies, all the wealth in the nation would eventually be held by fewer than 100 families. Thus, the goal of estate taxes is not to penalize the small or medium-sized estate but to help redistribute wealth from the large estates.

One of the changes brought about by the recent tax laws has been the liberalization of the amount of estate that can be transferred tax-free. In 1981, this was $175,000, but by 1987, only estates with net assets greater than $600,000 will be liable for estate tax. These changes effectively mean that the majority of Americans will no longer be subjected to these taxes. However, it is quite likely that the financial plan of a doctor could easily result in an estate greater than $600,000, and, therefore, it is important that you make plans to minimize taxes when this occurs. Even if you do not believe your estate is going to hit the $600,000 mark, it is worthwhile to develop a strategy in case inflation or a cyclical surge in your investments catapults assets into much higher valuations than you anticipate at this time.

BALANCING ASSETS

The basic goal of estate planning is to pass assets from parents to children with minimal taxation. Both parents can make use of the $600,000 exemption if they have planned well. Problems arise because parents usually do not die at the same time. When the first parent dies, an exemption "dies" as well and the surviving spouse is left with only a single exemption to apply to the entire estate. Estate planning strategies concentrate on "balancing the assets," that is, distributing ownership of parents' assets evenly between the spouses and children to ensure that both parental exemptions can be utilized. This is easiest to understand by looking at an example. Assume that Sam and Sara B. have combined property worth $1.5 million and that this property is held jointly with right of survivorship (the most common form of property ownership among married persons). Table 7.3 shows the effect of taxes without estate planning.

Suppose Sam dies in 1987. Since the family assets were held as joint tenants in common, they would pass directly (and untaxed) to Sara who now assumes total ownership of $1.5 million. So far things are not too bad. But in 1989 Sara dies. Since Sara's estate is quite large—$1.5 million—the $600,000 exemption does not go too far and the estate taxes are

TABLE 7.3 Total estate taxes without estate planning

Sam and Sara B.'s
assets held as joint tenants in common
$1,500,000

↓

Sam B. dies (1987)
Assets pass to Sara

↓

Sara's total assets
$1,500,000

↓

Sara B. dies (1989)

Gross estate	$1,500,000
Exempt from tax	600,000
Estate tax	394,639

Total estate taxes $394,639

$394,639. Although the children still receive a considerable inheritance, a significant amount of money is going to Uncle Sam.

Now let's look at the effect of a little estate planning on this same scenario. The basis of the estate planning is that Sam establishes a trust fund to which he wills some of the family assets (such as his life insurance). The beneficiaries of the trust fund are the children and not Sara. This maneuver creates a separate estate for Sam and his $600,000 exemption can be applied to these assets, which will pass directly to the trust fund in the children's benefit. This money will not be subject to further taxes when Sara dies. Sara retains outright ownership of the remaining family assets and, at her death, her $600,000 exemption can also be applied. If Sam sets up the trust so that roughly half the assets pass into it at his death only $111,000 will be paid in estate taxes rather than the $394,639 that would have been paid with no planning. Table 7.4 shows how this works assuming that Sam wills one-half of the family assets to the trust fund.

TABLE 7.4 Total estate taxes with estate planning

Sam and Sara B.'s
assets held as joint tenants in common
$1,500,000

Sam B. dies (1987)
Left to trust   Left to Sara

Children's trust assets   Sara's remaining assets

Gross estate	$750,000		$750,000
Exempt from tax	600,000		
Estate tax	55,500		
Trust assets after tax	694,500		

Sara B. dies (1989)

Gross estate	$750,000
Exempt from tax	600,000
Estate tax	55,500

$694,500
(free of further taxes)

Total estate taxes $111,000

There are many types of trust funds that can be used for the benefit of the children, and it is beyond the scope of this book to go into them. An attorney who specializes in tax and estate planning can provide all of the individual details and benefits. So that you can have a little information to take to the first meeting with the trust lawyer, we have included in Appendix E a brief list of the names of some of the currently available trusts and a brief descriptive statement about what they are intended to accomplish. However the list is merely meant to be a starting point and for general information. An important aspect of these trusts is that although the assets do not enter the estate but rather pass directly to the children, the surviving spouse does not have to be excluded from benefits. Although Sam B. willed his estate to the children's trust fund, the organization of the fund was such that Sara was able to directly draw money from it during her lifetime. Income produced by these trusts can be paid directly to the surviving spouse and is available to meet living expenses in much the same manner as if the assets were owned by the survivor. At Sara's death, the assets remaining in the trust fund would be distributed among the surviving children. (In practice, both Sam and Sara should set up survivor trusts in the event Sara dies before Sam.)

GIFTS

Another provision in the recent tax laws provides that each spouse can give $10,000 a year tax-free to as many individuals as he or she chooses. This means that a husband and wife can give $20,000 a year to each of their children without incurring a tax liability (although these gifts do decrease the estate tax deduction). This liberal gift allowance provides another means whereby parents can transfer ownership of funds to their children without incurring a tax liability. You may hesitate to consider giving each of your children $20,000 a year over the course of several years, but you must realize that you are almost certainly going to ultimately leave them all of your property anyway. By doling it out in relatively small parcels over a period of years, you simply avoid giving some of it to Uncle Sam as well.

Interest-free loans have been another popular technique used to decrease taxes. The method usually involves the issuance of an interest-free demand loan from the parent (50% income tax bracket) to the child (lower tax bracket). The interest earned on the money is thus taxed at a much lower rate than if the parent merely took the interest as income. The IRS has been actively pursuing ways to close or reduce the benefits of this technique and in the IRS information release 84-60, the IRS has established criteria for establishing the gift values of interest-free demand loans. As in all areas of tax law and tax policy, investors should work carefully with their tax advisors to keep abreast of this continually changing area which is so important to investment success. The status of interest-free demand loans to children and other family members will undoubtedly evolve throughout the decade of the 1980s, and those using this technique should be prepared for changes and perhaps reinterpretation of the status of previously made interest-free loans.

GETTING IT TOGETHER

Estate planning is probably the most individualized aspect of all financial planning. Not only do the sizes of estates vary, but attitudes toward inheritance (who gets what) and disposition of estates are an extremely personal matter. To further complicate matters, the probate and estate tax laws vary widely from state to state, and both state and federal laws are being continually modified. In dealing with estate planning, every investor should consult with an attorney who specializes in such matters. He will be able to advise you of the most effective plan for distributing your wealth at your death in a manner you most desire. Whether you give it to prodigal children or the Unification Church, your overall objectives should be to minimize taxation of your estate so that your beneficiaries will receive the largest nest egg possible.

8

STOCKS

Having looked at the time and money components of the financial independence equation, it is now time to turn our attention to judicious investments. In the next six chapters we shall take a look at a variety of investment vehicles that are available, see the mechanics of how they work, and attempt to get a perspective on when they are judicious and when they are injudicious. We shall begin by looking at stocks, since we believe that they will prove to be most judicious investments in the 1980s.

CORPORATE FINANCING

A corporation requires capital to operate, which it acquires through the sale of three basic instruments: bonds, common stock, and preferred stock.

When a corporation borrows money, it issues a bond to the lender. A bond is, in effect, a company's I.O.U. It is an agreement by the company to repay the loan on a fixed date in the future and, in the interim, pay a fixed amount of interest to the bondholder. Thus, a bondholder becomes a creditor of the company. He does not actually own the company, has no voting rights, and has nothing to say about how the business is run. In return, the bondholder has considerable security since the interest on a bond and its face value must be paid before a company can distribute dividends to common or preferred stockholders. Since the interest payment of a bond is fixed, the bondholder does not participate in the success or failure— short of bankruptcy—of the company directly. Bonds do participate indirectly, however. If the company is successful, the security of the bonds will be enhanced, and this will be reflected in a somewhat greater value; on the other hand, if the company fails, there may not be enough money to repay the loan. We shall take a more detailed look at bonds in the next chapter.

COMMON STOCK

The actual ownership of a company is represented by its common stock. The common stockholders are the owners of the company and have voting power and control over company management. The fortunes of the common stock are tied to the success of the company, and, if business goes well, it is the common stockholder who will do the best. Company profits are divided among the common stockholders and are usually paid quarterly in the form of dividends. As profits increase, dividends increase. On the other hand, if business is bad, the dividend may be cut or eliminated. Dividends and earnings establish the ultimate value of the common stock. In other words, the main reason for owning a company is to participate in its profits, and, over the long haul, this is the main investment value of common stock.

Of course, most of us are used to thinking of the value of common stock as its selling price rather than the dividend it commands. It is the current market price that is quoted in the daily newspaper and is the most readily apparent measure of the stock's worth. Although on any given day the market price of a stock may be much higher than warranted by its current dividend, such a relationship will not hold forever, and there are very few stocks that will maintain their price unless they also produce income in the form of dividends. Although this may seem to be an obvious point, it is easily forgotten by most investors who concentrate solely on a stock for its current market price. It is important to remember that a common stock can make money for its owner in two ways, either through capital appreciation in the form of increased market price or through sharing in the profits of the company through dividends.

Common stockholders, as owners of the company, stand to benefit most when the company does well, but they also risk the most should business be unprofitable. All other obligations and creditors of the company must be paid in full before any dividends can be paid to common stockholders. In the event that the company must liquidate, the common stockholder stands at the end of the line in his claim for proceeds. There is more risk and more reward in common stock than in other forms of investing in corporate America. There are times when the risks in stock outweigh the rewards, and there are times—we believe the 1980s decade is one—when the rewards outweigh the risks. Investments in corporate stock of sound companies operating in fundamental and profitable markets provide the promise of excellent long-term total returns (dividends plus market appreciation). The larger New York Stock Exchange companies have averaged greater than 12% annual total return over many years.

PREFERRED STOCK

Preferred stock is a hybrid security possessing some of the attributes of a bond and some of common stock. A preferred stock pays a fixed dividend, which must be paid before any common stock dividends. The preferred stock dividend is also usually higher than the common dividend, and most preferred stock dividends are cumulative; that is, all preferred dividends that were previously omitted (perhaps when the company was having some hard times) must be paid in full before any dividends can be paid on common stock. Preferred stock may sometimes also be convertible into shares of common stock at a specified price. Preferred stock, although somewhat safer than common stock, does not have the growth potential of the common and will not appreciate as much if the company prospers. The price of a preferred stock is not guaranteed by the company, as is the face value of a bond. Also, all interest on bonds must be paid before any preferred dividends. Therefore, preferred stock does not have as much security as a comparable bond from the same company. Finally, most preferred stock can be repurchased or "called" by the company for a predetermined price. This call price effectively limits the amount a preferred stock can rise in price.

We believe that preferred stocks are not good investments for individual investors; they have neither the growth potential of the common stock nor the safety of the bond. Most preferred stock is held by corporations. The Internal Revenue Service permits businesses to partially deduct dividends received from other corporations. This tax break makes preferred stocks attractive investments for businesses but less desirable for individuals.

WARRANTS

Many companies will issue warrants as a sales gimmick for their other securities. A warrant is an option issued by the company to buy common stock of a company at a specified price for a fixed period of time.

Suppose XYZ Corporation needs to raise some capital and decides to issue a 20-year bond. The officers estimate that in order to sell the bond in the present market they will have to pay 12% interest. But 12% is a high interest rate for the company to pay over a 20-year period, so instead they decide to offer the bond at a 9% interest rate and throw in a warrant. Each $1,000, 9% bond will come with a warrant that entitles the holder to buy

100 shares of XYZ common stock at $25 any time during the next 10 years. At the present time XYZ common stock is only selling for $20 a share, so the warrant has no value. However, should XYZ prosper and the common stock price rise above $25, the warrant will become valuable. Suppose in 5 years XYZ is selling for $30: the warrant will then be worth $5 a share since it entitles the holder to buy $30 worth of stock for only $25. Once issued, a warrant is freely traded in the market and behaves like a call option. We shall discuss the uses of options in Chapter 12.

THE STOCK MARKET

The price of any stock is determined in a competitive bidding market. A stock is worth only what someone is willing to pay for it. The daily selling price varies depending on the perception of investors as a whole (commonly referred to as the collective "market"). Over the long term, a stock's price will be governed by the quality of the company and the dividends it pays. However, the short-term, day-to-day value of a stock is not determined by the overall quality or long-term prospects of the company but rather by the "market's" perception of the company's value. Because of these market influences, on any given day, the price of a stock may bear little or no relationship to its long-term quality.

When there are more buyers than sellers, the price of a stock will rise regardless of any change in the fortunes of the company. Stocks that pay no dividends often sell for relatively high prices because most investors believe that the company will grow and prosper in the future and are willing to forgo present income to "get in on the ground floor." Similarly, stocks of established companies with good dividends may sell for very little relative to their dividends if most investors believe that the future of the company is poor.

The "market" is often capricious and volatile. In the fall of 1983, Digital Equipment Corporation announced that their third quarter earnings were lower than had been anticipated (the earnings were still good; they just weren't as high as everyone thought they would be). The effect of this announcement on the price of the stock was dramatic, causing it to drop over 30 points in less than a week. This sudden fall from grace was obviously not related to any fundamental change in the company but rather to a sudden change in the perception of the company by many investors.

The volatility can work both ways. In the early 1980s, biotechnology stocks were the darlings of Wall Street. A new company called Genentech offered its common stock for public sale. The company had no product, no sales, and no earnings. All it possessed was knowledge of gene-splicing technology. The original plan was to offer the stock near 20, but investor enthusiasm was so high that the original shares sold for 30. Investor demand for the relatively few shares available was so high that, within a week, the price had skyrocketed to over 70. And this was for a company with no product and no earnings. The froth did not last, of course, and the price settled back into the 30s in a few months.

Even companies with products and earnings can have their stock temporarily overvalued by the "market." Diasonics was a small company that made medical ultrasound scanners for radiologists and was developing some technology for digital imaging and magnetic resonance imaging (MRI). The company had been privately owned and had excellent growth for 3 years. In April, 1983, a public offering of stock was contemplated at $15 a share. However, investor excitement at the prospects of nuclear magnetic resonance caused the stock to open at 22 rather than at 15, and within 3 hours it had shot up to 29. By the next day it dropped to 27 and 9 months later it was south of 6. During this period there had been very little change in the basic operations of the company. There is a lesson here. Over the course of several years, it is the underlying value of a company as reflected in its earnings and dividends that controls the price of its common stock. However, between tomorrow and the long term, the price of the common stock can vary widely and often seemingly in no relation to the fortunes of the parent company.

It is these fluctuations that make the "market game." Although there are many investors who buy blue-chip stocks to hold only for the dividends, the majority of investors seek to increase their fortunes by anticipating changes in the selling price of the common stock. This type of transaction produces either a capital gain or a capital loss. If an investor has held the common stock for more than 6 months, the capital gain becomes long term and enjoys a significant tax benefit—only 40% of the gain is subject to tax. This tax shelter plus the frequent and often wide swings in the prices of common stocks are what attract the interest of the majority of investors. If you can consistently predict the price trends of stocks, you will have no trouble achieving financial independence.

HOW STOCKS ARE TRADED

There are no fixed prices for stocks; they trade in an open bidding market. The most recent price of a stock is simply the price at which someone who wanted to buy the stock was able to purchase it from someone who wished to sell it. When there are more buyers than sellers, the price of a stock will rise, and when there are more sellers than buyers, it will fall. If there is no one interested in buying a stock, it is theoretically (but not always actually) worthless. Thus, it is really the balance between the supply and demand for a stock that determines its price.

Although there are occasional private sales of stock, most sales take place on one of the major stock exchanges or in the over-the-counter market. The mechanisms are similar; prospective buyers and sellers are brought together by an agent who arranges the trade and who, in turn, receives a commission.

On a stock exchange, this agent is known as a Specialist. A Specialist is a member of the stock exchange who is granted an exclusive right to conduct transactions in certain stocks in return for maintaining an orderly market in their trading. Anyone who wishes to buy or sell a specific stock goes to the Specialist in that stock and places his order. The Specialist matches up the buy and sell orders and effects transactions. (Actually, an individual cannot go to a Specialist but must have an agent—his broker—conduct the transaction for him.)

The Specialist has the responsibility to see that there is an orderly market with no gross imbalance of buyers and sellers. If, for a brief period of time, there is a shortage of one or the other, the Specialist either buys or sells shares from his own personal account to keep the market moving. If there is a large difference between the bidding and offering price of stock, the Specialist may temporarily suspend trading until the imbalance is corrected, either by the appearance of buyers and sellers or by an announced dramatic change in the price of the stock. We do not need to go into the ins and outs of actual transactions; suffice it to say that the system of Specialists operating on the stock exchange serves to maintain a very liquid and orderly market where it is easy to buy and sell stocks. You may have noticed that when there is an imbalance in the market, that is, when there are more buyers than sellers or vice versa, the Specialist acts as a "contrarian"—he fulfills the function of the absent trader. One might suppose that this would put the Specialist at a disadvantage, since he would be forced to take a position that no other investors wanted. It is an interesting observation that Specialists do exceptionally well in their trading. We shall consider the implications of this in Chapter 15.

The over-the-counter market functions quite similarly to the stock exchange. One or more of the large brokerage houses maintains a market in a stock and fills the role of the Specialist. Theoretically, the over-the-counter (OTC) market should be somewhat less efficient than the exchange, but in practice this is rarely so. Sometimes the "spread"—the difference between the bidding and offering price for a stock—is larger in the over-the-counter market, but this is usually because companies whose stock trades over the counter are smaller; there are fewer shares and fewer potential buyers and sellers. In general, there is no reason to prefer a stock that is traded on one of the major exchanges to one that is traded over the counter (although listed stocks must meet standards not imposed on OTC issues). On the other hand, fly-by-night, flash-in-the-pan companies rarely make it onto the exchanges, but there is always someone willing to sell shares in them over the counter.

MARKET ORDERS

There are several different ways of buying and selling a stock, the most straightforward of which is the market order. After overhearing some favorable comments on XYZ Corporation in the tennis locker room, Sam B. decides to buy 100 shares. He calls up his broker and asks him to purchase 100 shares of XYZ for him "at the market." This means that the broker is authorized to go to the Specialist and purchase 100 shares at the best available price regardless of what that might be. If Sam is lucky, when his broker arrives at the Specialist's station, there will be more sellers than buyers, and he will get a lower price. If he is unlucky, there will be more buyers than sellers, and he will have to pay more for the stock. Regardless of the price, the broker must close the deal as soon as possible. On the large exchanges, under most circumstances, the price Sam gets will be very close to the recent price at which the stock has been trading; but there can be exceptions.

Suppose XYZ Corporation has been selling at 30 for several weeks but just announced that it had received a major government defense contract, which would double its earnings in the next 2 years. (This had been the source of the excitement at Sam's tennis club.) By the time Sam had called his broker, the stock exchange had closed, but the broker informed him the XYZ Corporation had risen 2 points that day on the basis of the good news. Sam was delighted and placed his market order for 100 shares. Unfortunately, the *CBS Evening News* carried a story about the new defense contract, and a lot of people around the country besides Sam became interested in XYZ stock. By 9:00 the next morning, orders for thousands of shares had been placed with brokers around the country, and the Specialist in XYZ was having difficulty. There were 10 prospective buyers for every seller, and the only way he was able to entice others to sell their stock was to allow the price of the stock to rise rapidly. The stock had closed at 32 the evening before, but the next morning trading was delayed and by noon, XYZ was trading at 38. Sam's order had been filled about 11:00 at 37.

When his broker called to tell him the news, Sam was shocked. He thought he would be buying XYZ at 32 but instead had paid 37. To make matters worse, later that day the company announced a correction in the previous day's announcement; instead of doubling the company's earnings, the new contracts would probably only increase earnings by 15%. Within 2 days, the price of XYZ had fallen back to 33, and Sam had an instant loss.

This is an overly dramatic example, but it does illustrate the potential dangers of market orders. Although a market order assures that the stock will be acquired, at times when the price of the stock is changing rapidly (usually because of some dramatic change or perceived change in the company's fortunes) an investor who places a market order may find that he is executing his trade at a price that is considerably different from what he anticipated. Sometimes this works to his advantage, but most of the time it does not.

Selling a stock using a market order is the same as buying; the only difference, of course, is that your broker is instructed to sell the stock for whatever price he can get at the time. In general, it is best to sell stocks using a market order; this ensures that your transaction will be completed, albeit not necessarily at the price you would have liked. Selling "at the market" protects you against being stuck with a stock as it rapidly declines in price.

Sam B. kept his $37 XYZ Corporation stock, and the price actually rose to 40 over the ensuing year. One afternoon at the tennis club, a friend asked Sam if he had heard about "the big investigation at XYZ Corporation." It seems that on the luncheon news it had been announced that the government was suspending all payments to XYZ Corporation pending the investigation of alleged faulty construction and design defects in the amphibious sleds it had ordered a year earlier. Sam was even more worried a week later when he heard on the morning news that three marines had drowned while performing maneuvers on the newly delivered sleds. He decided it was time to take his profits in XYZ Corporation and called up his broker to sell the stock. The broker informed him that, despite the gloomy news, XYZ had only dropped one point to 39 and might still do well. Sam hesitated. Finally he decided to sell when the stock reached 40, assuming that he could get yesterday's price of 40 (this is known as a limit order, to be discussed in a moment). But the broker found that no one was willing to pay 40 for the stock that day, and, unfortunately for Sam, the news continued to get worse. The next morning four more sleds sank, and so did XYZ stock. By 4:00 the next afternoon, the stock was selling for 32, and 2 days later it was down to 25. Sam still owned all his shares, but now instead of having a $3 profit, he had a $12 loss per share. When you decide to get out of a stock, sell it "at the market" to make sure you are out.

Buying is much different from selling. If you miss the buy point in one stock, there are hundreds of other stocks among which to choose. However, once you have decided to sell, you have only one stock to sell and if you miss out, you will be stuck with that stock. A good way to decide when to sell is to ask yourself, "If I had the money instead of the stock, would I still buy it?" If the answer is yes, hold on, but if you hesitate, sell!

This same advice can apply to buying a stock. If you are certain that the stock is going to go up, then buy it with a market order rather than trying to get a good price. Use market orders when you are confident about the prospects for a stock and want to be absolutely sure that your transaction is completed.

LIMIT ORDERS

We have already alluded to a "limit order" in the example of Sam's unfortunate dealings with XYZ Corporation. A limit order is similar to a market order except that the broker is constrained to make the trade at a previously specified price or better. If Sam B. had wanted to place a limit order when buying XYZ, he would have told his broker, "Get me 100 shares of XYZ at 34 or better." This means that the broker would execute the trade whenever he could buy XYZ at 34 a share or less. As long as the price was above 34 a share, the order would remain on the books but would not be filled. (We also saw how Sam's limit order to sell XYZ worked against him. In trying to get 40 for his stock, he was unable to sell it.)

In general, we believe it wise to use limit orders for purchases, since there is a price at which a stock is a good buy and a price at which it is not. When deciding to buy a stock, you should also decide how much you think it's worth, and use a limit order to make certain that you do not pay more than this. When placing a limit order, you will be asked to specify for how long the order is good. You may wish the order to be in effect for only that day or forever ("good until cancelled"). Most brokerage houses, however, will not hold limit orders for more than 30 days.

STOP ORDERS

Stop orders (also known as "stop loss" orders) are limit orders to sell a stock, not because the investor actually wants to sell it but to protect himself against a sudden decline in price. When the bad news about XYZ Corporation came out, Sam B. could have protected himself against a big loss by placing a stop order. Hoping that the company would weather the bad publicity but being unwilling to take the risk that it would not, he could have told his broker to "sell at 37." This means that if the stock price fell to 37, the broker would sell (execute a market order on XYZ), but, as long as it remained above that, Sam would still own the stock.

Stop orders are like insurance. You do not place a stop order because you really want to sell but because you want to be certain that, if your judgment is wrong, you don't get burned. Most successful investors use stop loss orders routinely, placing them arbitrarily 5 to 20% below the current stock price or, more commonly, on the 200-day moving average of the stock (the average price of the stock during the last 200 days of trading). It is a wise investment strategy, since it eliminates the possibility of taking big losses. On the other hand, you must realize that stock prices normally fluctuate from day to day, and you do not want to be in the position of selling your stock simply because it temporarily dipped in price. Therefore, we believe that when you use stop orders, you should keep them as mental stop orders (rather than on file with your broker) that you will faithfully execute if the stock closes below its 200-day moving average.

SHORT SALES

Short selling has a mystique that intimidates the nonprofessional investor. Most people assume that it is a complex investment technique beyond understanding and suitable only for high rollers. Actually, short selling is quite easy to understand.

The terms *long* and *short* have special meaning when used to describe investments. Long is a synonym for owned. Anything that an investor actually owns is said to be long. (You could think of yourself as being "long" flounder after a trip to the fish market. Anything that an investor does not own he is short. You were "short" flounder before the marketing.)

We generally think of selling only things that we own (or that we are long in): it is usually difficult to sell something you do not have. However, in security transactions, it is quite possible to sell something you do not own, and this is known as selling short. This is accomplished by borrowing the security you wish to sell (but do not own) and agreeing to replace it at some later date. The purpose of a short sale is to make a profit on a stock that you believe will decline in value. It is the reverse of a normal transaction. If you believe a stock is going to go up, you buy the stock today and sell it at a higher price tomorrow. On the other hand, if you believe a stock is going to go down in price, you want to sell it now and buy it later (to replace the stock you previously borrowed). This is what is accomplished by short sale.

Let us return to our example of Sam B., the XYZ Corporation, and their ill-fated amphibious sleds. Suppose that when Sam B. first heard about the potential troubles at XYZ, he called up an old navy friend who had worked with the sleds to find out what was afloat. His friend confirmed his worst fears; XYZ equipment was poor, and the government contract would likely be cancelled. Sam, sensing that other investors might start to perceive XYZ as a submerging rather than emerging growth stock, immediately sold his 100 shares for 39. If his judgment is right, he can also make a considerable profit by short selling XYZ. He calls his broker and tells him he wants to short 200 shares of XYZ at the present market price, which is 39. Brokers have access to large pools of stock, which they hold for their many clients. Sam's broker borrows 200 shares from the account of Joe K., transfers them to Sam's account, and sells them for 39. The proceeds are credited to Sam's account, and the broker makes note of the fact that Sam owes Joe K. 200 shares of XYZ Corporation. Six months later XYZ has sunk to 25, and Sam decides to replace the shares he borrowed for the short sale (this is called "covering the short"). He buys 200 shares of XYZ at 25 and has his broker transfer them back to Joe K., thereby settling the account. Sam was able to sell the shares at 39 and replace them with shares that he bought for 25, thereby pocketing a profit of 14.

Sam's profit is not actually that great, however. Despite its problems, the XYZ Corporation was still paying a $0.50 quarterly dividend, and, during the time Sam was short, two dividend periods elapsed. These dividends should have been paid into Joe K.'s account but were not because Sam had borrowed his stock. Therefore, Sam is responsible for paying Joe the lost dividends.

Short sales can backfire. Suppose Sam's pessimism was not warranted, and XYZ was able to solve its problems and salvage its big contract. If XYZ rose from 39 to 44, Sam would have been obligated to pay the higher price in order to replace his loan to Joe K.'s account and would have suffered a $5 loss rather than a $14 gain.

Selling short is a technique to take advantage of an anticipated decline in the security. Stock prices do not go up forever—they cycle. During a down cycle, a good way to profit is to sell short. There are risks, however. First, as with any investment decision, you may have judged incorrectly, and the stock may move up instead of down. In that case, you will lose money, and, if the stock moves a long way up, you can lose a lot of money. When you go long a stock (i.e., buy it), your risk is limited to the price you paid. Even if the original stock becomes totally worthless, you cannot lose more than your original investment. In a short sale, however, you can lose considerably more than your investment. If the shorted stock doubles in price, you will have lost your original investment, but if it triples in price, you will have lost 200% of your original investment.

In theory, the potential loss is limitless, but in practice it does not work out this way. When you sell short, you will be required to post some security with the broker to guarantee that you can replace the borrowed stock. This usually amounts to 150% of the current selling price (the cash from the short sale plus 50% from the investor). As the stock price changes, the amount of security required will also vary, but you will not be allowed to let it drop lower than 120% of the current market price. If a stock is moving up, your broker will require you to deposit more security money. If you cannot or will not do this, the broker will take the security deposit you have already made, repurchase the stock at the prevailing price, and close out your position.

Because of the security requirements (known as "margin"), your position will not move far away from you without your being aware of it. Your broker will call you. This is known as the infamous "margin call." Most investors either cannot or will not continue to ante up "margin" to cover a losing short position. There is an old axiom on Wall Street, "Never answer a margin call." It usually means that you were wrong. Whatever you thought was going to happen did not, and holding the position is just protecting your ego. It is also worth bearing in mind that money invested in a losing investment is worse than dead money.

Another disadvantage of short sales is that the IRS always treats them as ordinary income regardless of the length of time the position is maintained. If you are long a security for more than 6 months, you can take advantage of the long-term capital gains tax break. However, if you are short the security for 5 years, you still must declare any profits as ordinary income and cannot make use of the long-term capital gains deduction. This is an arbitrary and not particularly fair position, but it is the government's policy to discourage short selling.

Although short selling is a valid investment technique and is the best method for dealing with conditions that favor a declining market, we do not believe that the average investor should use it very often. In addition to the always present risk of having made a wrong decision on the future direction of a stock's movement, there are the added disadvantages of having to pay the dividends, the large margin requirements, the potentially unlimited loss, and the unfavorable tax treatment. As we shall discuss more fully in Chapter 15, there are less risky ways of dealing with times of market decline.

MARGIN

Margin is the financial term for a loan given by your broker using your stocks as collateral. In the previous section we saw how margin is required as security in a short sale. Margin is also used as collateral in long trans-actions. In order to promote sales, a broker will usually lend a client money to buy stock.

Suppose Sam B. has a good feeling about ABC Corporation, which is currently selling for $50. He would like to buy 200 shares of ABC, but because its price is high, he does not really have enough money to do so at the present time. However, if he buys 100 shares, his broker will lend him the extra money to buy an additional 100 shares. This is known as buying stock on margin or going "out on margin." Of course the broker will charge Sam interest for the loan (known as the "broker loan rate"), but the interest rate may be less than he would have had to pay to borrow the money from a bank.

In order to provide security for the loan, Sam will have to put up some collateral. First, he will have to let the broker keep the shares he purchased with the borrowed money and, in addition, he will have to deposit some money—usually 30% of the present value of the shares—to cover the possibility that ABC will suddenly decline in value. This extra money is referred to as the "margin." If Sam was correct in his assessment, and ABC Corporation increases in price, he will be making extra money, since he will be gaining the profit on 200 shares although he has only had to put up the cash equivalent of 130 shares (having borrowed the money for the other 70 shares from the broker). On the other hand, if ABC declines in value, the broker will give Sam a "margin call." This is a request for more collateral to cover the loss in value of the stock. If Sam is unable or unwilling to post more margin, the broker will sell some of the shares he holds as collateral to cover Sam's loan. Since margin calls on long stock positions only occur if a stock has declined in price, it means that Sam's shares will be sold at a loss.

Margin is a form of leverage; it moves the investor further out on the risk–return line. It is the method by which a broker makes it easy for his client to overextend himself. Although there are many highly successful professional money managers who make good use of margin purchases, we do not think the extra risks justify the potential rewards for the average investor. As we saw in Chapter 5, it is not easy to make a long-term profit borrowing money for investments during times of low and stable inflation. Some technical analysts even use large margin debt as a reason to get out of the market. Margin is best left for the professional investor.

COMMISSIONS

Every time a broker performs a security transaction, he will charge a commission. The size of the commission varies with the size of the transaction, the number of transactions a client makes, and the policy of the company. The so-called full-service brokers (such as Merrill Lynch, Shearson/American Express, E. F. Hutton, etc.) generally have the highest commissions, on the order of 5 to 6% for small transactions. In return for these high commissions, the broker provides a variety of financial advisory and consultation services for the client. There are also many "discount" brokers (they advertise in the financial pages of most newspapers and the *Wall Street Journal*). Discount broker commissions are usually 35 to 70% less than those of full-service brokers. They also provide fewer support services. They do not have personal stockbrokers, multitudes of research reports, flashy offices, advertisements during the Super Bowl, etc.

Commissions represent a significant cost to an investment program. They are dead dollars and should be minimized as far as possible. As we shall see later, for many investors most of the services of a full-service broker are unnecessary, and there is little reason to pay their higher commission rates; the commission rates of the discount brokers are high enough! In Chapter 15, we shall discuss methods to minimize the dead dollars that go into commissions.

FUNDAMENTAL STOCK ANALYSIS

Buying and selling stock is easy. The hard part is knowing what stock to buy and when to sell it. There are literally hundreds of theories for evaluating the future performance of stocks, and none of them is perfect. If there were a foolproof method, there would be no market, since everyone would be using it, and there would be nobody available to complete the opposite side of the transaction. Remember that for every buyer there must be a seller and that every transaction must have two parties. Therefore, every time a trade takes place, there are two presumably well-informed individuals who have exactly opposite opinions of the future course of a stock.

This is the essence of a market and the basis of the "market game." It is a lot like going to Las Vegas. Instead of betting against the house, you are betting against the other party in your transaction. Each of you believes he has the correct "system" for beating the odds. There is a difference, however. In Las Vegas, we all know (intellectually at least) that there is no successful system and that, if you play long enough, you will ultimately lose. However, in the stock market, there is every reason to believe that if you are clever and diligent (and lucky) you will be able to consistently do well.

This is not an unreasonable expectation. There are many investment decisions made on inadequate information. With a little forethought you should be able to outperform the average. There are two general categories of stock analysis: fundamental and technical. The vast majority of investment decisions are based on fundamental analysis.

The term *fundamental* refers to the fundamentals of the underlying company. That is, how well the company is doing its business, how good business is in general, how the company stacks up against its competitors, what the future prospects are for growth of the company, what the earnings are and whether they have been growing, whether the company is in debt, etc. Many books have been written on fundamental analysis, and we will not attempt to discuss it in any detail. We shall just have a quick look at the basic principles. If you wish to read further, begin with the books on fundamental analysis in the Bibliography.

The cornerstone of fundamental analysis is the price–earnings ratio or *P/E* ratio. This is the price of a stock divided by the company's earnings per share. The *P* part of the equation is easily determined from the most recent selling price, but the *E* portion is harder to get. The most conservative method is to use the actual reported earnings from the company's last fiscal year. These are called the trailing earnings. However, most analysts also try to project the company's earnings for the present year as well as future years. This gives rise to "estimated" *P/E* ratios.

The price–earnings ratio of a stock is a measure of the return on the stock's purchase price. A stock with a *P/E* of 5 is earning 20% per year, whereas a stock with a *P/E* of 50 is earning only 2%, and it will take you 50 years to get your money back. A company with no earnings has an infinitely large *P/E* ratio. In general, the lower the *P/E* ratio, the better is the value of the stock. Over the years, the average *P/E* ratio for the stocks that make up the Dow Jones Industrial Average has been around 14. Many analysts recommend that investors not buy stocks with *P/E* ratios of 7 or greater or stocks whose *P/E* is higher than half of the average *P/E* for all stocks with earnings traded on the exchange. In other words, if the *P/E* ratio for all stocks on the New York Stock Exchange was 18, one should pay no more than a *P/E* ratio of 9 for any given stock.

The return on equity is another piece of fundamental data. This indicates the amount of money a corporation earns relative to the amount it has invested in plant and equipment. A company should have a return on equity of at least 15% or better for the last 5 years to be considered for investment purposes.

When all is said and done, the ultimate value of a company boils down to net sales and profit margins. Of these two, the most important is an accelerating rate of net sales. It is always possible for a new management team to come in and get a handle on expenses or improve the efficiency of the operation, but the aggregate sales are often outside the control of corporate management. To be a candidate for purchase, an individual stock should have had at least a 10% net sales growth rate for the last 5 years.

If you, as an investor, feel generally favorable about the stock market and the industry group into which the stock falls, then you should look at these basic fundamental factors. If the stock has a *P/E* ratio of less than 7, a return on equity of greater than 15% for 5 years, and a growth rate of net sales of at least 10% for 5 years, your chances of having a sound investment are very high. Unfortunately, everyone else is looking for this type of investment as well, and they do not occur often. Usually, the "fundamentals" are mixed with some aspects which are favorable and others of which are unfavorable.

In the long run, "fundamentals" control the success of a company and its stock: fundamental analysis represents the basis for stock selection.

Obviously as an individual it is very difficult to get the necessary information to perform an adequate analysis of a particular stock. However, the large brokerage firms maintain research departments that do nothing but collect and analyze this type of data. Reams and reams of it, along with specific recommendations, are available to clients. There are also many professional advisory firms and advisory services that can provide insight into fundamental analysis. Perhaps the best known and certainly one of the most successful is the Value Line Investment Survey. Value Line uses primarily fundamental analysis to rate the prospects of many stocks on the major exchanges and many over-the-counter stocks as well. Over the years, the performance of stocks has generally followed Value Line's predictions.

There are two problems with pure fundamental analysis. The first is that there are many ways of interpreting data, and three stock analysts evaluating the same company may come to three quite different conclusions. Second, and more important, in the short and immediate term, the price of a stock may not reflect the status of the underlying fundamentals. There are no guaranteed systems for free lunches.

TECHNICAL ANALYSIS

Technical analysis is the other major school of stock evaluation, and its practitioners are referred to as "technicians." Some technicians grudgingly acknowledge that the long-term prospects of a company are controlled by the fundamentals, but they believe that the day-to-day price of a stock is controlled by a complex mix of market forces. By looking at the past history of a stock's price movements, one should be able to predict future prices regardless of what is going on in today's fundamentals. Technicians (and their computers) scan graphs or charts of a company's stock prices and trading volumes, searching to find a reproducible pattern that can be projected into the future. "Everything cycles," they will tell you, "and these cycles will repeat themselves if you know how to look. Don't waste time in trying to figure out what a stock *should be* doing, but look and see what it *is* doing. It is not important to know why a stock is moving up or down (in fact, this is probably unknowable); rather, one should concentrate on what happened to the stock in the past when it was in a similar setting."

Technical analysis sounds like black magic. Maybe it is. The fact remains that some technical analysts do very well predicting market and stock moves, and, regardless of how far out the theory sounds, the results are not to be sneered at. Just as they maintain fundamental analysis departments, most major brokerage houses also employ a staff of technicians who gaze into their crystal balls and computers in an attempt to foresee the future. Just as with fundamentalists, some technicians have success, and others do not. Even more common is the individual who will have a hot hand for a period of time and then seem to lose it.

Probably the most widely known technician is Joseph Granville, the flamboyant publisher of the *Granville Market Letter*. There have been periods of time in the past when Mr. Granville has been cannily accurate in his forecasts. There have also been times when he was out of the ball park. Martin Zweig, a frequent guest on *Wall Street Week*, is another technical analyst who is right more than he is wrong. (A stable of "elves" does the technical analysis on *Wall Street Week*, and although often wrong, they deserve credit for surviving the verbal barbs of Louis Rukeyser.) Alan Abelson, the terse and pithy writer for *Barron's*, has offered up his opinion on the staying power of technicians: "They are like second story men. They are only successful as long as no one notices them." Although there is undoubtedly some validity in technical market analysis, it too does not have all the answers.

TIPS AND INSIDE INFORMATION

The only universally successful stock market prediction device is inside information. If you know that XYZ Corporation is going to show a large and unexpected earnings increase that will be made public a week from now, you can buy some shares of XYZ today and be fairly confident of seeing them rise after the announcement. Similarly, if you had access to the books of Digital Equipment Corporation in the summer of 1983 and knew that the company earnings were far below predictions, you could have very profitably shorted Digital stock. Inside information is the best type of stock advice. There are two problems with inside information however. First, it is against the law to use this type of information to make trades (although the law is obviously extremely difficult to enforce). The second problem is that inside information is usually not available.

Inside information is only available to the "inside" person. By the time the individual investor gets to hear about it, it is no longer inside information. To get real inside information, you have to be lucky; you have to be in the right spot at the right time. You won't hear about it from friends, your broker, or the *Wall Street Journal.* What masquerades as inside information is usually no more than a tip.

Small investors love "hot tips," mistaking them for true inside information: "A friend overheard a little old lady in the supermarket talking to another woman about her nephew who works in the Bank of America with a man who handles the loans to ACME Corporation. This fellow saw a report on the desk of a colleague that mentioned that ACME was 6 months in arrears on interest payments and might default on a loan. He wanted to pass this information along to a few close friends."

Needless to say, this type of "inside information" usually produces a loss rather than a gain. The important thing to remember is that people with true inside information do not go broadcasting it about. First, it is illegal; and second, it would lose its value if it were widely known. It is generally safe to assume that any "hot tips" you hear are no more than gossip and rumors. Even worse, it may be deliberately misleading information that is being disseminated by people who have already taken an opposite position on the stock. Although it is tempting to act on such tips, we think you will be happier in the long run if you do so with imaginary money rather than your real dollars.

EVERYBODY HAS A GOOD STORY

Everyone in the investment services business, that is, brokers, financial advisors, bankers, and your friends, all have detailed and plausible sounding explanations for their recommendations. Everybody has a good story. After all, if it didn't make sense, they wouldn't be interested in it in the first place. So how does the average John Q. Public investor go about deciding which story to believe? Where and when should you invest your money? Which is a judicious stock, and which is a loser?

We believe that the best way to do this is to look at the story teller's track record. There are many financial advisors and investment analysts who know what they are doing and do get consistently good results. There are others who have their ups and downs, and there are some who are consistent losers. Rather than listening to their present story, you are better off looking at their record. If most of their past recommendations have been profitable, it is not unreasonable to assume that they will continue to be so. If your stockbroker has consistently made money for you, then by all means stay with him. However, if he has as many failures as successes (there is always a good story for each failure, of course), you will probably be better off looking elsewhere for advice. There is no dearth of available financial advice: stockbrokerage firms, bank trust departments, investment advisory letters, financial newspapers, and well-intentioned friends. Keep an open mind and listen to as many as possible. More important, look at their past performance and keep track of their recommendations to see how you would have done if you had followed their advice. When you find a winner, stick with him. We will discuss more about investment advisor selection in Chapter 15.

STOCKS AS JUDICIOUS INVESTMENTS

Over the course of the years, investments in common stocks have been very judicious. The overall trend of stock prices and dividend payments has been continuously upward. But it is not a smooth upward road, and there are many dips and peaks in common stock performance. For example, it was almost impossible to lose money in the stock market in the late 1960s and early 1970s, but it was also virtually impossible not to lose money in 1974. From late 1980 until mid-1982, it was tough to avoid losses in the stock market, but from August, 1982 until May, 1983, everything, including the kitchen sink, went up. Despite some rather nasty downward slides, the general course of the stock market has been up, and we believe that this will continue in the future. In fact, as we shall discuss in more detail in Chapter 14, we believe that the 1980s will be the decade of common stocks and that they will represent the most desirable investment vehicles during this period.

9

BONDS

Bonds are confusing to most people. There is widespread belief that they are "safe" investment vehicles, best suited to widows and orphans. Although bonds can be safe, dull investments, they can also be as volatile and risky as a speculative stock. In this chapter we shall look at bonds and see how they work and how they can be used in an investment program.

Bonds are a "fixed-return" investment; that is, the owner of a bond receives a fixed amount, the *face value* of the bond (usually $1,000), on a specified date, *the maturity*, in the future. In addition, a bond pays a fixed amount at periodic intervals (usually 6 months or a year) as "interest." These two payments are the only aspects of a bond that do not change. The value of a bond on any day but the maturity date will be determined by the competitive market (just as the value of a stock on any given day will be determined by its price in the market). The market value of a bond depends on the length of time remaining until maturity, the quality or safety of the bond, and prevailing interest rates.

The nearer a bond is to maturity, the closer its price will approach the face value. This is because, on the maturity date, the bond will be redeemed for this value. Conversely, if the maturity is several years in the future, the face value has little effect on the price (since most investors will not hold a bond for many years). Thus, very short-term bonds will sell at very close to face value, whereas for long-term bonds (25 or 30 years), the face value will have little effect on price. The face value will have some, but not complete, influence on the price of intermediate-term issues.

In general, the longer the term of the bond, the higher the yearly "interest" payment or yield. In bonds that are otherwise comparable, each 5 years of term will usually add ½ to ¾% to the "interest" the bond pays. This is because the investor must wait longer to get his money back and must therefore take more risk of default or devaluation.

Higher quality bonds cost more than the lower quality ones. The quality rating (calculated by Standard and Poor's and Moody's bond services) measures the risk of default on either the periodic interest payments or the face value of the bond itself. The highest rated bonds carry very little risk— the prospects of the issuer are excellent, and the fixed payments will almost certainly be made. Low-rated bonds, on the other hand, carry a real risk of default: the issuer may go broke before the bond matures, rendering it worthless. To compensate for the increased risk, the price of a low-rated bond will be less than that of a comparable higher-rated issue, and the longer the term of the bond, the greater the discount. Similarly if a bond's rating increases, its price will also increase.

BONDS AND INTEREST RATES

The main factor controlling the value of all but short-term bonds is the prevailing interest rate. Bond prices are inversely proportional to the current interest rate; as rates go up, prices go down. In order to understand this relationship, we must distinguish between the "interest" rate printed on the bond and the prevailing interest rates in the economy.

Every bond carries a nominal "interest" rate known as the *coupon*, which specifies what the fixed, periodic payment will be. The face value of the bond multiplied by the coupon gives the yearly "interest" payment. This is a fixed, constant amount that will be paid throughout the life of the bond regardless of its current value. For example, consider a $1,000 face value bond with a coupon of 10%. This bond will pay $1,000 × 10% = $100 per year to its holder regardless of its current selling price. If the bond sells for $1,000, it will pay $100 a year. If the same bond is selling for $2,000, it will still pay $100 a year. If it sells for $500, it will still pay $100 a year. Although the coupon is expressed as an interest rate, it actually is not. Both the coupon and the face value are fictitious or "paper" figures; to have meaning, they must be multiplied to obtain the yearly payment. This payment is a real, absolute value, which will not change over the life of the bond (unless it defaults, of course).

The actual "interest" a bond pays is known as the *yield* and is determined by dividing the yearly payment by the current price of the bond. Let us consider again the $1,000 face value with a coupon of 10% that pays $100 a year. Suppose you buy this bond on July 1 when it is selling at its face value of $1,000. You will pay $1,000 for the bond, and it will pay you $100 a year. The payment divided by your cost is 10%; this is your yield on the bond. On the other hand, suppose that on July 1 the bond was selling for $500 instead of $1,000. In this case, you would have paid only $500 but would still receive the same $100 a year payment, and your yield would be $100 divided by $500 or 20%. In this situation, the bond is yielding more than its coupon (in investing parlance, this is known as "selling at a discount"). Now suppose that on July 1 the bond is selling at $2,000. If you pay $2,000, you will still receive only $100 a year in payment, and your yield will be $100 divided by $2,000 or 5% (this bond is "selling at premium"). The yield of a bond is the expression of its rate of return or its "interest rate." The yield varies continuously and depends on the most recent selling price. (Often financial newspapers will also print a figure called "yield to maturity," which is a calculation based on the coupon payment and the difference between the current selling price and the face value of the bond when redeemed at maturity.)

What happens to an investment in this bond as its selling price changes? Let's suppose Sam B. bought a bond on July 1 when it was selling for $1,000. His yield is 10% and will remain constant as long as he holds on to the bond. Suppose on December 1 the bond price has risen to $2,000. The current yield (that is, the yield on December 1) will be only 5%, but Sam's yield is still 10% since he paid $1,000. If on April 1 the bond price has fallen to $500, the current yield will be 20%, but Sam's yield will still be 10% since he invested $1,000.

The point to remember is that your yield on a bond is set when you buy it and does not change as long as you hold it, regardless of the variations in the selling price and current yield. The *capital value* of your bond does change as the selling price varies, and you will have either a capital gain or loss if the current yield is different from your yield. In the example we have been considering, on December 1 Sam would have had a $1,000 capital gain if he had sold the bond. If he did not sell but held until April 1, his bond would have been worth only $500, and he would have had a capital loss if he sold on that date. As long as he held the bond, however, his capital gains and losses are only "paper," and his yield is the same, constant amount that it was on the day he purchased it.

How do interest rates cause the bond price, and, hence, the current yield to vary? We have been considering the current yield as if it were a passive, independent variable when actually it is the factor that controls the selling price. On any given day an investor purchasing a bond will expect to receive a current yield that is competitive with current interest rates. If the prime interest rate is 18%, no one is going to pay $2,000 for Sam's bond because he would only be getting a yield of 5% on his investment! They might pay $500, however, since then their yield would be 20%, more in line with the prevailing interest rate. The important concept here is that the selling price of a bond is the dependent variable. On any given day a bond will sell so that its yield is comparable to the prevailing interest rates. As the interest rates rise, the price of bonds will decrease, and as interest rates fall, their price will increase.

We can see that although bonds are a "fixed-return" investment, they can be far from a safe investment. The price of bonds will fluctuate as interest rates change. If you buy a bond when interest rates are low, you can experience a considerable loss of capital value as interest rates rise! The only way to recoup this loss may be to hold the bond to maturity, and if you paid a "premium" for the bond, even this won't work!

LONG-TERM BONDS

Bonds behave differently depending on the time remaining to maturity. Let's first consider long-term bonds, that is, bonds more than 15 years from maturity. The majority of these bonds will not be held until they mature, and, therefore, the face value has little effect on their selling price. Interest rates are the predominant factor here; long-term bond prices move up and down in very close association with current interest rates. It is best to think of them as you would a stock. The price of a stock varies, and so does the price of a long-term bond. There is a difference, however. You cannot always know what will cause the price of a stock to move, but you do know what affects bonds—interest rates. You can be certain that if interest rates rise, the price of a long-term bond will fall, and vice versa.

Long-term bonds can be excellent investments when interest rates are high. Their price will be depressed (they will sell at a discount), and the current yield will be high. Buying at this time will give the investor an excellent rate of return. Moreover, when interest rates fall, the price of the bonds will rise, and the investor will have a nice capital gain. Even though interest rates are falling, the bond owner still maintains the high yield he established on the day he purchased the bond, so he wins two ways: a high yield and a capital gain.

When interest rates are low, long-term bonds are a poor investment. The current yield will be low because the price is high (the bond may sell at more than face value—a premium). Not only will the investor have a poor rate of return, he will suffer a capital loss when the interest rates rise again and the price of his bond falls. Long-term bonds are basically an interest rate play; buy when rates are high and sell when rates are low. If you can predict interest rate changes, you can do very well in long-term bonds! If you ignore interest rates, you will likely get cleaned!

VERY SHORT-TERM BONDS

Next, let us consider the opposite of a long-term bond—the very short-term bond. These are usually referred to as "bills" or "notes" and have maturities of no more than a year and usually less than 90 days. Because the term is so short, the value of these instruments is not so sensitive to interest rates. The value of short-term bonds will change very little even if interest rates change dramatically. The reason, of course, is that they will be redeemed for their face value in a very short time. No one will sell something at a discount when he can redeem it for face value in 90 days! Similarly, no one would be willing to pay a premium for such a bond. Money market funds invest in very short-term notes. This enables them to obtain a guaranteed interest rate with no risk of capital loss.

Of course, the yield from short-term bonds will vary with interest rates. In 1981, the interest rates were high, and very short-term bonds sold to yield 15%. In 1983, interest rates had dropped, the 1981 bonds had long since matured, and new short-term bonds yielded only 8%. When interest rates rise again, so will the yield of new short-term issues. (Most very short-term bonds do not actually pay interest; rather, they sell at a discount. The difference between the face value and the discounted selling price is the "interest.")

INTERMEDIATE-TERM BONDS

Intermediate-term bonds have some features of both extremes: their yield is somewhat higher than prevailing interest rates but not as high as that of long-term bonds. On the other hand, their capital value fluctuates with the interest rate changes, although not as widely as do long-term issues. The greater the time to maturity, the more they behave like long-term bonds. As the term shortens, their selling value approaches the face value, and the yield approaches the coupon.

TYPES OF BONDS

Another factor in the price of bonds is the issuing agency. From time to time certain types of bonds are more or less in favor, and this directly affects their selling price. There are usually good reasons for these changes in sentiment on the part of the investing public, and it is important to be aware of the unique features of different types of bonds.

United States Treasury Bonds

The closest thing to a risk free investment in the world today are debt instruments issued by the United States Treasury. Treasury obligations have never suffered a default, and interest payments are routinely made; they are backed by the full faith and credit of the United States Government. Because of continuing need for government financing and the fact that the government has the power to tax and print money, United States Treasury bonds are the most secure of all investment alternatives.

There are three types of treasury obligations, which are categorized according to term. Short-term obligations are called treasury bills and range in maturity from 31 to 181 days. Treasury bills are initially sold by auction through the Federal Reserve Banks. The selling price is determined by competitive bidding and is usually governed by the current interest rate. Anyone can buy treasury bills directly from the Federal Reserve System by submitting a noncompetitive bid. It is also possible to buy treasury bills in an aftermarket maintained by brokerage firms and banks, who charge a small commission for handling the transaction.

Treasury notes have intermediate maturities ranging from 1 to 5 years, and treasury bonds are securities with maturities of greater than 5 years. The main difference between bonds or notes and bills is that the former have a face value and make regular interest payments throughout their life, whereas the latter do not make any interest payments but sell initially at a discount. Because of their short term, once they are sold, treasury bills are little affected by interest rates, whereas the value of treasury notes and bonds will fluctuate with interest rates as described earlier. The income from any treasury security is not taxable by state or local governments.

The dominant feature of government securities is their safety. They are essentially risk-free and, as such, have the lowest yields of all types of fixed income securities. In comparing various investment possibilities, it is always wise to relate them to the current price of a United States Government bond. Unless the alternative investment, adjusted for the time value, yields more than the bond, forget it.

State and Local Bonds

Long-term bonds are also issued by states and municipalities. They have been attractive in the past because the interest they pay is exempt from Federal income tax. They are also usually free from state taxes in the state in which they were issued. Because of the tax-exempt status, the yield of these bonds is lower than that of fully taxable instruments. Their investment attractiveness increases as the investor's marginal tax bracket increases. In other words, to someone in the 50% income tax bracket, a taxable bond yielding 10% is essentially equal to a nontaxable municipal bond yielding 5%.

There are some hazards with municipal bonds. Although all state bonds are rated by Moody's and Standard and Poor's, only a few municipal bonds are, and these ratings are not based on as thorough and exhaustive a review of municipal balance sheets as are the ratings of corporate bonds. The security of state and municipal bonds is considerably less than that of U.S. Government obligations. The electorate may resist further taxation or, as in the case of Proposition 13 in California, may take significant revenue-generating potential away from local government. In the late 1970s, New York City nearly defaulted on its bonded indebtedness, and although the city bonds were backed by the "moral obligation of New York State," it was not clear whether the legislature in Albany would translate this obligation into hard dollar support. Since the New York City bond crisis, things have become even worse for municipalities. Populations have moved out of the bigger urban centers, and many states have passed tax-restricting measures (such as Proposition 13 in California and Proposition 2½ in Massachusetts). The tax-free interest of a municipal bond may be small compensation if the bond defaults or must suspend the interest payments. We need look no further than the 1983 default of the Washington Public Power Supply (W.P.P.S.) bonds. The State of Washington itself was awash in red ink and was either unwilling or unable to bail out the bonds.

In summary, state or municipal bonds have some tax advantages but are less secure than United States Treasury bonds. They should be purchased very selectively and then only after consultation with one of the rating services.

Corporate Bonds

As we saw in Chapter 8, most corporations issue bonds to raise capital for their operations. The interest rate these bonds pay depends on the public's perception of the creditworthiness of the corporation and the current interest rate. The risk associated with a particular corporate bond is directly related to the financial integrity of the issuing corporation. Large companies with small amounts of debt provide bonds that are nearly as risk-free as the United States Treasury Securities. Bonds of smaller, unproven companies run a much higher risk of default, however. To assist investors in assessing the risks of a particular corporate bond, there are investment agencies that provide a complete financial analysis and rate all bonds for their safety. All aspects of the parent corporation are closely scrutinized, and projections are made regarding the salability of the corporate product, the strength of the management, corporate objectives, capital structure, past performance, manufacturing, technology, and so on. Table 9.1 shows the ratings used by Moody's and Standard and Poor's, the two largest rating agencies.

As you can see, the rating systems are nearly the same, differing only in the size of the letters used. In general, the more and larger the size of the A's, the better. It is something like the high school grading system: A's are good; anything containing a B is worse than something without a B, unless it's a C; C's aren't very good, but they are better than D's. Speculators usually get D's (which is probably all you need to know about D's). The fewer the B's, the worse it is. Corporate bonds down to the level of BBB are considered investment grade. Any ratings below this can be pretty risky, and some are frank speculations.

There are two broad groups of corporate bonds: secured and unsecured. If a particular asset, say a piece of property or a claim on a particular income stream of the corporation, stands behind a bond, it is said to be secured. A corporate mortgage bond, for example, would be secured by a lien on part or all of the corporation's property. In the case of default, such bonds would have first claim on the proceeds from the sale of the property (in the same way as the bank has first claim on your house if you default on your home mortgage). Other bonds are frequently secured with equipment or collateral. This is similar to the bank holding the title on your car until you have repaid your car loan.

Bonds that are unsecured by any tangible assets are called *debentures*. They are covered only by the general faith and credit of the issuing corporation. Should the company default or go bankrupt, the debenture holders are general creditors of the corporation and will receive the proceeds from any bankruptcy proceedings after the secured bondholders have been paid. However, they are the next in line and will be paid before either the preferred stock or common stockholders.

TABLE 9.1 Bond ratings

Standard & Poor	Moody	Comment
AAA	Aaa	Highest grade investment bond
AA	Aa	
A	A	
BBB	Baa	Lowest grade investment bond
BB	Ba	Very risky bond
B	B	Speculative
CCC–D	Caa–c	Speculative to in default

Another type of corporate bond is called the *subordinated debenture* and is a class of unsecured bonds that stands behind regular debentures if the company liquidates. (They are sometimes referred to as junior securities.) Because of their slightly increased risk, subordinated debentures usually carry a slightly higher rate of return than regular bonds.

The prices, and therefore the yields, of corporate bonds move like a herd of elephants in response to changes in the interest rate. Nearly all bonds of the same rating will yield nearly the same rate of return for corresponding maturity dates. Since highly rated corporate bonds virtually never default on interest and principal payments, one is nearly as good as another and almost as safe as buying a government bond.

Preferred Stock

As we saw in Chapter 8, preferred stock is a hybrid security that possesses some of the attributes of a bond as well as some of equity. It is like common stock in that it is included in the equity section of the corporate balance sheet and does not have a guaranteed redemption price by the issuer. It is like a bond in that its dividend is constant and usually does not change with the fortunes of the company. If times are bad and there is not enough money to pay the dividend, it accumulates and will be paid in full before any dividends on common stock are paid. However, the dividends on preferred stock cannot be paid until the interest on the corporation's bonds has been satisfied, and, therefore, preferred stock carries a higher risk than the bonds of the same corporation. Although the dividend of a preferred stock is usually somewhat higher than the interest rate on the bonds, it is usually not enough higher to justify the extra risk. Preferred stock is usually purchased by other corporations, since they are exempt from paying taxes on the dividends received.

Zero Coupon Bonds

During the heady days of the late 1970s, when interest rates were sometimes sighted north of 17%, some companies and brokerage houses, always interested in new commission-generating products, hit on the idea of a zero coupon bond. These bonds were structured like treasury bills in that they did not pay interest but were sold by corporations at a deep discount from their face value. They were appealing to investors because they permitted them to "lock in" their total return at the time of purchase (when interest rates were high). This contrasted with the uncertainty of a traditional bond, which forces the investor to reinvest his interest payments at whatever rates are prevailing at the time. In addition, since no interest payments were made, the entire yield of the bond could be viewed as long-term capital gain and might be eligible for the 60% tax exclusion. Because of these advantages, investors were willing to accept a slightly lower return on these bonds than on more conventional issues, and this, of course, was beneficial to the issuing corporation. For example, a 5-year "zero" with a face value of $100 was offered for $49.72; the $50.28 difference between the purchase price and the redemption value works out to a compound annual rate of return of 14.5%. To make matters sweeter, it was hoped that this would be taxed at long-term capital gains rates. This bond sold well when other, more conventional bonds were yielding 18%.

The decline in interest rates has decreased the popularity of zero coupon bonds. In addition, it is unlikely that the Internal Revenue Service will allow the proceeds to be taxed at long-term capital gains rates. The IRS views the "shadow" interest as taxable and it is unwise for investors to assume that they will receive a tax break with this type of security; they are thus best suited for tax-deferred accounts, such as IRAs.

LIONs and TIGRs and CATS (Oh My!)

A variation on the zero coupon bond theme was sprung on investors by Merrill Lynch in mid-1982 when they issued their Treasury Investment Growth Receipts (TIGRs). Next, Salomon Brothers unleashed their Certificates of Accrual on Treasury Securities (CATS). In order to keep pace, Lehman Brothers swallowed their pride and issued the Lehman Investment Opportunity Notes (LIONs). These and others of their genre are something like corporate zeros but are designed for investors who want the security of a U.S. Treasury bond. The sponsoring institution packages groups of treasury bonds such that the interest payments are retained by the company and the repackaged bonds are sold to investors at a discount from face value reflecting the prevailing yield to maturity. The bonds are placed with a major bank as custodian, and the brokerage house sells receipts entitling investors to specific portions of the portfolio.

For the individual investor, these vehicles offer the advantages of automatic reinvestment of interest at a guaranteed rate and the ability to purchase the security of a treasury bond in small denominations (the standard treasury bond is issued in $10,000 amounts).

The greatest attraction of the LIONs, TIGRs, and CATS is the ability to "lock in" a high rate of return. They make most sense when interest rates are high and are less attractive when rates are lower. Of course, this is the general pattern with all bonds and fixed return securities.

INVESTING IN BONDS

It is important to realize that, from an investment standpoint, bonds are nothing like stocks. Individual stock prices rise and fall on the merits, or perceived merits, of the individual companies. Bond prices are controlled primarily by interest rates, secondarily by the term, and ultimately by the quality of the underlying company.

Short-term bonds, bills, or notes are used as "cash equivalents"—a place to deposit money at the highest current interest rate compatible with nearly total safety. Money market funds are merely pooled investments in very short-term issues.

Long-term bonds can be very volatile vehicles used to take advantage of high interest rates and with the expectation of returning capital gains when interest rates decline. Long-term bonds are very risky investments when interest rates are low.

Intermediate-term bonds are used for special purposes, usually as part of a tax strategy to defer receiving gains until some specific time in the future. They can also provide a reasonably safe intermediate-term investment if liquidity is not necessary. For example, if you know you will need $20,000 to send junior to college 12 years from now, you might buy bonds with a face value of $20,000 that mature in 12 years. If these bonds have a coupon less than the current interest rates, they will be selling at a discount, and you will be able to buy them for less than $20,000. In the next 12 years you will be receiving "interest" on the bonds and will also have a capital gain when they mature. However, you sacrifice liquidity, since, in the 12 years before the bonds mature, their value will decline if interest rates rise. Investing in intermediate-term issues must be carefully matched to individual requirements and tax needs; it is best done only in consultation with a professional advisor.

Investors must also be aware that some bonds are not actively traded (have a "thin" market); this can cause problems in liquidity and rather wide swings in prices because of the lack of sellers and buyers. This usually occurs when the original bond is several years old or is very deeply discounted from its face value. Because of the imbalance in buyers and sellers, these markets are "inefficient," meaning that it may be necessary to depart considerably from the generally prevailing price to actually execute a trade. When a bond is thinly traded, it is always wise to use limit orders rather than market orders to avoid having a transaction executed at an unfavorable price.

Finally, investors desiring increased safety in bonds should consider investing in a bond mutual fund rather than in individual corporate bonds. The advantage of a mutual fund is that for a relatively small investment one can own a portion of a large portfolio of bonds, thereby virtually eliminating the risk of any significant loss from a single missed payment or default. However, bond funds usually charge commissions and concentrate on the income and safety of bonds and less on capital gains. You can tell the difference between an A and B rating as well as a bond mutual fund manager. If your primary goal in buying bonds is to achieve capital gains, it is better to skip the fund and invest in individual, deeply discounted long-term bonds.

10

REAL ESTATE

During the 1960s and 1970s, no investment captured the attention of the average investor like real estate. If your next door neighbor had not made a killing in real estate, he certainly knew someone who had. In addition, during the 1970s housing prices skyrocketed, far outstripping inflation and all other investments. By 1979, it was nearly impossible to find a person who sold his house for less than he paid for it, and it appeared as if housing prices would go through the roof forever.

Most people are familiar with real estate transactions, at least the techniques pertaining to the purchase of a family residence. (On the other hand, a much smaller percentage of families own stocks, bonds, or any of the other types of investments.) It is ironic how little thought and research precede the purchase of a house, the largest investment the average American will make. We have had clients who spend 6 months researching the nuances of competitive models of automobiles in order to shave an extra $800 off the purchase price while, at the same time, they plunk down $200,000 for a house without even having the roof inspected. The purchase of a personal residence is a very emotional decision, and this, coupled with the prevailing belief that "real estate prices always go up," makes it seem unnecessary to be cautious. In this chapter, we shall look at the principles of real estate investment and the prospects for real estate in the 1980s.

REAL ESTATE AS A BUSINESS

One of the most important aspects of considering an investment in real estate is to clearly separate the business and investment aspects from the personal and emotional ones. For most investors, their personal residence will be their first and only investment in real estate. Many people can find very good reasons to spend $50,000 on a Masserati or a Mercedes, but few would claim that it is also a good business decision. However, in real estate, personal and emotional decisions often predominate, and it is taken as an article of faith that these also represent "good investment decisions." There is certainly nothing wrong with heavily weighing your emotional feeling about a piece of real estate (particularly your personal residence), but it is also important to look at the business prospects with a heart of stone. You may well decide to spend a small fortune on your anchorage, but at least be certain you do it with your eyes open and without the illusion that you are also making a brilliant business decision unless you have gone through some careful analysis.

One of the characteristics of the real estate market in the 1970s (and, for that matter, a characteristic of any strong bull market) was that it was hard to tell the smart from the lucky. There were a lot of people around in the early 1980s who had brilliant track records in real estate in the 1970s and who stumbled as the real estate market began its downward slide. It is not safe to assume that real estate prices will always go up. They, like everything else, cycle.

There have, in fact, been major real estate crashes in the United States. In the early 1800s, prices of eastern real estate began to soar. Subsequently, people began to be attracted to the cheaper land to the west. The Government wanted to develop this area and began to provide loans and other Government subsidies to a backwater area called Chicago. The Federal Government also planned to build the Illinois–Michigan Canal joining Lake Michigan with the Mississippi via the Illinois river. The mining, agriculture, livestock, and forest products potential was huge, and the speculators poured in. Land prices soared. The same 80- by 100-foot parcel of land at South Water and Clark streets that sold for $100 in 1832 sold for $3,000 in 1834 (which was a fortune in those days). One year later, the same lot brought $15,000 (as reported by the *Chicago American*). In the mid-1830s, Chicago seemed to be more a real estate lottery than a city. At the peak of this overheated period, the canal operation was cancelled, and the real estate market collapsed. Before it was over, it precipitated the "Panic of 1837" which mushroomed into a full-blown, economic depression. People did not lose everything, but an acre of land selling for $11,000 in 1836 could not be sold for $100 in 1900! Everything cycles, of course, and for those who held on, their acre was worth several hundred thousand in 1979.

There are other examples of boom and bust in real estate: southern California circa 1875, Florida circa 1925. In Dade county, people actually lined up to purchase lots in new subdivisions, and a winning lottery option on the purchase of a new house was often worth thousands of dollars. A perverse twist to the Florida real estate crash of 1926 was that one of the influences fueling the boom had been the mild and balmy weather that had prevailed for a generation. Just at the peak, two hurricanes hit the state, accelerating the real estate crash of the late 1920s.

The fact that "they're not making any more land" does not mean that anybody will buy the piece of land that you happen to own. Profits in real estate are not guaranteed. In fact, we believe that in the 1980s real estate profits that outperform inflation may be difficult to come by, and these investments must be made very selectively.

There are two ways to make a profit in real estate: investing and speculating.

INVESTING IN REAL ESTATE

It is important to remember that, as an investment, *real estate has no intrinsic value*. Your personal residence has an intrinsic value as a shelter, but the deed for the condo building lot at Vail is just a piece of paper. The investment value of real estate is strictly a function of how much income it produces. It should be viewed much as you would view a bond or a stock, as a vehicle for producing an income stream in your program of financial independence. Like all other investment vehicles, it will produce a certain rate of return and will have an associated risk (either a failure to produce that rate of return or a loss of investment capital or both). Therefore, in evaluating the investment merits of a piece of real estate, you should first calculate its expected rate of return (rent) and then its anticipated risk. Having done this, you should then determine if the risk–return relationship compares favorably with that of other available investment vehicles.

Suppose, in July, 1983, Sam B. was offered an opportunity to purchase a duplex apartment for $100,000. This property was estimated to produce an average annual net cash flow of $12,000 (after considering all expenses, rents, depreciation, and tax breaks). Sam has carefully gone over all the calculations. He has made certain that the property is indeed in good shape and that the estimated expenses are realistic. Furthermore, he has looked at the rental history and is satisfied that the projected rents are indeed realistic; that the city council is not considering a rent control law; and that it is likely he will be able to keep the property fully occupied. He has calculated his tax savings using both the regular tax and the alternative minimum tax and believes that he has a realistic estimate of his true tax break. Having taken care of all the caveats, he is reasonably confident that his $100,000 investment will indeed produce $12,000 a year in income. Thus, he will be getting a 12% annual rate of return. Of course, he cannot be completely certain that things will go as he has calculated, and there is some risk associated with the purchase. To put the risk in perspective, he checks the current yield of a 20-year treasury bond or high-quality corporate bond and finds that it is 11.5%. He then asks himself whether it is really worth the extra 0.5% return to accept the risk of the duplex. Sam B. calls the real estate broker and politely rejects the offer.

SPECULATING IN REAL ESTATE

There is, of course, another way to make money in real estate: capital gains or speculating. Cautious folks and real estate brokers alike shun the term *speculation* and always refer to the process as "rapid appreciation" or "capital gains." Although it is true that, from the viewpoint of pure semantics, any profit realized on the appreciation in price of an asset is capital gains, it is also true that when you invest in real estate with a negative cash flow and the hope that its price will go up you are speculating.

We all agree that buying undeveloped land in Western Utah with the hope that oil will be discovered is speculating. We can probably even agree that buying swamp land 50 miles from Disney World is also speculating. It may be a little harder to believe that the brand new two-bedroom condominium on the ski slopes at Aspen is speculating. And, of course, it is unthinkable that we won't be able to sell our new $250,000 house for $300,000 6 months from now (after all, the same house sold for only $150,000 a year ago).

Unfortunately, a spade is a spade. Any time you are anticipating a profit from appreciation in real estate without regard to its cash flow, you are speculating. You are speculating that when you want to sell there will be a buyer willing to pay your asking price. Just because the condominium salesman assures you that the present $200,000 units "won't last long; they will be selling for $300,000 next year" does not mean that this will occur. He is just speculating that it will occur. We are concentrating on real estate here, but the principles are just as useful in any overheated market. For example, computer programs were developed in the late 1960s which justified paying *P/E* ratios of 40 to 80 for "growth" stocks. But chutzpah was really redefined by realtors of the 1970s who found ways to justify a negative cash flow for the real estate investor.

The reason it is important to understand that looking for capital gains in real estate is really just speculation is that this is potentially a risky business.

There is far less risk associated with misjudging an income stream than there is in misjudging a future resale price. If the potential profit in a real estate deal consists mainly of appreciation in price, it represents a very risky investment and should produce a very high rate of return to justify the risk.

Sam B.'s real estate broker was not easily put off. When Sam called to reject the duplex offer, he countered, "Wait a minute, Sam! After-tax cash flow is only one of the advantages of this deal. The big kicker is the long-term capital gains you will get. We have carefully analyzed the population trends, new building starts, demographic–Sunbelt–baby-boom–ecology–lifestyle–megatrends, and I can assure you that you will be able to sell this place for a minimum of $200,000 in 10 years. Think about it and give me a call back."

So Sam thinks about it: "Maybe the guy is right. He is, after all, a long-time friend and very reputable fellow and has certainly made a considerable amount of money for himself. He is probably right that I will be able to sell the duplex for double my money in 10 years."

Sam then uses formula 4.4 from Chapter 4 and calculates the rate of return on the capital appreciation as 7.2% a year. This, added to the 12% from the income stream, brings the total annual rate of return to 19.2%. In addition, Sam can anticipate excluding at least some of the capital gains from taxes, which might make the actual rate of return closer to 21 or 22%. This return is more in line with the assumed risk, and, viewed in this perspective, the investment may be indeed be reasonable. Sam must re-member, however, that nearly half of his return is predicated on capital appreciation, which is really speculation and is much riskier than most of us generally believe.

Should Sam buy the duplex? Only Sam can answer the question. He will have to take a hard look at the assumptions behind the income and capital appreciation projections and decide if he feels comfortable with them. If he can sleep at night with this risk, he should probably buy the duplex, since a 22% annual rate of return is good.

Real estate as an investment, then, has two components: its income-producing potential and its speculation potential. By far the most important is the income, since the ultimate value of any investment is always a function of its income-producing potential. It is particularly important to keep this in mind when considering real estate, since it is very easy to be seduced by the potential of significant capital appreciation. Ask the people who invested in Houston's Garden Apartment limited partnerships going condo in 1979. Everyone in the country got the same idea and the vacancy rate soared to 30%. Real estate buyers who purchase property that produces little or no positive cash flow and justify the purchase with the expectation of huge capital gains several years in the future have stepped beyond the stage of investment and entered the world of speculation. They are betting that, in years ahead, they will find a greater fool than they to take the property off their hands.

Now we are not saying that the price of real estate never goes up, nor do we claim that substantial amounts of money cannot be made in this speculative aspect of the investment. However, if you pay a price that is unrelated to the underlying income-producing potential of the real estate, you are living in the fast lane. Even if you are successful and do realize a large capital gain, if it takes several years to do this, your annualized rate of return may not be significantly greater than that which could have been obtained with a much less risky investment.

YOUR HOME AS AN INVESTMENT

Chances are you already have an investment in real estate—your personal residence. It is an informative exercise to evaluate the business quality of this investment. Set aside, for the moment, any emotional benefits you are receiving from your home and consider only whether it represents a good or bad use of your investment dollars. In other words, would you be better off renting your housing or owning it?

Let us assume that Sam B. moved to a large western city 4 years ago at the height of the real estate frenzy. He was able to find a house that suited the family's needs (and provided a little luxury on the side) for a mere $300,000. The family also looked at some rental properties including condominiums and single-family detached houses and found that similar quality properties were available by lease at approximately $1,200 per month. Like most American families, they decided to buy the house. Let's also assume for the moment that they were able to completely finance the $300,000 purchase price at a relatively modest 12% fixed, assumable, no-points mortgage (actually, this type of mortgage was extinct in the early 1980s). The monthly mortgage payments were approximately $3,000, nearly all of which was tax-deductible interest, so that Sam estimated his out-of-pocket monthly mortgage expense was $1,500. Compared to the $1,200 or $1,300 it would cost to rent a similar piece of property, this seemed to be a bargain. "After all, renting gives you no tax break, and you are not building up any equity," reasoned Sam. This is true, but renters may get tax deductions and mortgage payments are structured so that the buyer really doesn't start building up significant equity until after the first half of a 30-year mortgage.

There are considerably more expenses to home ownership than the monthly mortgage payment. There are taxes, insurance, repairs, assessments, and so on. Sam's actual monthly cost was closer to $2,200 than $1,500. The real gap between his ownership cost and rental cost was nearly $800 per month. This $800 represents very lazy investment money. All Sam can hope to receive from this "investment" is some capital gain when he ultimately sells the house. From a financial point of view, Sam would be considerably ahead by renting and investing the $800 a month in treasury bonds at 12%.

Of course, Sam could not finance the entire $300,000 purchase price; he had to put some of his own equity into the home at the beginning. Suppose he made a $100,000 down payment and financed the other $200,000. This would reduce his monthly mortgage payment to slightly under $2,000 or slightly under $1,000 after taxes. He would still have the same $700 a month in other costs, but now his total monthly payment of $1,700 is not so much greater than the rental expense. It is tempting, in contemplating a home purchase, to calculate the out-of-pocket expenses based only on the financed portion of the property. But we must look more closely. It is not reasonable to ignore the earning potential of the money tied up in the down payment. If Sam was able to obtain a mortgage for 12% interest he could certainly have found a safe 12% investment for his down payment (such as a Treasury Bond). By making the down payment, he was forgoing $12,000 of potential annual income, which, after taxes, translates into $500 a month. In actual practice, the percentage of down payment makes very little difference in the final, monthly after-tax cost of home ownership. A large down payment makes the out-of-pocket monthly expenses seem smaller, but it represents a loss of potential monthly income from other investments. Also, if Sam decided to rent, he would retain the use of his $100,000 and thus further decrease his monthly rental expenses by $500 per month.

Contrary to what many investors believe, the method of financing has little to do with an investment's profitability. If a given investment yields 10%, that is its return regardless of whether it is financed with debt, equity, or a combination of the two. What is affected by financing is the nominal rate of return on the investor's equity—the amount of money initially paid into the investment. The less equity, the greater the leverage. As we saw in Chapter 4, the greater the leverage the greater the risk. Leverage is simply a multiplier; if things go favorably, leverage will increase the rate of return. If things go unfavorably, leverage will increase the loss. But leverage will not change the probability that an investment will be a success or a failure!

In general, leverage is an advantage if it is possible to borrow money at an interest rate lower than the rate of return of the asset. If you can get a 12% mortgage and the property is earning 16% a year, you are better off with a small down payment and lots of leverage. On the other hand, if you have to pay 16% for the mortgage and the property is producing no income and only appreciating 10% a year, the financing is working against you. Another important point to remember is that leverage increases risk. Since most real estate investments already have a considerable element of risk, the use of high leverage can easily push the investment beyond what is prudent for the average doctor investor.

How does this effect Sam B.'s analysis of his decision to buy rather than rent? After he has completed his monthly cost analysis and comparison with rental cost, he needs to consider the leverage. If he has made a small down payment, he must realize that he is taking an even bigger investment risk than the monthly figures might indicate. If he guesses right, and his house continues to appreciate in value, he will be ahead of the game. On the other hand, should a housing slump set in and prices stabilize or even fall, he will have many dead dollars.

The purpose of this example was to illustrate some elementary ways of analyzing a real estate investment with a familiar example. Even though Sam B.'s decision to purchase a house was not the best investment decision, it was still probably a good decision, and we are not advocating that you go out and sell the family residence. In addition to its investment potential, home ownership provides considerable emotional satisfaction, and these factors must definitely be taken into account. Silas Marner was wrong. You should not be so devoted to your financial independence plan that you deny yourself a satisfying lifestyle. Being 70, rich, and unhappy is not what this book is about. Emotional values certainly have a place in evaluating the real estate investment in your home. However, emotional factors should be vigorously purged from any other real estate investment decisions.

RAW LAND

When they are thinking of real estate investments, undeveloped or "raw" land is the first thing that comes into most people's minds. It is by far the most glamorous and potentially profitable form of real estate speculation. At the same time, it is also the riskiest, and profits are rare. Although it is true that "they aren't making anymore land," it is also true that there is still plenty of surplus on hand, and simply owning land is no guarantee of a profit. We all know of the cattleman who made a windfall fortune when the interstate highway was built next to his ranch and the alligator farmer who owned 1,000 acres of swamp on the future site of Disney World. But we never hear from the owners of the millions and millions of acres of raw land in this country that just sits, doing nothing, still awaiting the arrival of an interstate highway. The key to making money in raw land is having the land in the correct location, and this invariably involves a lot of guesswork and risk. If you guess correctly, you will make a fortune. But if you guess wrong, or if you guess right but are 20 years too early, raw land will become an albatross around your neck.

There are several disadvantages to investments in undeveloped land. First, raw land provides no income but is simply a source of continuing expense. There are property taxes, liability insurance, and real estate transaction costs. All these are in addition to the interest charges if you are able to finance a portion of the land (many banks will not finance undeveloped land). Second, it is usually necessary to invest a sizable sum of money to realize any potential profit in raw land: $10,000 is usually a minimal amount, and $50,000 or $100,000 is a more common sum. Third, you must have deep pockets. Raw land often sits for years before appreciating in value, and all the while, the meter is running on the carrying costs. Finally, raw land (as is all real estate) is among the least liquid of investments. If you decide you have made a mistake and want to bail out, you may find it impossible to do so at anything but a distressed price.

Because of these disadvantages—primarily the negative cash flow and high risk—we believe that raw land does not represent a judicious investment for most doctors. Unless you are absolutely certain of the appreciation potential of the property, your money will be better off elsewhere.

INCOME-PRODUCING PROPERTY

Another common form of real estate investment is ownership of small units of income-producing property such as small groups of rental housing or a small piece of commercial property. When carefully selected, these investments can produce a useful income stream, but for the small investor, they usually are not feasible. The problem is that although the gross rate of return may be 15 or 20% a year, the expenses of managing and supervising small units of property are relatively high and significantly decrease the net return. It is almost as difficult and expensive to manage a four-unit apartment house as it is the 70-unit model. When the costs are spread over 70 units, they are manageable, but when spread over only four units, they may devour the profits. If you are a handyman or simply like the concept of being a landlord, it is possible to make modest profits in small income-producing properties, but we think most doctors will find the earnings not worth the hassle.

LIMITED PARTNERSHIPS

Limited partnerships are the most sensible way for the small investor to participate in real estate. Limited partnerships are business organizations composed of two groups: the general partners and the limited partners. The general partners are professionals who organize and run the business, and the limited partners are the financial backers. The general partners operate the business and take a small percentage of the profits, whereas the limited partners risk most of the financial loss but receive most of the profits.

Typically, a real estate limited partnership would manage a fairly large income-producing property such as a group of garden apartments, a shopping center, a high-rise apartment complex, or a large piece of industrial property leased to a major corporation. The general partners are professional developers and managers of such properties and handle all of the operations. The limited partners have no knowledge or experience in real estate but contribute most of the capital for the operation. The partnership is "limited" because each limited partner is liable only to the extent of his investment. This is in contrast to the conventional partnership, where all partners are totally liable for all debts of the partnership. A limited partnership is a mechanism whereby a small investor can get access to professional management and operation of a large real estate investment.

In the past, limited partnerships were an important tax shelter, since a limited partner was able to deduct all of the potential liabilities of the partnership even though he was not actually legally responsible for them. For example, Sam B. and 29 other limited partners could each have put up $10,000 to organize the "Sunbelt Vista Garden Apartments." Using this $300,000 initial capitalization, the general partners might have borrowed another $2.7 million from banks and insurance companies to provide a 10:1 leverage for actual construction of the apartments. Each of the limited partners would have been entitled to claim 1/30 of the total capitalization as his expenses and would have been able to deduct the carrying charges on $100,000 from his income tax even though he had only initially invested $10,000. Thus, it was possible to generate tax losses that far exceeded the initial investment. However, because Sam B. is a "limited" partner, he would not actually have been liable for the loan if the project failed. (He would, of course, have lost his original $10,000.) Because of this generous tax break, it was a bull market for limited partnerships, and many poorly conceived and ineptly managed limited partnerships were sold, not on their investment merit but simply because of the tax advantage. The "at-risk" rules of the new tax laws mostly eliminated the excess tax write-offs, and limited partnerships are no longer the tax windfall they once were.

A well-managed limited partnership with skilled general partners can still represent an excellent investment opportunity for participating in real estate, however. We believe that they are the only really practical method for the small investor to become involved, since real estate management is no place for an amateur. Only by coupling forces with skilled general partners can the average doctor hope to come out ahead. In evaluating a proposed limited partnership, the most important factor is the past performance record of the general partners. If they have a history of successful operations, it is reasonable to assume that their present offering will also be profitable. It is unwise to throw in with anyone who does not have a proven track record, however. It is also important to make certain that the actual cash flow of the partnership will be positive. That is, the partnership should provide a positive income stream and not depend solely on tax write-offs for its benefits.

Because of the complexity of the field and the variety of offerings available, we believe you should consult with a professional financial advisor before investing in any limited partnership.

THE VACATION CONDOMINIUM

Vacation condo "opportunities" are everywhere and are hyped without even lip service to their actual value and with no trace of shame. This is the used car lot of the real estate world!

Buy a vacation condo if you want to use it, but do not expect to make any money. The price of these units is usually so inflated that all profit potential for the next 25 years is gone. Contrary to what the sales force may tell you, the units are *not* going like hotcakes (if they were, there would be no need for the vigorous promotion and hype). The fastest way we know to turn vacation gloss to investment dross is condo time sharing! *Caveat emptor!*

REAL ESTATE INVESTING IN THE 1980s

The past 15 years has been a time of rapidly appreciating real estate values, and, in general, investors in real estate have done very well. However, real estate profits are not inevitable, and, like any other investment vehicle, real estate cycles. Generally speaking, real estate is a timely investment at the beginning of a period of accelerating inflation. The incredible bull market of the 1970s was fueled by a fortuitous combination of favorable demographics (the coming of age of the post-war baby boom), the existence of many favorable tax benefits for real estate investments, and rapidly increasing inflation. Government funds were subsidizing low- and middle-income housing, and the addition of a second income from a working spouse enabled more families to qualify for mortgages. The widespread publicity given to the rapid acceleration in single-family housing prices further fueled the demand for housing and created almost frenzied buying in the late 1970s.

Most Americans fail to realize that, in historical terms, the average value of real estate in the United States has simply indexed inflation. In other words, you could buy just as much bread with a house in 1925 as you could in 1978. In inflation-adjusted terms, over the long term there really has not been a tremendous appreciation in real estate values. The real profits in real estate during the 1970s were made because of the rapid acceleration of interest rates. Homeowners with mortgages at low, flat interest rate levels could make a handsome profit by transferring the mortgage to a buyer in return for an increased selling price.

As real estate entered the decade of the 1980s, nearly everything that had been favorable in the early 1970s had shifted to neutral or unfavorable. First, the baby boom had pretty much been absorbed by the market, at least in terms of demand for entry-level housing. Thus, most of the new activity represented trading up from original houses. Trading up adds very little to the overall aggregate value of real estate, since it does not bring any new buyers into the market. When new buyers stop coming in, those wishing to trade up have no one to sell their existing house to, and the cycle begins to slow down. Some economists believe that recent high interest rates and housing prices have produced a deferred (or "pent-up") demand, which is waiting to swamp the housing markets now that prices have stabilized and interest rates have lowered. Although it is true that some would-be buyers may have been shut out of the market, many of them may have turned to other sources of housing. The housing futures project at Harvard–MIT estimated that 2.7 million new housing units were added in the early 1980s through so-called nonconventional sources (such as a conversion of commercial buildings to residences, rehabilitation of abandoned homes, breakdown of larger homes into smaller housing units, etc.). This group has estimated that in the 1980s these types of conversions may rise to 4.5 million and effectively absorb any deferred demand for new housing.

Real estate values have traditionally been linked to inflation rates. In the 1980s, we have seen inflation stabilize and decrease, and this is likely to make real estate a relatively average investment during the decade of the 1980s. Even if housing prices were again to begin an accelerated upward climb, it will probably not be the individual homeowners who profit in this cycle but rather the banks. In the upsurge of the 1970s, commercial banks were mostly shut out, since they were locked into low-yielding flat-rate mortgages at a time when the cost of their money was going through the roof. Having been burned by this experience, banks have responded by lessening their risk to rising interest rates in the form of variable-interest-rate mortgages. Thus, the flat-rate mortgage, which was the major money maker for most investors in the 1970s, will be less available during the 1980s. It is ironic that banks have introduced variable-interest-rate mortgages at a time when, in all likelihood, interest rates will continue at a low level or decline.

Another reason for concern in the real estate market is the current conservative political climate and the frequent discussion of lower taxes or even a flat-rate income tax. Most proposals for a flat-rate income tax eliminate the current deduction for interest payments. If this interest deduction were eliminated, it would have a serious negative impact on real estate prices, since it would, in effect, greatly raise the cost of real estate financing. We do not feel that this change in tax policy will go into effect in the near future, but just the fact that it is being discussed will introduce a new element of caution in the forces controlling real estate prices.

Finally, as we shall see in Chapter 14, there are many reasons to believe that the 1980s will be a period of steadily decreasing inflation rates or deflation. Real estate has historically not performed well during such periods.

In summary, we do not believe that the real estate bonanza of the 1970s will continue through the 1980s. There will be some good investment opportunities in selective locations during this decade, but opportunities will be harder to find, and investors will need to be more selective than in the past. Real estate will probably have a place in your financial plan at some point. The important overall principle to remember is that real estate is no different from any other investment and must be critically evaluated on the basis of its current income stream and its relative investment risks. Since the types of investment available in the real estate world are varied and complex, we do not believe you should undertake them without first consulting with a professional financial advisor.

11

TANGIBLE ASSETS

The inflation of the late 1960s and 1970s caused a serious erosion in the value of financial assets and currency and generated massive shifts of funds away from these instruments and into tangible assets. We all can remember gold topping $800 an ounce at the height of the inflation-era hysteria. Many investors and brokers made substantial amounts of money dealing in gems, metals, and other tangible assets, and there are many who predict a resurgence of inflation within the next few years. There is no question that in times of runaway inflation, tangible assets do very well. However, they are not very rewarding investments during periods of stable inflation or deflation. Our view is that there will not be runaway inflation during the 1980s and that this will be a period for financial assets rather than tangible assets. However, there are many investors who are interested in balancing their investment portfolio and providing a hedge against the inflation risk. There are others who are interested in combining esthetics and investments in a single package. For these people, there may be a place for investments in tangibles.

PRECIOUS GEMS

There are a wide variety of gems that are touted as "investments." However, only diamonds have widespread acceptance as a store of value, and unless you are hopelessly addicted to emeralds or some other stone, you should confine any gem investments to diamonds. To have investment value, a gem must have three attributes—beauty, durability, and rarity. The diamond is the only gem stone that possesses all three of these qualities. Perhaps its most important characteristic is its rarity. Only 1% of all the diamonds mined in the world will yield a gem stone at least 1 carat in size. (A carat is 2/10 of a gram and should not be confused with the karat, which is a measure of the purity of gold—24-karat gold being 100% pure.)

Another reason for the popularity of diamonds is their portability. A great amount of wealth can be stored in a small object that is easy to transport and conceal. Although this may not be of much concern to Americans, in most of the world, this attribute is of considerable importance and accounts for the continuing popularity of diamonds as a store of wealth. Diamonds are recognized throughout the world and have international liquidity.

Finally, as with any tangible asset, diamonds possess a hard value, which is relatively immune from the ravages of inflation and cannot be printed out of existence by free-spending politicians. When inflationary expectations increase, money inevitably flows into diamonds and other tangible assets, driving up their prices. Diamonds are one of the few investment items that can be used in day-to-day life as admired jewelry and a much-appreciated gift.

There are four determinants of diamond value: cut, color, clarity, and carat weight. Each of these has been standardized by the Gemological Institute of America, and you should never buy a diamond that has not been rated by this organization in these four areas. As a general concept, colorless diamonds are the most valuable, and value decreases with hue. When an extremely deep shade is reached, value may again increase, and the diamond is then labeled "fancy." Clarity is a measure of the internal perfection of a stone and is graded from flawless to imperfect. Only rarely is a diamond completely flawless, and even the top grades usually possess some modest irregularities that do not materially affect the value of the stone. The cut of the diamond has only a minor bearing on its value, but any stone with an imperfect cut or a cut that is inappropriate to its size will lose value. The importance of carat weight is obvious.

If you decide to invest in diamonds, it is very important to deal only in certified gems and only with long-established, reputable dealers. If you are buying a diamond simply as a present with no eye to investment value, this may not be so important, but when you are picking a stone as an investment, you want to be certain that it will appreciate in value along with other diamonds and, more important, be marketable if and when you decide to sell it. It is very difficult for an amateur to have any understanding of the inherent value of a given stone, and getting an education on the subject is a tall order. Opinions differ from one expert to another, and the market is heavily influenced by personal taste, even among the experts.

There are gem market letters available that can provide some insight. One that we have found helpful is the *Gem Market Reporter* by Kurt Arens of Phoenix, Arizona. Mr. Arens has also written a pamphlet, *Guide to Successful Gem Investing*, which is published by the Western Monetary Consultant of Fort Collins, Colorado. In the end, however, you will be at the mercy of the dealer, and the only way to be sure you are not being taken is to work with reputable professionals. Gem dealers are rated by Kurt Arens's *Gem Market Reporter*, and you should always obtain references (and check them out) before making a purchase from a dealer.

As is the case with many tangible assets, there is the buy-retail/sell-wholesale trap, the market is very thin, and the "spread" is usually quite large. Commissions as high as 30% are not uncommon in these transactions. Therefore, you should not make an investment in diamonds with the thought of turning it over rapidly. Diamonds are most suitable as an insurance policy against runaway inflation or social and political upheaval. Since neither of these situations seems likely in the United States in the rest of the century, we suggest that you confine your diamond purchases to those that enhance your lifestyle.

INVESTOR METALS

Just as diamonds are the standard of the gem industry, gold is the standard of investor metals. The reasons for investing in gold are similar to those for investing in gems with only minor differences in flavor. Gold does not have the esthetic rewards of a diamond (you cannot wear a gold bar on your finger), nor is it as compact and portable. On the other hand, it is universally accepted throughout the world and is a much more liquid investment than a diamond. Because there is a well-organized market, it is easy to execute trades with small spreads and small commissions. We believe that gold is the only metal that deserves serious consideration as an investment.

You may be surprised that we do not include silver as a suitable investment. One of the problems with silver is that at some periods it trades like gold and at other times it trades as an industrial metal such as copper or iron. Silver is not as rare as gold, and there are huge above-ground supplies in such countries as India and Russia. This easy availability of supplies effectively puts a ceiling on the ultimate price appreciation, and therefore silver does not make a secure hedge against runaway inflation. There is also a large industrial market for silver, and this also exerts considerable influence on the metal's price. Over 85% of silver is used for industrial purposes rather than as a store of wealth. Any change in industrial usage patterns will have a major effect on the price of the metal. Over 40% of silver is used for photographic purposes, and the emergence of computer and digital information systems makes it possible that this industrial use will decline in the upcoming years, thereby freeing a large source of silver for other uses and thus keeping a ceiling on prices.

History has taught us that the silver market can be manipulated. Although Bunker Hunt lamented in March of 1980 that "a billion dollars isn't what it used to be," he, his brother Herbert, and a group of rich Saudi Arabians almost succeeded in pulling off one of the greatest financial coups of all time by cornering the world's silver market. They drove the price from $2.90 an ounce in 1973 to $50 an ounce by January of 1980. When the scheme fell apart on March 27, 1980, the quick looked pretty much like the dead, and the resulting crash in the price of the metal not only wiped out silver speculators but caused all of Wall Street to teeter on the edge of a 1929-style financial panic. We believe serious investors in metals should stick to gold.

INVESTING IN GOLD

There are many ways to participate in the gold market, including gold mining stocks, gold coins, gold bullion, gold commodity futures and options, and gold mining ventures in limited partnerships. Of these, we believe that gold mining stocks and gold coins are the most judicious investments for the average doctor.

Shares of gold mining companies are traded on the major stock exchanges, and there are several mutual funds that invest primarily in mining companies. (The mutual funds offer geographical diversification and generally decrease the risk associated with owning gold mining stocks.) Gold mining stocks are an attractive way to participate in the market because their price usually lags slightly behind the price changes in the metal itself, giving the investor an opportunity to observe the market before taking the aurous plunge. In addition, gold mining shares usually outperform the bullion price movements, providing some degree of leverage. The shares usually pay a dividend, which in the past has run as high as 10 to 14%. They are extremely liquid investments, can be purchased with little commission, and do not require carrying expenses such as insurance, assay, and storage fees. The disadvantage of owning mining shares is that you do not really own gold, and you are not as thoroughly hedged against inflation or political upheaval as you would be by having the metal itself. In addition, gold mining companies are susceptible to other market risks, as outlined in Chapter 4, which do not affect physical gold.

Gold coins are the best way for the average investor to participate in direct ownership of gold. The advantage of coins is that they are legal exchangeable tender and are very liquid. Coins such as the 1.0-ounce South African Krugerrand, the 1.2-ounce Mexican peso, or the 0.98 ounce Australian krona are currently exchanged in most developed countries of the world. The market price of the coins varies directly with the underlying gold market. They are small and easy to store and require no assay at the time of trading. Because of these advantages, gold coins usually sell at a slight premium over the value of the metal they contain, and if you sell them, you will probably have to do so at a small discount. However, these differences are usually small compared to the movements in the value of the metal itself, and we believe it is a worthwhile price to pay for the other conveniences of owning the coins. If you purchase gold coins in the United States, you should be aware that many states consider them real property rather than currency and will impose a sales tax. You should therefore buy your coins in a state that does not have a sales tax or in a state that does not charge the tax for out-of-state purchases.

It is also possible to invest in gold bullion, but there are extra expenses associated with this that are not associated with coins. Bullion must be assayed every time it is traded, is large and difficult to transport, must be insured and stored, and is usually only available in fairly large denominations. Investors should consider gold bullion only if they are buying a large amount of gold and plan to leave it on deposit in a bank and never take possession.

Gold is considered a commodity, and future contracts are traded on the commodities' exchanges. As we shall explain in the next chapter, only those with a death wish should deal in commodities. Occasional fortunes are made there, but the majority of commodity investors lose their shirts. Steer clear of gold commodity futures.

The same can be said for fooling around with gold exploration, gold mining ventures, and limited partnerships to explore for gold. In trying to analyze these mining investments, it is sometimes hard to tell a golden calf from a golden shaft. Gold is very difficult to find, and these investments are usually sold only on the basis of their tax benefits. You will almost certainly lose your money if you invest in them.

Gold is not for every financial plan. However, it does provide some security against runaway inflation or complete financial collapse. If you are the type of person who cannot sleep at night without having some sort of security blanket, you might wish to have a small amount of your assets in gold coins. If you are just a little uneasy about the future course of the economy, you might want to take a small position in gold mining stocks.

However, for most doctors, we feel that there are better opportunities in the years ahead than gold.

COLLECTIBLES

The term *collectibles* is applied to a broad range of tangible goods that usually have some elements of rarity or scarcity, artistic value, age, or esthetic qualities. Collectibles include rare coins, stamps, books, antiques, artwork, oriental rugs, etc. Although people make collections of nearly anything from string to baseball cards, the simple fact that an item is collected does not make it an investment-grade collectible.

Investing in collectibles is generally very speculative and should mostly be done for its personal rewards. It is an extremely difficult undertaking because of the expertise required to ascertain market value and to develop any feel for appreciation value. Sotheby Park Bernet maintains an index of collectible prices, which provides a rough gauge of the general state of the market in various types of objects. Table 11.1 shows the values of the *Sotheby Index* for 1975, 1980, and 1981. The base index year was 1975, and we can see that there was a rapid appreciation in price of many collectibles in the latter part of the 1970s. However, between 1980 and 1981, many categories declined in value.

There are other difficulties to be considered when investing in collectibles. The *Sotheby Index* provides no help in choosing a specific item from a class of collectibles. Even if you decide that Chinese ceramics are in a bull market, after you have charged into the china shop, you have no

TABLE 11.1 The Sotheby Index

Category	Weights[a]	1975[b]	1980	1981
Old Master paintings	17	100	255	199
Nineteenth century European paintings	12	100	225	176
Impressionist and postimpressionist paintings	18	100	206	239
Modern paintings (1900–1950)	10	100	204	232
American paintings (1800–pre-WWII)	3	100	350	424
Continental ceramics	3	100	336	299
Chinese ceramics	10	100	462	259
English silver	5	100	205	160
Continental silver	5	100	179	143
American furniture	3	100	172	209
Continental furniture	7	100	232	218
English furniture	7	100	256	270
AGGREGATE		100	253	244

[a]The higher the number, the greater the influence on the Index.
[b]Base index year.

way of knowing which ceramic tea set to purchase. The collectible market is extremely inefficient (meaning that if you are a seller there are often times you can't find a buyer, and vice versa), and spreads of 30 to 40% between the bid and asked prices are the rule rather than the exception. Sales tax is usually added to the sale of any collectibles. In addition, they pay no dividends and often entail considerable upkeep costs in the form of shipping, insurance, restoration, and taxes. Finally, fraud is very common, and a single instance of fraud can depress the value of even the genuine articles in the same general field.

On the positive side, collectibles, like diamonds, can provide a good deal of lifestyle enhancement and provide a way of turning a personal hobby or collection into an area of investment. We believe that no one should consider investing in collectibles unless he is personally very knowledgeable in the specific category of item he is purchasing.

TANGIBLES AS INVESTMENTS

Tangible assets and financial assets represent opposite poles of the investment spectrum. Whether one or the other is the most judicious investment at any given time is most directly correlated with the rate of inflation, but there are other factors that also come to bear. Factors that favor tangible assets include:

1. Rising rate of inflation
2. Rising taxes
3. Increasing government regulation
4. Political instability
5. Policies favoring consumption
6. Fear of personal harm.

The factors which are favorable for financial assets include:

1. Declining rate of inflation
2. Reduced government intervention in the private sector
3. Sustained economic growth
4. Improving productivity
5. Political stability
6. Policies favoring savings and investment.

We believe that in the 1980s there are more factors favoring financial assets than tangible assets. This was not necessarily true during the 1970s. Table 11.2 shows the compound annual rates of return for a variety of different types of investments for the 10-year period from 1972 to 1982 and for the one year from 1981 to 1982. During the 1970s, the highest

TABLE 11.2 Compound annual rates of return[a]

	10 years (6/72–6/82)	Rank	1 Year (6/81–6/82)	Rank
Oil	29.9%	1	6.3%	3
U.S. coins	22.5	2	−27.8	13
U.S. stamps	21.9	3	−3.0	9
Oriental rugs	19.1	4	−16.2	11
Gold	18.6	5	−34.0	14
Chinese ceramics	15.3	6	−0.5	6
Farmland	13.7	7	−0.9	7
Silver	13.6	8	−44.5	15
Diamonds	13.3	9	0.0	5
Housing	9.9	10	3.4	4
Old Masters	9.0	11	−22.0	12
CPI	8.6	12	6.6	2
Stocks	3.9	13	−10.5	10
Foreign exchange	3.6	14	−1.9	8
Bonds	3.6	15	11.4	1

[a]Data provided by Salomon Brothers Inc.

rates of return were generally experienced by tangibles, but there has been a change favoring financial assets in 1981. Tangibles were given another low blow by the Tax Equity and Fiscal Responsibility Act of 1982, which prohibited pension funds from investing in tangible and collectible assets. This eliminated a huge potential pool of investment dollars from these items and further decreased their liquidity and demand.

In the 1980s, tangibles may have a place in an investment plan for individuals near retirement who need a degree of high security. However, for the majority of financial independence programs that are growth oriented, tangibles do not represent a judicious investment at this time.

12

COMMODITIES AND OPTIONS

Commodities and options are the fast lane of the investment highway. They both involve very high leverage, which gives the investor the potential for a very high return and the chance to lose big. The action is fast, with price changes occurring almost daily. The game is usually won or lost in days or weeks. Brokerage firms love commodities and options. They charge (relatively high) commissions for executing the trades, and because of the fast action, trades are frequent. There are some legitimate investment reasons for dealing in options and commodities, but the entire area has a greater resemblance to Las Vegas than it does to sound financial planning. On the other hand, at some time all of us like to take a spin in the fast lane, and there will probably be some point in your financial dealings where you may consider taking a flier in commodities or options. If you select this option, however, your investment is more likely to be deductable than taxable.

COMMODITIES

Commodities are real items such as grains, eggs, pork bellies, heating oil, gold, plywood, cotton, and so on. They are traded by means of futures contracts. The buyer of the contract agrees to pay a certain amount for a certain quantity of the item at some date in the future, and the seller agrees to provide that item in the required quantities on that date. Although the ultimate exchange of the commodity on the settlement date involves farmers or industries that deal in the products, a futures contract may go through many hands before reaching this point, usually among people who have little idea of what the final product even looks like. Many commodity traders do not know a soybean from a cocoa bean, yet they buy and sell contracts worth millions of dollars in these items. The great attraction of commodity future contracts is their extremely high leverage and volatility—fortunes can literally be made and lost overnight. In Chapter 8 we saw how margin is a down payment or security deposit for a future transaction. The margin requirements for commodity future contracts can be as little as 5 or 10% of the value of the underlying contract, which generates the large leverage.

It is January and Sam B.'s Uncle Seymour has just returned from Colombia and reports that the cocoa weevil is running rampant, destroying thousands of acres of the cocoa crop. Sam figures that this means there will be a cocoa shortage in 6 months and decides to buy a cocoa future contract for delivery in July. Today that July contract is selling for $2,500 a ton in 10-ton units for a total price of $25,000. Sam figures that with cocoa shortage coming up in July, the price of cocoa will be three times what it is today, and his contract will be worth $75,000. To make it even easier to play the game, Sam does not have to pay the full $25,000 of his contract today; all he has to put up is 10% margin or $2,500.

All during the winter and spring, the cocoa weevil continues to ravage the beans, and by May it appears as if there may be total failure of the crop. The price of 10 metric tons of cocoa for delivery in July shoots up to $80,000. Sam sells his contract for $80,000 and pockets a $55,000 profit in 3 months' time. Considering that he only had to invest $2,500 of his own money, this represents more than a 2,000% return. Such is the allure of the commodities' market. Occasionally, it even works like this. It is much more likely that, in a favorable situation, Sam's contract might have appreciated from $25,000 to $30,000. Still, the $5,000 profit would represent a 200% return on his initial $2,500 investment—not a bad 3 months' work.

But things can go sour in a hurry in commodities. Suppose that just a week after Sam bought his contract, a sure-fire cure for cocoa weevils is discovered. Not only does the new spray kill cocoa weevils, it stimulates cocoa bean growth, and within 2 months the Colombian crop is robust, and growers are predicting the largest harvest in history. By May, the price of the July future contract has fallen to $15,000. Sam would have lost not only his initial $2,500, but would have had to ante up another $7,500 to pay for his contract. He would have had a 400% loss in 2 months.

This type of rapid loss can occur in any margin transaction but usually does not get out of hand because of margin calls from the brokers for more security. After one or two margin calls, most investors will cut their losses and liquidate their losing position. However, it is not always possible to do this in commodities transactions because of the daily trading limit.

The daily trading limit is a statutory price range within which trades may occur on a particular day; it is usually set at a fixed amount above and below the previous day's closing price. On any day when the price of contracts has reached a limit, no further trades may occur until the next day. If, on the next day, the first few orders reach that day's limit, trading is again halted. This can be extremely hazardous to your wealth.

Suppose the daily trading limit on cocoa futures is $500. This means that when the price of a contract changes $500 (either up or down), trading is suspended for that day. Let us assume that Sam's cocoa contract had stayed pretty much constant and was still selling for $25,000 on the day of the announcement of the cure for cocoa weevil. Sam wasn't the only owner of a cocoa futures contract who could see that this news boded ill for those long in cocoa, and the next morning the commodities exchange was flooded with sell orders. Within 15 minutes the price of the cocoa contract had dropped to $24,500, reaching the trading limit, and all trading was suspended. Sam had been unable to sell his contract. The next morning the cocoa contracts continued their plunge, and within three trades the price had fallen to $24,000. Trading was again suspended. By this time, every owner of a July cocoa futures contract knew that cocoa was going into the drink and was trying to sell. There was even more downward price pressure. Sam had to sit helplessly by, watching his contract lose $500 every morning, unable to get out of it. (This situation is called being locked in "limit down.") It was not until the price of the contract had fallen to $15,000 that the supply and demand again came into balance and Sam was able to extract himself from the situation. Commodities are high-risk investments.

If you have any lingering doubts about the wisdom of investing in commodities, consider this fact: over 85% of investors in commodities lose money! Commodities is a tricky game, and probably most successful trades are made on the basis of blind luck or inside information. If you play the commodities game, you will be playing against pros, and, unless you are extremely lucky, they will pick you clean. We can think of no reason why any doctor should include commodities trading as part of his financial plan. If you are a compulsive gambler, go to Atlantic City or Las Vegas—the odds are much better.

OPTIONS

The concept of options has been around for a long time. The first recorded transaction occurred in Biblical times when Jacob took an option with

Laban to marry his daughter Rachel. In the United States, a thriving over-the-counter put and call option market has existed for over a century, with the buyers and sellers being brought together on an *ad hoc* basis by brokerage firms. Options came of age, however, with the creation of the Chicago Board Options Exchange (CBOE) in 1973. For the first time there was an options market with standard striking prices, expiration dates, and listings. Subsequently, all major U.S. stock exchanges have listed both put and call options, and options are even traded on commodity future contracts, stock exchange indices, and interest rates. There is no end to the creativity of those who sell securities.

Options are contracts to either buy or sell an item, such as a share of stock, a piece of real estate, or a futures contract, before a given date at a specified price called the "striking price." The cost of the option is called its "premium." An option to buy the item in question is known as a "Call"; an option to sell, a "Put." The buyer of a call option on 100 shares of XYZ stock pays the seller a premium, for which he receives the right to buy 100 shares of XYZ from the seller at a specified price for a certain period of time. The buyer of a put option obtains the right to sell 100 shares of XYZ stock at a specified price for a given period of time.

Options are easiest to understand by looking at a sample transaction. Suppose Sam B. wants to take a flier in options and has a good feeling about SWY Company. SWY is currently selling for 40, but Sam does not have $4,000 to invest in 100 shares of stock at this time. However, the April 40 call option on SWY is selling for $3. An "April 40 call" means that the option owner has the right to buy (call) 100 shares of SWY any time before April. (Actually, options expire on the Saturday following the third Friday in the listed month.) "40" is the exercise price or "striking" price of the option. (Options at other striking prices are also traded on SWY stock.) Since SWY stock is selling for $40 today, the option to buy it for $40 has no inherent value. However, if SWY stock goes up to $45 before April, the option to buy it at $40 will be worth an instant $5 profit. Therefore, the April 40 call option does have some potential value, and Sam must pay $3 a share to obtain it. However, at $3 a share he only has to put up $300 rather than the $4,000 it would cost him to buy the stock outright.

Suppose Sam was right, and SWY stock rose 6 points to 46 by early April. The value of Sam's option increased almost the same amount as the stock and was worth $900. He would have realized a $600 profit on a $300 investment for a 200% gain! Options are just leverage instruments. They magnify the gain, but they also magnify the risk. Suppose Sam had been wrong, and SWY stock declined slightly to 39. The value of Sam's option would still all be potential, and on the expiration date, it would be worthless. Sam would have lost his entire investment, a 100% loss. If he had bought the underlying stock, he would only have lost $100 or 2.5%.

Put options work exactly like call options but in the opposite direction. If Sam had anticipated a decrease in price in SWY stock, he would have bought a put option rather than a call option. If the stock declined, the value of the put option would increase. If, on the other hand, the stock increased in value, the put option would be worthless.

Options on stock are continuously traded, and in practice, very few options are actually exercised. In the example in which Sam made a profit on his SWY call option, he would not, in all likelihood, have exercised the option and bought the stock (which he would have had to resell to earn his profit). This would generate three transactions and lots of commissions. He would simply sell his appreciated option contract in the option market. If Sam had a loss on the option, he would have had to do nothing, since it would quietly expire worthless without any help from him.

Option Premiums

Usually, several options are available on a stock. There are put and call options on both sides of the selling price, and the options extend for 3, 6, and 9 months into the future. The current price for all of the options is listed in the financial pages of most large daily newspapers. Table 12.1 is an example of how the listings for options on SWY stock might appear.

The first column lists the name of the stock on which the option is traded, and this is followed by the expiration month of the option and the striking

TABLE 12.1 Puts and calls on SWY stock

Option		Sales (100s)	Open interest	Last	Close
SWY	April 35	247	704	10½	42
SWY	April 35 p	2	29	½	42
SWY	April 40	314	1,250	5	42
SWY	April 40 p	45	113	3	42
SWY	April 45	175	947	2½	42
SWY	April 45 p	30	54	6	42
SWY	July 35	123	52	11	42
SWY	July 40	152	67	6	42
SWY	July 45	98	41	3	42
SWY	Oct. 35	7	4	11⅛	42
SWY	Oct. 40	14	7	7½	42
SWY	Oct. 45	23	17	3⅛	42

price. Usually there will be both a put and a call option at each striking price. Put options are identified by a small p following this price. (To shorten the table, we have only shown the put options for the month of April; in actual practice, there would also be put options for the months of July and October.) The extreme right-hand column shows the most recent closing price of SWY stock. Notice that options are traded at striking prices near the closing price. Striking prices are generally fixed at 5-point intervals if the underlying stock is trading below $50 per share and at 10-point intervals if the underlying stock is trading between $50 and $200 per share. Options are available at 3-month intervals up to a maximum of 9 months in the future, and they expire on the Saturday following the third Friday of the listed month. The column labeled "sales" shows the day's trading in a particular option. The column labeled "open interest" shows how many of the options are still outstanding in the market. The column labeled "last" shows the most recent price—the premium—of the option.

Look first at the April 45 call, which is selling for 2½. Since SWY stock is selling for 42, the option to buy at 45 has no intrinsic value. The $2.50 premium represents the speculative value of the option, that is, the price you must pay for the possibility that SWY stock will rise to 45 before April. Next, look at the April 40 call, whose premium is 5. Since the stock is selling 2 points above the call, this option does have 2 points of intrinsic value. In this case, the premium is composed of two components: 2 points of intrinsic value and 3 points of speculative value. Any option with intrinsic value is said to be "in the money," whereas an option with no intrinsic value is "out of the money." The April 40 call is "in the money," and the April 45 call is "out of the money." Next, look at the April 35 call selling for 10½. This call is said to be "deeply in the money," since it has 7 points of intrinsic value. Notice that it also has 3½ points of speculative value. The speculative values of all three options are similar but not identical. Option prices are fixed by the competitive bidding market, and because the options market is relatively thin, there are often some variations in the premiums of options that are otherwise similar.

Now compare the April 40 call, the July 40 call, and the October 40 call. All three options are 2 points in the money, but the premium increases the greater the term of the option. In general, the longer the term of an option, the greater the premium. This is logical, since there is more speculative value in a longer-term option than in a shorter one.

The April 35 put, the April 40 put, and the April 45 put have the same characteristics as the call options, only in reverse. In this case, the April 45 put is 3 points in the money and has 3 points of speculative value, so that it sells for 6. The April 40 put has only 3 points of speculative value.

The far "out of the money" April 35 put does not even have much speculative value.

Looking at the sales and open interest columns gives an idea of how much liquidity an option has. In general, there are far fewer options contracts traded than shares of the underlying stock, and options are relatively less liquid. This means that there may be a considerable spread and that you may have to depart considerably from the listed price to execute a trade. Notice that the open interest and sales increase as the term of the option shortens. It is also generally true that put options are less popular than call options and have correspondingly smaller sales and open interest.

Suppose tomorrow SWY stock rises to 43; what will happen to the price of the call options? At first glance, one might suspect that they would all rise $1 in price as well. However, this is not generally true. It is quite likely that the deeply in the money April 35 call would indeed rise 1 point, since the intrinsic value of this option seems fairly secure (it is unlikely that SWY will fall below 35 before the expiration date of the option). However, the premium on the out of the money April 45 call will probably go up only a quarter or half a point. This is because an out of the money option still has no intrinsic value; the fact that the underlying stock went up a point did nothing to change its intrinsic value. The further out of the money an option is, the less its price changes with changes in the underlying stock price. At the other extreme, deeply in the money options tend to move in lock step with the underlying security.

Because of the discordance between the movements of out of the money options and the underlying security, we believe that investors should confine their option buying to in the money options with the longest possible expiration dates. This is the best guarantee that if the stock moves as you anticipate, the option price will follow suit.

Uses of Options

The most common reason for investing in options is the increased leverage. Sam B. felt certain that SWY stock was going to go up but did not have enough money to take a significant position in the underlying stock. He could, however, participate in the stock's rise by buying an option.

Some investors sell options (called "writing" an option) on a stock they own when they believe that the stock is not going to go up significantly in price. This procedure is known as covered call writing because the call that is written is "covered" by ownership of the stock. The stock owner will write a slightly out of the money call, for which he receives 2 or 3 points of premium. If his prediction is correct, the option will expire worthless, and the premium will simply represent additional income from the stock.

Brokers frequently recommend this to clients who have a portfolio of lack-luster stocks that they do not want to sell. It is offered as a way of increasing the yield of stock with minimal risk. (One thing is certain: it increases the commissions to the broker.)

Another common use for options is to limit the down-side risk in a stock. Suppose you are interested in XYZ stock for a long-term investment and yet are uncertain about the general market atmosphere. One approach would be to buy XYZ and simultaneously buy a similar put contract. Assume that XYZ is selling for $40 a share and a 9 month at-the-money put contract has a premium of $4. By spending $400 to buy the put, you have established a floor below which you cannot lose money. If XYZ fell to $30 a share, you would have lost $10 on the stock, but this loss would be offset by a $10 appreciation in the value of the put contract. Conversely, if XYZ rose to 60, the put would expire worthless. You would have paid $4 a share for "insurance" on your basic investment decision.

The above examples barely scratch the surface of possible option uses. Because options generate lots of commission dollars, brokers have been very clever in thinking up "option strategies" for their clients. There are "spreads," which involve simultaneous purchase and sale of an option on the same stock, and "ratio writing," which involves selling a covered call option as well as one or more uncovered call options. Perhaps the most interesting of all is the "straddle." This involves simultaneously buying a put and a call on the same stock at the same striking price. The investor is simply hoping that the stock will move in one direction or the other but does not really care which.

Should You Invest in Options?

There is no doubt that options are a growth industry. Not only has the volume of trading of conventional options soared, but options are now available on such things as commodity futures contracts, interest rates, and stock market indices. When listed options first became available, it was anticipated that they would be mainly used by fund managers and institutional investors; however, they have been far more popular with small individual investors who account for approximately 85% of the options trading volume.

Although options have considerable superficial appeal and occasionally make sense in a financial plan (buying put options is probably the most economic way for a small investor to profit in a declining market), our feeling is that options should not generally be used in the financial plan of most doctors. For one thing, options are a "zero-sum game." An option contract is really a bet between two individuals, the seller and the buyer.

There is no underlying security to give the transaction any inherent value. Every time an option is traded, one of the parties will win, and the other will lose the same amount. The only consistent winner is the broker, who makes commissions from both players in the game.

In addition, the price of options is set in the market and is regulated by supply and demand in the same manner as the price of stocks. But options markets are generally much thinner than stock markets, and this often causes uncomfortably large price spreads. Although options prices will vary in a general relationship to the underlying stock, as we have seen, this is not a perfect relationship and it is quite possible that an investor will have guessed right on the direction of the stock movement and find that the option does not follow the stock price. Options are a depreciating asset, since they will expire and be worthless in no more than 9 months' time. An investor may have correctly foreseen the direction of a stock movement but have underestimated the time frame in which the movement will take place. He may see his option expire worthless only to find that the stock takes off the next week. We have known investors who have made the right decision on the stock but lost money on the option.

As we shall see in Chapter 15 we believe that the only consistent way for the small investor to profit in the market is to copy the activities of the successful professional investors. Martin Zweig has done an extensive study of the use of options by professional money managers. His studies have found that mutual funds that make use of option strategies generally underperform those mutual funds that do not use options. If the professionals cannot make a consistent profit here, realistically, what chance do you have?

When all is said and done, however, there remains that gut level appeal. Options are glamorous. We all need an occasional trip in the fast lane. Undoubtedly, there will be some time in your financial program when you will take a small fling at options. There is nothing wrong with this as long as you remember that options trading is much closer to gambling than to investing. Use only a small amount of your assets for options trading and look at it as an entertaining part of the game. You may do all right. The odds are certainly not as poor as with commodities trading. Even more satisfying is the fact that when an option goes well, the profits are usually quite large. Most of the time you will have small losses however. Whether you win or lose, you will certainly keep your broker happy!

13

MUTUAL FUNDS

The adage that "you can't see the forest for the trees" is particularly appropriate for investing. Most small investors concentrate only on the trees (e.g., AT&T, IBM, KATY INT., Coleco) and have little perspective on whether they are in the right forest (e.g., financial versus fixed assets). They are always on the lookout for the "next IBM." Keeping their ear peeled for the latest tip from E. F. Hutton or *Wall Street Week*, they concentrate on individual issues without deciding whether the general class of investment vehicle is appropriate. Even the most judiciously selected individual stock will not perform well if the market is in a serious decline. It is better to be in the wrong stock in the right market than the right stock in the wrong market. Even a gilt-edged AT&T bond will lose value as interest rates rise, and the debenture of a fly-by-night company will appreciate as interest rates fall. When inflation is chugging along at 13%, it is difficult to make an after-tax profit with almost any common stock; fixed assets or cash is a more judicious investment at these times. The most important thing the small investor can do is appreciate the distinction between the investment forest and the individual trees in the forest.

Ironically, it is much easier to select the correct investment forest—the general class of investment vehicle that will be most successful—than it is to select an investment tree—a specific stock, bond, or piece of real estate. In the previous chapters we have looked in a general way at classes of investment vehicles and have seen what types of economic and inflationary environments favor and hurt them. This book is about the forest. Although

143

picking the right investment forest is not easy or guaranteed, it should certainly be possible for most intelligent investors.

On the other hand, picking the individual tree—a specific investment—is extremely difficult and requires thorough knowledge not only of the particular asset (stock X, bond Y, piece of real estate Z, etc.) but also of the general industry, the social and economic forces affecting that particular type of investment, and probably a good deal of luck. Of the many thousands of "knowledgeable" investors (including professional stockbrokers, bank trust officers, fund managers, investment letter writers, and financial columnists), fewer than a third consistently make profits. Fewer than 5% make consistent, *high* profits year after year. It is a very difficult business, even for the knowledgeable professional. It is nearly impossible for the smaller, part-time investor to consistently profit unless he also has good professional advice.

Just as it's wise to beware of the doctor who knows all the biochemistry of bile salts but does not know when to take out your gall bladder, one should avoid the analyst who knows how many people fly from Montana to Miami on Martin Luther King Day but not when to sell Braniff. The problem is how to obtain good investment advice. Garden-variety investment advice is easy to come by, but what we are seeking is the advice of the 5 to 10% of professionals who consistently do well. Enter the mutual fund.

THE REGULATED INVESTMENT COMPANY

The regulated investment company, popularly known as a "mutual fund," is a special class of corporation designed to allow investors to pool their resources and hire professional money managers. The concept is straightforward. Consistently successful investing results require not only full-time management but also a large amount of capital, both beyond the means of the average small investor like Sam B. However, if Sam B. and a large group of people like him get together and pool their investment resources, they not only can generate a pot of money large enough to be effectively invested but can also afford to hire investment professionals to manage the money for them. If the investments do not perform well—if the professional manager is not a consistent winner—they can replace him with someone whose track record is better.

Moreover, the pool of funds can be concentrated in specialty areas—small forests. A mutual fund might specialize in real estate with managers selected for their real estate expertise. A fund could concentrate in stocks with returns consisting of both dividends and capital gains; alternatively the fund might concentrate in more speculative stocks, those with little to no current dividends but prospects for explosive growth. Investors wishing to buy gold or other hard assets would join a fund that specializes in these types of investments. The mutual fund is a vehicle whereby the small investor can obtain access to professional management and advice that would otherwise be beyond his means.

Mutual funds are actual corporations whose business is investing, a special class of corporation operating under subchapter M of the Internal Revenue Service Code. This subchapter provides that the income of the investment company is not taxed directly but flows through to the individual investor and is reported on his tax return. Suppose the "Supergrow Fund" has a good year, and its investments earn $500,000 in dividends, $200,000 in short-term capital gains, and $300,000 in long-term capital gains. The Supergrow Fund itself would not pay any taxes on these gains; rather, they would be apportioned among the shareholders of the fund (in proportion to the number of shares owned), and each shareholder would report the income on his individual tax return. Suppose Sam B. had 1,500 shares of Supergrow, which was 1% of the total shares. He would receive 1% of the earnings—$5,000 of dividends, $2,000 of short-term capital gains, and $3,000 of long-term capital gains—which he would report on his individual income tax return. Mutual fund shareholders must report and pay taxes on income as it is accrued. (A conventional corporation might choose to "plow back" profits into the company rather than paying a dividend. In this case, the shareholder would not have any individual tax liability, because the company profits were not distributed.) Thus, shareholders of regulated investment companies are not subject to the "double taxation" that occurs with most corporations. In return for this tax treatment, mutual funds are "regulated," meaning that they operate under strict limitations as to their operations and, in particular, the types of investments in which they may or may not engage.

Investors in mutual funds own actual shares of stock of the corporation. However, the value of a share of stock is not directly determined by a competitive bidding market as is the value of ordinary stocks. The price of a share of mutual company stock is known as the *net asset value* (NAV) and is determined by taking the total net assets of a company and dividing them by the number of outstanding shares of stock. For example, suppose Supergrow Fund is invested in 50 different common stocks. In addition, the fund has 10% of its assets in treasury bills and another 5% in long-term bonds. Supergrow has 150,000 shares of its own stock outstanding. At the end of each business day, the net asset value of a share of Supergrow is calculated by taking the current market value of all of the 50 common stocks that Supergrow owns, adding to it the current value of the bonds and treasury bills, and dividing this figure by 150,000.

Suppose, on August 20th, the net asset value of Supergrow was $20 per share. On August 21st, the value of many of the common stocks that

Supergrow owns will change, and at the close of the business day, the net asset value will again be computed. It was a good day for Supergrow, and four of its stocks went up several points, whereas only two declined. The remainder were essentially unchanged. The net result was that the value of Supergrow's portfolio increased $15,000 or the equivalent of $0.10 per share. Thus, the net asset value of a share of Supergrow increased from $20 to $20.10. Of course, had the value of Supergrow's portfolio declined, the net asset value of a share of its stock would also have decreased.

Whereas shares of most corporations trade in the open market, either on one of the stock exchanges or through brokerage firms, shares of most mutual funds are bought and sold directly with the company. When Sam B. wants to buy shares of Supergrow, he will buy them directly from the mutual fund at the current net asset value. When Sam wishes to sell his shares, the mutual fund will buy them back from him at the current net asset value. Thus, shares of mutual funds are very liquid. In theory, mutual funds are not required to provide instant liquidity and may legally take between 7 and 30 days to redeem shares. These provisions exist to prevent "runs" on a fund that would force it to liquidate some of its portfolio at unfavorable prices. In actual practice funds virtually always redeem shares on the same day as requested.

The professional management of a mutual fund is compensated by a fee based on a percentage of the total assets under management. Most management fees range from ¼ to 1% of the total value of the fund. Thus, an individual investor is paying between ¼ and 1% of his investment money for the services of the professional advisor, which is by far the cheapest method of purchasing such services.

In addition to the management fee, some mutual funds also charge a commission for purchasing or redeeming shares, known in the trade as a "load." Loads are used to pay salesmen and some operational expenses of the funds and range from 1 to 8%, with 3 to 5% being average. As with any commission, a load represents dead dollars and can only be justified if the value of the investment advice is superior. Several studies have shown that there is no correlation between the presence or absence of a load and the general performance of a fund. Of the most consistently successful mutual funds, some have loads and others are "no load." The fact that a fund has a load charge does not guarantee that it will perform better than its competitor. Since there are many no-load funds with excellent performance records, we see no reason for the average investor to deal with load funds. Rather, they should convert these dead dollars to active investment dollars.

MUTUAL FUND ADVANTAGES

Mutual funds have several advantages for the small investor: liquidity, diversification, commission-free reinvestment, and variety.

Because mutual funds will continuously sell and redeem shares at the current net asset value, they are extremely liquid investments. Most funds will accept orders for purchase or redemption over the telephone, will accept direct transfer of money from the client's bank account for share purchase, and will wire proceeds from redemptions directly to the same account. Most money market funds allow redemption by check writing. Most management groups allow switching of assets from one individual fund to another (within their group) without charge.

Diversification is an important principle for any investment program, since it helps decrease risk. Not all investments, regardless of how well reasoned, prove successful, and only by including variety in a portfolio can an investor guard against a large loss. This is simply a manifestation of the "don't put all your eggs in one basket" philosophy and is fairly self-evident. The problem faced by a small investor is that he does not have enough assets to diversify widely. If you have only $10,000 to invest, you are not going to be able to take a position in many companies, and you will not be able to diversify much; thus, your investment risk will increase. Because of their large pooled resources, mutual funds are able to diversify investments and help decrease risk.

Because they buy in large quantities, mutual funds also have the advantage of lower transaction costs. If Sam B., as an individual investor, buys 100 shares of IBM, he will have to pay 3 to 5% in commission costs. If Supergrow buys 10,000 shares of IBM, they will be able to do so for less than 1% in commission costs.

Paradoxically, if a mutual fund becomes too large, diversification can work against it. As a fund's total assets increase, it may have so much money to invest that it is forced to purchase stock that it would not otherwise consider. This most often happens to funds that are very successful. Supergrow Fund started 7 years ago and initially was a small fund with only about $25 million in total assets. The managers were sharp, however, and Supergrow lived up to its name; the value of fund shares appreciated at an annual compound rate of return of nearly 35%. Not only did this increase the total asset pool, but the success of the fund attracted attention, and more and more investors put their money in. Now the total assets of the fund are $1.5 billion, over 60 times what they were 7 years ago. This success makes it more difficult for the fund to operate. When the managers had only $25 million to spend, they were able to be selective in the stocks they purchased, diversifying over 50 or so highly selected companies. Now that the managers have $1.6 billion to spend, they cannot be so selective.

In fact, mutual funds are legally constrained from owning more than 5% of the stock of any one company, and, therefore, in order to invest all of the assets, the fund manager will have to buy 900 or 1,000 stocks rather than concentrating on a highly selected few. This means that he will also have to put money into companies he might not otherwise wish to. Having large stock positions also makes it more difficult for the manager to move in and out of a stock without altering the price. It is easy to sell 1,000 shares of stock without upsetting the market, but buying or selling 100,000 shares is another matter. This is difficult to do without seriously disrupting the market price of a stock. Thus, as mutual funds are successful and grow larger, it becomes more difficult for the managers to continue to maintain their pace of growth. Sometimes funds try to limit their size by imposing load charges to discourage new investors or even by limiting the number of shares they will sell. More commonly, a successful management team will organize new funds whenever the assets in one of the old ones reach a certain level.

As we have seen in earlier chapters, the most important factor in guaranteeing investment success is time. Investment dollars must be as active as possible and continually at work. Mutual funds make it easier for the individual investor to accomplish this by providing for automatic reinvestment of earnings. As mutual funds earn money through dividends or capital gains, they will either pay the earnings out to their investors or will continually reinvest them in additional shares of mutual fund stock. This reinvestment is usually done without a load, and it provides a convenient way for the individual investor to keep his money active.

Mutual funds come in all varieties, and this permits the small investor to participate in selective categories of investments. There are funds that concentrate on high-quality long-term bonds, whose goal is to provide continuous income. There are funds that invest only in tax-exempt bonds for shareholders who need a source of tax-free income. Some funds invest only in common stocks of established companies that pay high dividends; their goal is to maximize current income with a secondary emphasis on capital gains. At the other extreme, there are funds that invest only in small, emerging growth companies having no prospects for immediate dividends with the potential for explosive capital gains. Some funds invest in gold bullion. Some funds invest in stocks of foreign companies. Some limit their investments to one region of the country or one class of industry. There are even funds that restrict their investments to corporations with certain social or political goals. "Money market" funds invest solely in treasury bills and other very short-term debt instruments and function essentially as bank accounts. There is a mutual fund with a philosophy for almost any investor. (A list of no-load mutual funds is available from the No Load Mutual Fund Association, Valley Forge, PA, 19481.)

Most of the larger mutual fund management companies run several different types of funds covering many different investment goals. For example, the Fidelity Group of Boston operates many different funds, providing enough variety for even the most finicky investor. Most management groups allow investors to switch their assets among various funds with no charge. This enables the investor to easily switch his investment forest without having to worry about the individual trees. If Sam B. has been in the Supergrow stock fund, but now believes the stock market is headed "south," he can call up Supergrow and tell them to switch his assets into the money market fund for a while. If interest rates shoot up to 17%, he will call and tell them to move him into their bond fund. Each of these switches requires only a telephone call and usually no commission or load charges. This ability to switch between types of funds is an important advantage to the small investor. If he owned the individual stocks or bonds himself, he would have to pay a 3 to 5% commission each time he made a purchase or sale, considerably decreasing the profits on the transaction.

PERFORMANCE OF MUTUAL FUNDS

Perhaps the greatest advantage of mutual funds is that their performance is a matter of public record. The daily net asset values and distributions are carried in the financial pages of larger newspapers, and Lipper Analytic Services publishes quarterly, in *Barron's*, an exhaustive analysis of all mutual funds including a listing of the top performers for the past quarter, past year, past 5 years, and past 10 years. Nowhere else in the investment world is it possible to see so clearly the track record of investment managers. Your stockbroker or the trust officer of your bank may assure you that "he makes a lot of money for lots of people," but you do not really know his performance record; the only way to find out is to see how well he does with your money, and this can be an expensive lesson. (On the other hand, if your present investment advisor has been doing well for you, by all means sit back and let him carry the ball.)

Because mutual fund performance records are available not only for the past quarter, but for as far back as 10 years, it is possible to select a winning investment management team. If a group of fund managers has consistently outperformed the market for several years, it is a safe bet to assume that they will continue to do so in the future, and you would be well advised to place your money with them. This has been a consistently observed pattern in mutual fund performance; those funds that performed well in the past generally continue to do so in the future. It is also worth noting that those funds that are performance leaders during the early stages of major market reversals generally are the performance leaders throughout the duration of that cycle. This is worth knowing, because bull and bear markets, once established, tend to continue for many months or years.

The results of the best funds can be quite impressive. Because of their large diversification of stocks, the net asset value of mutual funds nearly always follows the same trend as the major stock averages, such as the Dow Jones Industrial Average or the Standard and Poor's 500 average. However, the best growth funds usually outperform the market averages by a factor of 3 to 5 and produce annualized returns during major bull markets of well over 20%. Of course, when the general market is declining, these same mutual funds will also fall in value and sometimes will fall by greater factors than the popular market averages. Nevertheless, the best fund managers somehow consistently do much better than the market on the upswing and no worse than the general market average on the downswing.

You may be wondering why, if these guys are so sharp, don't they get out of stocks when they think the market will decline? There are two reasons. The first is that the incorporation rules of mutual funds rigidly define the types and extent of investments in which the fund may engage. (This is to the advantage of the potential investor since it defines the character and potential behavior of the fund.) For instance, a growth-oriented common stock fund may have the requirement that at least 70% of its assets always be invested in growth-type stocks. Sometimes the fund manager may be 100% invested, but, when he believes a market decline is imminent, he may only be able to shift 30% of the investments out of stocks without violating the bylaws of the corporation. A second reason is that fund managers attempt to manipulate their portfolios to maximize the possibility of long-term capital gains with their subsequent favorable tax treatment. This means they will often sit on stocks during a period of general market decline with the anticipation of later rises and greater net after-tax return.

Table 13.1 shows the performance of some selected growth-oriented mutual funds for the period from January 1, 1975 to January 1, 1982. This table assumes that all fund distributions were reinvested in shares. It also assumes that a similar dividend reinvestment would have been made in the Dow Jones Industrial Average at an average dividend rate of 8%. You can see that these funds outperform the market in general from four- to nearly tenfold.

TABLE 13.1 Fund performance January 1, 1975 to January 1, 1982

Fund	Percent change in NAV
Scudder Development	+620
V/L Special Situation	+543
Lexington Growth	+361
B/B Capital Shares	+306
S/R Capital Opportunities	+303
DJ Industrials	+ 67

TABLE 13.2 Fund performance in the 1973– 1974 bear market

Fund	Percent change in NAV
Scudder Development	−72
V/L Special Situation	−62
Lexington Growth	−56
B/B Capital Shares	−53
S/R Capital Opportunities	−48
DJ Industrials	−37

Table 13.2 shows the performance of the same funds during the bear market period from 1973 to 1974. During this time, the Dow Jones Industrial Average decreased 37%, and the funds decreased from 48 to 72%. Although the funds decreased more than the industrial averages during the bear market, they more than made up for this loss by their exemplary performance during the ensuing bull market period. In Chapter 15, we will describe a technique by which the individual investor can minimize the effects of market declines.

DISADVANTAGES OF MUTUAL FUNDS

Mutual funds are an investment technique rather than a specific investment vehicle. Although the majority of mutual funds invest in common stocks, there are funds that invest in cash equivalents (money market funds), interest and income plays (corporate bond funds), tax-exempt income (municipal bond funds), security (government bond funds), and tangible assets (gold funds). They present the small investor with an opportunity to only have to pick the general category of investment without having to worry about specifics. Since it is much more difficult for the small individual investor to pick a specific investment than it is to select a category of investment that will be successful, we believe that, regardless of which investment forest you choose, you should have most of your assets in mutual funds and then leave the selection of the individual trees up to the professionals.

There is a disadvantage to mutual funds: boredom. They just are not action packed. When you are sitting around the lunch table and the conversation turns to investments, it is much more glamorous to talk about individual stocks, options, or limited partnerships. Nothing quite matches the glamor of announcing that you have recently gone short a popular issue. Admitting that your money is in mutual funds is like saying you are too chicken to play the game. Somehow mutual funds seem to represent an investment cop-out. Even when you are alone with the morning paper, it somehow is not very exciting to check the net asset value of your mutual fund: it takes all the excitement out of reading the *Wall Street Journal*. After all, new business trends, merger rumors, sales reports, and so on lose their immediacy if you cannot rush right out, call your broker, and get in the latest game. Although you can be reasonably certain that you are, in the long run, making more money, there is no denying that mutual funds take some of the excitement out of investing.

The diversification of mutual funds, which decreases their investment risk, at the same time somewhat limits the potential reward. It is difficult to get rich overnight in a mutual fund; they do not usually double in 6 months' time. On the other hand, if you are lucky and get your money in the right individual stock, you may be an instant winner. We do not believe that you should be striving for overnight success. Our goal is long-term financial independence, not a windfall profit. To be an overnight winner requires considerable luck, but to acquire financial independence over the course of 10 to 20 years takes only common sense and some patience and discipline. If you have the kind of personality that demands rapid gratification, you are probably better off going to Las Vegas or Atlantic City, where you can find out if you will succeed or fail in a few hours' time. Most of us enjoy the heat of this type of action, but we also realize that this is not the road to financial independence.

Although the bulk of your assets should be invested in mutual funds, there is always some place for individual investments. Take a small portion of your investment dollars, say 10 to 15%, and try your hand at individual investments. Taking a flier in an individual stock or option can help alleviate the boredom of mutual funds, and as long as you do this only with your "gambling money" from the lifestyle portion of the pie, you shouldn't derail your long-term financial plan.

14

INVESTMENTS FOR THE 1980s

The value of various investment vehicles changes with time. Everything cycles. Bonds are not always conservative, and stocks are not always speculative. A hedge against inflation is the worst kind of investment in deflationary times. Similarly, personal investment requirements will change. A young professional may be more interested in rapid asset growth and would undertake high-risk investments, whereas an investor nearing retirement will be more interested in conservative vehicles that preserve capital and provide current income. One of the biggest mistakes you can make as an investor is to lose flexibility. It is important to avoid the tendency to fight the last war. Blue chip stocks were rather lackluster performers for many years but have done extremely well in the early 1980s. Bonds were a disaster between 1975 and 1981 but were the leading investment vehicles in 1981 and 1982. Collectibles and real estate performed spectacularly in the late 1950s and the late 1970s but have been poor performers in the 1980s.

You cannot play tennis with a hockey stick. It will be very difficult to make money using an investment vehicle that is out of phase with the current economic conditions. Similarly, it will be difficult not to make money if you are in the right category of investments at the right time. Probably the most important factor in separating a judicious from an injudicious investment is timing. As you formulate the investment tools for your financial plan, it is vital that you make some assessment of the upcoming economic environment so that you can utilize your investment dollars in the most judicious manner. If you want to win the Davis Cup, by all means try to get Connors and McEnroe on the team. But even they will not do well if the team is warming up in Transylvania while the game is being played in Tahiti. Predicting the future is a tough business, of course, and there are no sure-fire methods for success. In this chapter, we shall look at some trends in inflation, the economy, and the capital goods cycle with an eye to predicting which type of investments will be most successful in the 1980s.

INFLATION

Probably the single most important factor in determining the value of investments is the inflation rate. Not only does the inflation rate determine the relative value of hard assets versus financially denominated assets, but it ultimately controls prevailing interest rates, and this, in turn, directly affects the rate of return on bonds versus the rate of return on stocks. Therefore, in attempting to predict the upcoming investment environment, you must first decide what inflation will be doing.

Because the 1970s and early 1980s were periods of accelerating inflation, many people believe that continuing inflation is inevitable. This is probably not so. In the past there have been periods of high inflation that have been followed by deflation and price stability. There is reason to expect that this type of pattern will occur in the United States again. In order to arrive at a judgment concerning future inflation, it is important that we understand its cause. The Carter Administration told us it was because of OPEC. The Republicans said it was because Democrats tax and spend. Nearly everyone in public office says it is too complicated for "us" (voters) to understand. That simply is not true! Intelligent folk as well as politicians can understand it. It's just that there are many politicians who stand to lose if the public understands that inflation is caused by government policy. It's not caused entirely by the Arab oil embargo. It's not entirely the fault of the Japanese auto makers who have contributed to our negative balance of trade. And it's not because of the underground economy.

Inflation exists because the government spends more than it earns (collects from tax payers) and makes up the difference by printing money. This excess money is generally not supported by an offsetting increase in real goods and services but is simply created out of thin air. As such, it has no real value, and when it is added to the pool of money already in existence, it causes a dilution of the value of all money. We tend to think of inflation in a backwards fashion. That is, we have a tendency to think that inflation exists because the price of goods and services is rising. In actuality, the price of goods and services is not rising; rather, the value of money is decreasing! A loaf of bread is still a loaf of bread. If that loaf of bread costs $1 today and $1.10 in 6 months from now, it does not mean that the loaf of bread has changed. The loaf of bread is still the same, and it is still a reality. What has changed is the value of the dollar. The dollar has decreased in value by 10% because it has been diluted by other dollars created in Washington.

Think for a moment of the United States as a family. Just a small, typical family except that it has access to a printing press that can print money. Each year one of the family members is selected to use the press to print the amount of money the family will have to spend during the upcoming year. Let us next consider a hypothetical year in which the family has $10,000 to spend and that they spend $2,000 of that money in the various aspects of their lives that are concerned with the consumption of energy, such as driving, heating their home, using electricity, using plastic or other petroleum-based products. The remaining $8,000 is spent on all of their other needs, which we shall lump together under the general title *lifestyle*. Now, at the beginning of the next year, suppose that OPEC doubles oil prices, and the cost of energy doubles so that this year the family will have to spend $4,000 on energy consumption instead of $2,000. We have been told that this causes inflation, but this is not necessarily so. An increase in any one component of the cost of living does not have to increase the overall inflation rate. The fact that the price of oil has increased does not necessarily mean that our family will experience an increase in the aggregate inflation rate.

Let us assume that the father was elected to run the printing press the year of the oil price increases, and he again printed only $10,000 for the family to spend. That year, since the price of oil had doubled, the family spent $4,000 on energy and had only $6,000 to spend on "lifestyle." This necessitated some hard decisions, since $2,000 of lifestyle money had to be eliminated. The family was not able to buy as many items as they could in the previous year and had to forego a new TV set and video game and chose to repair the family car rather than buying a new one. The effect of the decreased consumption by the family meant that there was less demand for video games, TVs, and new cars. This decrease in demand will, in a free market, cause the price of these products to decrease slightly, compensating for the increased price of all petroleum-related products. Therefore, even though the internal distribution of resources has changed, the value of the money itself has not. The price of oil increased, the price of TV sets decreased. That's good for oil and bad for TV, but it is not, in the aggregate, inflationary.

There is an alternative way the family could have dealt with this situation. Instead of spending $4,000 for energy, they might have decided to cut their energy expenses by driving less and not heating the home as well. They might have chosen to spend only $2,000 on oil, thereby keeping the other $8,000 intact so as not to change their "lifestyle." By doing this, they would have decreased the demand for oil, which would ultimately decrease the price of oil (this is just what happened in the United States in the early 1980s). More importantly, there would have been no net inflation.

Now let us assume that instead of electing the father to run the press, one of the children was put in charge. Instead of printing $10,000, the child, not wanting to give up the TV and video game, decided to print $12,000 to make up for the difference in the price of energy. Using this money, the family consumed exactly what they had in the previous year, spending $8,000 on lifestyle and $4,000 on energy. They had consumed the same amount of goods and services but had spent $12,000 instead of $10,000. In this case, there was a 20% inflation rate, since more dollars were spent on the same total amount of goods and services.

The point is that an increase in the price of any single component of an economy does not mean there will be inflation. Inflation only occurs when the aggregate of all prices rises. Viewed in another way, inflation occurs when the total number of dollars increases but the amount of goods and services produced stays the same. By way of practical illustration, during the time of rapidly escalating prices for crude oil after the OPEC embargo in 1974, there was a large increase in inflation in the United States. During this same period, Japan, which imports virtually all of its crude oil, had a relatively stable and low inflation rate. The United States monetized the oil problem; Japan did not. The United States elected to print money; Japan did not.

Actually the cause of inflation is the expansion of the money supply rather than the simple printing of money. When the supply of money is expanded more rapidly than the supply of goods and services, inflation is a direct result. The Federal Government, through its fiscal and monetary activities, has several ways of increasing the money supply in addition to printing money. It can increase the supply of money by establishing credits and guaranteeing loans. It can expand the money supply by reducing the reserve requirement for banks and lending institutions. It can expand the money supply by lowering short-term interest rates. It can expand the money supply by creating jobs in which no useful work or services are provided. (An individual expands the money supply when he receives a raise but does not increase his work output.) A common thread here is deficit spending. When the government spends more than it earns, inflationary pressures are increased.

The general effect of government policy since the 1930s has been the same as when the child was elected to run the family printing press—inflation. Inflation ultimately benefits debtors, since they can repay their debt with less valuable dollars. And who is the largest debtor? You guessed it, the Federal Government. It's much easier for politicians to create straw men to blame for inflation than to risk annoying the electorate by increasing taxes or decreasing government spending. Since most politicians believe that for every solution there is a problem, and since this whole process aids reelection and costs money, there is really no mystery why inflation and politics started at about the same time.

The trend in the inflation rate is important because it indicates the type of investment that should do well. In its simplest terms, inflation can be thought of in terms of the balance between the number of dollar bills on the one hand and the amount of goods and services on the other. During periods of accelerating inflation, the investment vehicle of choice is some form of hard asset (i.e., real estate, gold, silver, diamonds, oil paintings, commodities, etc.). During times of relatively stable inflation rates (these periods usually follow periods of accelerating inflation), dollar-denominated or financial assets such as stocks and bonds usually perform better. And during periods of deflation, the investment vehicle of choice is dollars. This is how you find the right forest:

Inflationary Trend	*Corresponding Investment*
Accelerating inflation	Tangible assets
Stable inflation	Financial assets
Deflation	Treasury bills or dollar bills

MONETARY POLICY AND INTEREST RATES

There is a widespread misconception regarding the factors affecting the level of interest rates. As Federal budget deficits mounted during the early 1980s, it became very fashionable to claim that increasing federal deficits would cause an inevitable rise in interest rates. The theory behind this statement was supply and demand—increasing federal deficits would require an increase in federal borrowing, and this increased demand would cause an increase in the cost of the money, i.e., interest rates. The theory sounds superficially attractive. Over the long term, fiscal deficits are inflationary and may cause interest rates to rise; however, for the short term, this relationship does not apply.

The supply-and-demand/cause-and-effect determination of interest rates is predicated on a level supply of money and a resulting free-market determination of interest rates. In the United States, this does not exist. Because the Federal Reserve Board can dramatically alter the supply of money and the interest rate at which that money is available, free-market forces do not come immediately into play in determining short-term interest rates. By tightening or loosening the availability of Federal Reserve Funds, the Fed is able to effectively set short-term interest rates.

This control of money supply by the Federal Reserve Board is the basis of monetary economic policy and this policy usually emanates from the current political administration. Although, on paper, the Federal Reserve Board is independent of the White House, historically, it has never behaved as such. Thus, in the short term it is quite possible for the Federal Government to keep control of interest rates and raise or lower them at will.

Long-term interest rates are usually determined by inflationary expectations. Investors purchasing a 20-year bond will expect a yield that will outperform the anticipated inflation rate. Thus, when inflation is running at 15% a year, it will be impossible to sell long-term instruments to yield less than 15%. On the other hand, if inflation is 3%, investors will buy long-term instruments that yield only 6 or 7%. Thus, the anticipated inflation rate is ultimately the main determinant of intermediate- and long-term interest rates. Although the Federal Reserve Board can keep a cap on rising short-term interest rates by increasing the available money supply, this action is, in itself, inflationary and, if continued for a period of time, will simply increase the rate of inflation and consequently the intermediate- and long-term interest rates. The goal of monetary policy is to manipulate short-term interest rates to smooth out fluctuations in the general economy and help stabilize the volatility of inflation.

Keeping short-term interest rates low by increasing the money supply is generally an inflationary policy. However, if there is high unemployment and relatively high idle plant capacity in the country, large increases in the money supply can be sustained without an appreciable change in inflation. Such a period occurred during the early 1980s. However, if large increases in the money supply and Federal deficit spending occur during a period of relatively low unemployment and low, idle plant capacity, this could translate into rapid increases in the rate of inflation.

It is important for investors to watch the relationship of the Federal Reserve discount rate to economic activity. If monetary policy is keeping interest rates low by increasing the money supply during periods of expanding economic activity, decreasing unemployment, and high plant utilization, increases in the inflation rate should be anticipated. On the other hand, if monetary policy is tightened as economic activity increases, it is quite possible to maintain a stable or decreasing inflation rate.

Although it is true that continued expanding Federal deficits will ultimately lead to increases in interest rates, this will not occur in the short term. Rather, it will occur because high Federal budget deficits are ultimately inflationary, and inflationary pressures inevitably cause a rise in interest rates. If the Government is able to maintain a stable rate of inflation by balancing short-term interest rates against economic activity, it will be possible to go for a considerable time without causing a rise in interest rates. The unanswered question in the 1980s is whether the policies of the Reagan Administration, or its successors, will be able to accomplish this. Our personal feeling is that it will, and therefore we believe that the next 2 to 3 years and perhaps the rest of the decade will be a time of stable or decreasing inflation and relatively stable interest rates—in other words, a time for financial investments such as stocks.

CAPITAL GOODS CYCLE

Another method of predicting future inflation rates and economic activity is the use of historical patterns of inflation, interest rates, and their relationship to the capital goods cycle. The best description of inflationary cycles in industrialized countries was published in the 1920s by Nicholai D. Kondratieff and has become known as the Kondratieff Wave Theory. Kondratieff was a Russian economist who wrote on the boom and bust cycles in capitalist systems. His theories were based on observations of commodity prices in industrialized countries during the 19th century. Kondratieff correctly predicted that a major depression would occur in the United States beginning in the late 1920s. (Unfortunately for him, he also predicted that the United States and other industrialized Western countries would survive the depression. This view was extremely unpopular with the Russian rulers of that era and resulted in Kondratieff spending the remainder of his career in the East.) The basis of the Kondratieff theory is that economic inflationary pressures move in long cycles, which will continue into the future. The theory has achieved a wide current popularity because it has generally been correct in predicting inflationary and economic cycles during the twentieth century.

Kondratieff observed that industrialized economies move in long waves or cycles of approximately 40 to 60 years' duration, on which are superimposed smaller cyclical moves. He also observed that there was a relationship among wars, social political trends, and the troughs and peaks of these cycles. A stylized cycle wave is based on commodity prices and interest rates and consists of three phases. The first phase is a 15-to-30-

year up wave associated with booming economic growth and accelerating rates of inflation. The up wave ends with a brief but severe recession and subsequent recovery. This is followed by a plateau or transition period, usually lasting between 8 and 10 years. The transition period is followed by another 15-to-30-year down wave, which is initiated with a deep deflation or depression. Beginning with the Revolutionary War, the United States has experienced 3½ long wave cycles.

Wars recur with regularity in both the up and down portions of Kondratieff waves and have some similar characteristics depending on their location within the cycle. Wars occurring in the troughs or at the beginning of an upswing are usually (relatively) popular and definitively settled. In the United States, wars occurring during the troughs of the waves have been the Revolutionary (ca. 1780), the Mexican–American (ca. 1845), the Spanish–American (ca. 1898), and the Second World War (ca. 1943). These wars have ushered in the start of the upswing portion of the cycle, which has historically lasted between 15 and 30 years. Recessions occurring during this upswing are usually minor, and the beginning of this period is generally characterized by relatively low prices for goods and services, low interest rates, low levels of debt in both the public and private sector, and generalized increasing productivity and economic activity.

Wars that occur near the peaks of the up cycle have tended to be expensive, prolonged, and have enjoyed considerably less popular support than wars occurring in the troughs. In the United States context, peak wars have been the War of 1812, the Civil War, the First World War, and the Vietnam War. The nature of these wars has often accentuated economic distortions and helped terminate the upward leg of the economic cycle. A recent example would be the "guns and butter policy" of the Johnson administration during the Vietnam escalation. This resulted in a sharp increase in wholesale prices and launched a 15-year period of rapid inflation. Peak wars have usually resulted in accentuated inflation as a consequence of misallocation of resources.

The end of an upswing cycle is followed by a plateau period approximately 10 years in length. Kondratieff referred to this as the time of "secondary prosperity." This period is initiated by a sharp and deep recession, deeper than any previous ones in the up cycle. The recession is relatively short-lived and is followed by stable economic growth and an apparent return to the previous up cycle conditions. Characteristically, during these periods there is a swing to the right in politics and social practices, a movement toward disentangling the government from private life, stable to slightly declining prices, declining interest rates, tax cuts, and an increasing trend toward protectionism. This period is terminated by increasing deflationary forces, large liquidations of private, corporate, and government debt, and subsequent deflation. These changes initiate the downswing leg of the wave cycle, during which the conditions of the upswing are generally reversed. Deflation is followed by decreasing economic activity, a fall in the price of goods and services, rising unemployment, and a shift to the left in politics. Interestingly, the down leg is not a time of complete stagnation; it is a period of technological innovation and realignment. Many important discoveries and efficiencies are made, but they are not economically and commercially exploited until the beginning of the next up cycle.

In the United States, the most recent transition period was the 1920s. The end of World War I marked the end of an up cycle that had begun during the late 1800s around the time of the Spanish–American War. Between 1896 and 1920, wholesale prices tripled in the United States. The 1920s were a plateau phase, a time of high economic prosperity but no real sustained growth in the economy. The stock market crash of 1929 initiated the beginning of the deflationary down cycle, which was not completed until the mid-1940s, corresponding with World War II. The subsequent upswing began in the late 1940s. By the end of this last upswing in 1979 and the associated Vietnam War, the United States Wholesale Price Index had risen over 800%.

In general, the basic assumptions of Kondratieff seem to fit well with the economic experiences in both the United States and other industrialized countries. Other economists have observed similar long wave-cycle patterns in capital investments such as office buildings, manufacturing facilities, plant equipment, and applications of technology.

The implications of the Kondratieff wave theory for the stock market are significant. In general, corporate earnings and subsequent stock prices have quadrupled during the upswing of the cycle, and this increase has usually extended into the plateau phase. During the plateau phase of Kondratieff waves, stock prices have historically risen dramatically: the price of the average stock was six times higher in 1929 than it was in 1921. Therefore, the plateau phase of a Kondratieff cycle can be a very fortunate time for investments in common stocks.

How do current economic conditions in the United States fit in with the Kondratieff cycle? Where are we in the 1980s? The current wave began in a trough at the end of World War II, and the up cycle started in the late 1940s. There is no question that this up cycle has terminated, but the exact timing is somewhat questionable. Some authors believe that the up cycle terminated during the early 1970s and that the ending of the Vietnam War followed by the 1974 recession marked the initiation of the plateau phase.

If this is correct, the 10 years from 1975 to 1985 should represent the plateau phase, and the downward cycle should begin sometime in the mid to late 1980s. If this scenario is correct, stocks and financially denominated investments should continue to do well until the mid to late 1980s but will become poor performers by the end of the decade; the remainder of the century will be a time of deflation and a time for dollar assets.

However, there are some compelling reasons to believe that the up cycle continued until the early 1980s and that the plateau was initiated by the sharp recession of 1980 and 1981. The main reason for this belief is that general economic activity and productivity continued to rise during the late 1970s and that the period following the 1974 recession behaved more like previous terminal upswing periods with continued increasing production and rapidly increasing inflation. The actual peak of economic activity in the United States occurred in 1978 and 1979. Also the 1980–81 recession was considerably deeper than the 1974 recession. In the past, plateau phases have been initiated by the steepest recession since the beginning of the up cycle.

Of course, it is possible that the 1980–81 recession was actually the beginning of the deflationary or downswing part of the cycle, but this seems unlikely for two reasons. First, if this were the beginning of the down cycle, the plateau phase would have been only 5 years in length, and this is shorter than has been historically observed. Second, the recession of 1980–81 has been followed by a fairly sharp recovery in 1983, suggesting that it is not the beginning of a long-term down trend. Finally, the late 1970s was a period of rapidly increasing inflation, and this has characteristically been seen at the end of the up cycles rather than during transition periods. The essence of the transition period is stability both in terms of economic activity and in terms of inflation and interest rates.

Detractors of the Kondratieff wave theory have pointed out that exact timing of the cycles is very difficult and we would agree. However, we also believe that most evidence suggests that the early 1980s was the beginning of a Kondratieff plateau phase and that the remainder of the decade will be a period of stable inflation and interest rates and appreciating stock prices. In the past, stocks have appreciated between four- and sixfold during a plateau phase. The Dow Jones Industrial Average was in the general region of 800 during the early 1980s, and, if this represents the beginning of a plateau phase, it would suggest that the Dow Jones Industrial Average might be between 2,500 and 3,500 by the end of the decade!

It is important to remember that the capital goods or Kondratieff cycle is just a theory. It is based on past observations of economic activity, mostly in the nineteenth century. Obviously, a Russian economist in 1920 would not be able to get very accurate estimates of economic activity in industrialized countries in the early 1800s. Nevertheless, Kondratieff was able to propose a model of economic activity that appears to have generally predicted the trends of the twentieth century.

There have been many changes in the United States in the past 50 years, which may well invalidate any comparisons with prior history. The most striking has been the major involvement of the government in the economy. Earlier Kondratieff waves were based on a free-market economy, which exists only partly today. Government regulations, taxation, and spending are major influences in our modern-day economy, and these are more subject to political considerations than traditional supply-and-demand relationships. For example, the existence of legislative entitlement programs and the entire social security system has an unprecedented effect on the entire national economy. It is well known that, as the social security program is now configured, it will be unfundable. The political decisions that evolve from this situation may have such a far-reaching impact as to completely invalidate any cyclical comparisons with the past. For example, the existence of extensive entitlement programs makes a 1930s-style depression unlikely in the 1980s. Similarly, there has never been as great a burden of Government debt as exists today. This debt will ultimately have a major effect on inflation and interest rates, which may well obscure all other influences.

We believe that it is unreasonable to expect that the 1980s will be exactly like the 1920s. Nevertheless, to whatever extent the historical trends of prior capital goods cycles still exist, they point toward a period of prosperity for financial assets, especially common stocks.

THE CASE FOR STOCKS

We have seen how the decrease in inflation of the early 1980s is bullish for stocks. Assuming that the Reagan Administration can keep the federal deficit from renewing inflation, there is reason to be optimistic for stock prospects in the 1980s. We have also seen how the historical capital goods cycle as outlined in the Kondratieff wave theory suggests that the common stocks will do well at least until the mid-1980s and probably until 1990. There are several other factors that also suggest that the 1980s will be the era of common stocks.

In terms of relative value, the stock market is undervalued. Dividends and profits of Corporate America have increased steadily since 1972, but stock prices, as measured by the Dow Jones Industrial Average, have not kept pace. This is reflected in the price/earnings ratios of common stocks, which historically have averaged around 14. Throughout the 1970s and the early 1980s, the *P/E* ratio of the stocks in the Dow Jones Industrial Average has been approximately half of this historical norm. In effect, this means that stocks in the early 1980s are "cheap." Merely reestablishing the his-torical *P/E* ratio of 14 would imply a doubling of stock market prices from the late-1970s levels. However, during bull markets there has usually been some overshoot, and for a period of time the *P/E* values have gone above 14, which suggests that stock prices could more than double in the next few years.

Stock prices have also lagged far behind the prevailing inflation rate. From 1966 to 1981, inflation averaged 9% in the United States; yet, the Dow Jones Industrial Average remained essentially flat, trading between 500 and 1,000. If stock prices simply catch up to inflation, they would have to more than double.

Compared to the minor appreciation of stock prices, the cost of building and equipment has increased dramatically. Replacement costs of capital equipment have increased approximately 13% during the last 10 years, more than twice as much as the average stock price. Therefore, it is cheaper to buy a company than to build your own plant. This has been a major reason for a large number of corporate stock repurchases and corporate acquisitions and takeovers that occurred during the 1980s. As long as this continues, this should be a clear message to us that "stocks are cheap." Stocks would appear to have a favorable position on the risk–reward line relative to other investment alternatives. Real estate and hard assets have added significant appreciation since 1966, whereas financially denominated assets such as stocks and bonds have not. It is a general rule of thumb that there is more risk in buying something that has had recent, significant appreciation than there is in buying something that has not run up in price. This is an obvious point. The secret of investment success is to "buy low and sell high." It is difficult to make money if you "buy high."

Stock prices are set by bidding in the competitive market and are con-trolled by supply and demand. It would appear that there is a large reservoir of inherent demand for stocks at this time. In the early 1980s, the amount of financial resources in assets other than stocks was at a historical high. Stock ownership by mutual funds was a historical low. Pension funds with over $600 billion in assets entered the decade with the lowest percentage of stock ownership in 15 years. When pension fund managers return to their historic levels of stock ownership, over $30 billion will be redirected into the stock market. Similar large amounts of cash and cash equivalents are on the sidelines in mutual funds, money market funds, and insurance companies. Individual investors may well exceed their levels of previous stock ownership. For one thing, the creation of IRAs and Keogh plans has provided a great impetus for savings and investment on the part of individuals. (Even if an individual places his IRA money in the local bank, it represents cash that is now available for investments in stock ownership.) The general aging of the "baby-boom" population is moving greater numbers of Americans into the 40- to 60-year age group, which is historically the group that has invested in stocks. The leading edge of this post-war baby boom is now approximating this age. Finally, the unprecedented accumulation of cash by trading partners of the United States and by oil-producing countries represents a large reservoir of funds that will ultimately have to be reinvested. It is likely that a large percentage of these funds will find their way into American investments.

There are also a number of technical market-forecasting techniques that predict that the Dow Jones Industrial Average will be between 2000 and 3000 by the end of the decade. These include such factors as a return to historic *P/E* ratios coupled with a generalized increase in corporate earnings. A particularly interesting technical indicator is the so-called Federal Reserve Board rule. It has been observed that when the Federal Reserve Board eases the monetary climate by increasing the money supply and decreasing interest rates two times in succession, there is a resulting major increase in stock prices. The converse also holds: when the Federal Reserve Board tightens the monetary climate three times in succession, stock prices fall considerably. These changes in Federal Reserve Policy are known collectively as the Federal Reserve "buy" rule and the Federal Reserve "sell" rule. Since 1914, the Federal Reserve buy rule has been activated 17 times. Following each of these, the stock market, as measured by the Dow Jones Industrial Average, has risen. The smallest rise was 18%, and the largest 500%. During this same period, the Federal Reserve sell rule has been activated 12 times, and following each of these the Dow Jones Industrial Average decreased. The smallest decrease was 3.5% and the largest was 90%. The most recent Federal Reserve signal was a "buy," activated in August, 1982. Although the discount rate has since been increased, a sell signal has not been given to date.

SUMMARY

We believe that the direction of most indicators is clear: common stocks represent the most judicious investments for the next few years, at least through 1985 and probably through 1990. The Dow Jones Industrial Average should approach, or top, 3,000 during this period, and this is the investment arena (the forest) in which the major profits will be made. Regardless of the specifics of your financial plan, be it high-risk aggressive growth or low-risk income-producing capital preservation, you should have the majority of your assets in common stocks or mutual funds that own common stocks. The early 1980s represented an excellent environment for bonds, but we believe that in 1980–81 interest rates probably bottomed out, and that bonds will represent a relatively less attractive investment in the remainder of the decade. Similarly, unless there is a renewal of inflation (which we think unlikely), real estate and other hard assets will not provide a rate of return sufficient to justify their risk. Dollar-denominated investments (such as certificates of deposit, money market funds, and short- or intermediate-term bonds) should provide a modest income stream that, after taxes, will approximately index inflation. As such, they will not provide nearly as high a return as common stocks. By the end of the decade, there should be a secular change in the investment environment, which will make cash-equivalent assets such as treasury bills the most judicious investments. For the present, however, go with the best risk–return relationship. Go to common stocks.

15

A PERSONAL INVESTMENT PROGRAM

In this final chapter we shall reiterate the main principles for financial independence and see how they can be incorporated into a successful personal investment program.

First, you must define a financial independence goal in terms of both time and assets. Once this is defined, you can structure your investment program to get you to your goal on time using the financial independence (FI) equation:

Financial Independence = Time (Money + Judicious Investments)

$$FI = T (M + JI)$$

Time is the single most important factor in any financial security plan. Because of the compounding principle, even a mediocre investment will generate a considerable return given enough time. At the other extreme, even the most spectacular idea will bear no fruit if it is never implemented. Any financial independence program you formulate should make maximum use of time.

Generating money for a plan is primarily a matter of personal discipline; nearly all professionals have adequate resources to implement a successful investment program, but many lack the resolution or do not take the time to do so. Mobilizing money is more a change in outlook than a change of lifestyle. Remember that all money falls into or.e of three categories: dead, lazy, and active. You must learn to automatically classify every dollar under your control and, when you identify dead or lazy dollars, take steps to move them into the active category.

There is no perfect investment; each type of investment vehicle has its strengths and weaknesses. In the 1980s, we believe that the greatest opportunities will exist in common stocks but that there will also be times when the most judicious course is to have your assets in cash equivalents. Periods of high interest rates represent a unique opportunity to lock in a high level of steady income. Real estate and tangible assets will not be strong unless the inflation rate increases. The small investor should never deal in commodities and use options only as occasional sport.

THE MONTHLY FINANCIAL INDEPENDENCE PAYMENT

We described the monthly financial independence payment (MyFIP) in some detail in Chapter 5. This is the cornerstone of any successful investment program regardless of the investment vehicle that is subsequently utilized. If you are unwilling to make a monthly commitment, you will be squandering the time factor and will have difficulty in obtaining your financial goal. Therefore, before even considering specific investment vehicles, you must decide how large your MyFIP needs to be and take whatever steps are necessary to insure that you actually make the payment.

The size of the MyFIP will vary with your individual goal. If you have very few present assets or only a short time in which to obtain your goal, the MyFIP will have to be large. On the other hand, if you already have a significant start on your goal and have 25 years in which to work, your monthly payment can be considerably smaller. For our clients who are less than 45 years of age, we have found a good general ballpark figure is 30% of their gross income *inclusive* of any retirement plan contributions.

Sam B., with a gross income of $100,000, should try to contribute $30,000 a year to his investment program. (Remember that this contribution includes all types of deferred income including retirement benefits.) Sam will try to have as many of his investment dollars in a retirement plan as possible because these plans are tax deferred. In fact, he has stopped thinking of them as "retirement" plans and instead refers to them as his "tax-deferred investment" plans. (Since they are not taxed, tax-deferred retirement plans are not the place for tax shelters, municipal bonds, or real estate deals when part of the value of the investment is in the special tax status.) In addition to his gross income, Sam has contributions of $24,000 a year to his retirement plan at work. This leaves only $6,000, or $500 per month, to be made up from his "lifestyle" money. Some of this money will be generated in the savings Sam will receive when he converts his whole-life insurance to term insurance and increases the deductibles on his casualty insurance. The remainder will not be missed because he will look at it as one of his fixed monthly bills, the same as the telephone bill or the mortgage payment. The only difference is he will make his MyFIP payment before any others: he **pays himself first**. Sam elects to have his bank transfer the MyFIP payment directly from his bank account each month to an aggressive growth stock mutual fund.

If you do nothing more than institute a monthly financial independence payment and put it into any of the money market funds, you will achieve a modest degree of financial security with virtually no risk. However, by taking a little extra care and positioning your assets to take advantage of the best current investment possibilities, you will be able to take far more rapid strides toward your final goal. Money market funds provide an annualized return about 3 to 4 percentage points higher than the inflation rate. With very little extra risk, you should be able to easily generate a return of double the inflation rate, and we believe your target should be an annualized return of triple the present inflation rate. Generating this extra return requires only a slight increase in risk and should not cause even the most nervous investor to lose an extra minute of sleep.

TYPES OF INVESTMENT PROGRAMS

In managing accounts, we have found that most professionals' needs can be filled with one of three basic program types.

Most professionals should use a growth program that is designed to yield an annual return of at least triple the inflation rate with very modest risk.

Investors with less demanding goals or those with modest current assets should utilize an established income program that is designed to provide at least double the current inflation rate with more safety than the growth program.

Investors who are very close to their financial goal or near retirement should utilize a capital preservation program that will provide a steady income of 4 to 5 points above the inflation rate with minimal risk. If at first you succeed (become financially independent), stop! Don't take any more chances! Regardless of your age, when you have achieved your goal you should use the capital preservation program.

In general, all of your assets, both those in the tax-sheltered retirement plan and those outside of the tax shelter, should be in the same program. For tax record-keeping purposes it will be necessary to maintain separate accounts for the retirement funds and the other assets, but they should usually be in the same investment vehicle.

All three programs have several aspects in common. First, they rely heavily on the use of mutual funds for the reasons outlined in Chapter 13. Generally, at least 80% of the total assets will be in a mutual fund, and no more than 20% will be in individual investment vehicles. Second, each program utilizes a money market mutual fund as a cash reservoir. Because of their ready liquidity through either check writing or direct bank transfer, these funds provide the best storehouse for transitional dollars. In addition, these funds are a place to shift assets when prospects for other types of investments worsen. Such situations might include a rapidly rising inflation rate or the prospects of a short- or long-term bear market. Third, when interest rates are very high, all programs shift much of their assets to deeply discounted bonds, which present a profitable investment opportunity. The differences among the programs are in the type of mutual funds they utilize.

Growth Program

The growth program is recommended for the majority of investors under age 45. In addition to a money market fund, it consists of one or more top-performing growth or aggressive-growth mutual stock funds. When the investment climate suggests a rising stock market, the investor should move his assets totally into one of the stock funds, since they have historically outperformed the general market by factors of 3 to 5. Some of the aggressive-growth funds perform even better. However, when there is significant risk of market decline, investors should "switch" the assets out of the stock funds and into "cash" (money market fund). Switching is particularly important if an aggressive growth approach is used, since aggressive growth funds can often decline dramatically during bear markets. (We shall discuss a method for determining the appropriate time to switch in a moment.) The Columbia Fund and the Nicholas Fund are examples of growth funds that have performed well over the past five years. The Fidelity Select Technology and Magellan Funds, the 44 Wall Street Fund, and the 20th Century Ultra Fund are examples of aggressive growth funds whose performance has been exemplary in the early 1980s.

Established Income Program

This is a more conservative program recommended for older investors, those with less ambitious financial goals, or those wishing to lessen investment risk. This program is designed to provide both capital gains and modest current income. In addition to the money market fund, assets are placed in one or more growth-equity-type mutual stock funds. Some of the assets will also be in tax-exempt or corporate bond funds when interest rates are favorable, and there are usually some individual utilities or a utility mutual fund. As with the growth program, the total yields will be increased if the investor "switches" the assets from the stock fund to the money market fund when there is high risk of stock market decline. The Fidelity Equity Income Fund and the Price New Era Fund are two growth-equity funds that have performed well in the past few years.

Capital Preservation Program

This program is for the investor within 10 years of retirement or who is near his financial goal. It stresses high current income with minimal risk levels. In addition to the money market fund, it consists of an established growth or "blue-chip" mutual stock fund, a long-term bond fund, some Treasury Bonds, a utilities mutual fund or selected individual utilities, and possibly some gold (depending on the current inflation). Switching funds from stocks into cash is not as important with this program as with the others since the mutual funds recommended are not as volatile, and capital gains are a secondary consideration. Periods of high interest rates represent a unique opportunity for this type of program; they permit the purchase of long-term deeply discounted bonds, which can "lock-in" a high rate of return for many years. Zero coupon bonds can also be useful.

THE IMPORTANCE OF TIMING

Throughout this book we have stressed that everything cycles. Even in a general environment that favors stocks there will be times when the stock market declines. Even when interest rates are low and generally stable, there will be periods of 1- or 2-point interest rate rises that can cause the value of bonds to temporarily decrease.

August, 1982 was the beginning of a major bull market. In the ensuing 10 months, it was almost impossible to lose money in the stock market, and everyone became an expert. Throw a dart at the stock listings, buy, and relax. This is the beauty of a major bull market—nearly everyone wins. Unfortunately, every bull market has been followed by a bear market in which many people lose nearly all of what they won. The "instant expert" of the bull market can be the "instant loser" in the bear market. Now, the total gains of the bull markets are usually greater than the total losses of the bear markets; that is, the overall trend of the stock market is up. Although the overall trend is up, it is not a smooth line but rather a series of peaks and valleys, and these slopes can be steep; investors who stay in a bear market can take a terrible mauling. A long-term "buy and hold" strategy will likely make money, but at a considerably slower rate than could be obtained by listening to the market trends. Every investment cycles, and financial success is easier to obtain if your assets are riding with, rather than bucking, the trend of the market. The whole trick is identifying the trend, easy in retrospect but difficult prospectively.

There is no lack of available advice on the future. On any given day there are experts who predict that interest rates are going up, that interest rates are going down, and that interest rates will stay the same. Similarly there are market analysts who predict a bear market, those who believe a bull market is imminent, and those who think the market will be flat. It is a rare edition of *Wall Street Week* in which all of the guests agree as to what will happen next. Call three stockbrokers from three different brokerage houses and you will likely get three different projections as to upcoming market action. There are a multitude of investment advisory services, and it is very unusual for more than two-thirds of them to agree on even the general trend of the market, let alone which stock groups or individual stocks will be most successful. Given so many "expert" and conflicting opinions, how does Sam B. go about deciding where to put his money and when to do it?

Our investment management company, The Professional Financial Security Corporation, has devoted considerable market research to analyzing and predicting market trends. From the performance records of a variety of forecasting systems, we have identified one rather simple technique that produces consistently good results. It is based on the observations of Vilfredo Pareto (1848–1932), an Italian economist who wrote a fascinating treatise on economics and human success and failure entitled *Mind and Society*. Best known for his theories on social welfare and competition, Pareto based one part of his thesis on observations of many different competitive human tasks and this can be expressed in simple form as the "20–80 rule."

THE 20–80 RULE

The 20–80 rule states that in any competitive activity that is undertaken by a large group of people, 20% of the people will achieve 80% of the positive results. The type of activity has little effect on the rule; it applies to playing golf, answering test questions, meeting sales quotas, and investing money. Any businessman can tell you that only one-fifth of his operations really contribute most of the profits of the company. In football, 5 of the 26 teams in the NFL have won 80% of playoff and Super Bowl games. Eighty percent of successful investment decisions are made by 20% of investors. A corollary to the 20–80 rule states that 20% of people account for 80% of the negative results.

The 20–80 rule is intuitively correct if we think about it a moment; it is just another way of expressing the familiar "bell-shaped curve" of performance. In school there were the "smart ones" at the upper end of the curve, and in investing there is the "smart money," which consistently does well. In school, if you copied the test answers from one of the "smart ones," you could improve your score; in investing if you copy the "smart money," you will improve your return. Copying test answers in school is against the rules of course, but copying "smart money" in investing is fair game.

Who are these 20%, the so-called smart investors? They are a diverse lot, difficult to find as individuals but identifiable in groups. Members of the stock exchange invariably do well in their personal accounts (not always as well for their customers). Portfolio managers of mutual funds either do well or are soon out of work. Certain underwriters and venture capitalists always seem to land on their feet. Some pension fund managers greatly outperform the average. Many of the activities of these professional investors are published in *Barron's* and *The Wall Street Journal*. In other words, they leave some tracks to follow.

We have analyzed the activities of this group of smart investors (as well as those who seem to comprise the lower 20% of Pareto's classification) over the years and found that certain combinations of selling and buying activities reflect, at times, extremes of bearish or bullish anticipation. This collective sentiment usually correctly anticipates actual changes in stock prices. On occasion, extreme sentiment readings have not resulted in stock price movement; nevertheless, we have found that it is best to be investing with this group and not against it.

In *D*ℝ *INVESTOR*, our monthly advisory, we compile the activities of these successful professional investors into a composite index, which we call the *Professional Sentiment Index* (PSI). As PSI becomes positive, it indicates that, as a group, these investors are becoming more bullish. When PSI reaches +5, it indicates that the great majority are bullish and it is a time to join them and move into equities. As these investors sour on the market, PSI becomes negative, and when it dips to −5, the majority of professional investors are "out of the market." We believe that you should be too.

Table 15.1 shows the Dow Jones Industrial Average on the dates of major PSI signals from August, 1979 to March, 1983. There were 10 signals given during this period, and following 9 of these signals, the market moved in the direction indicated by the Professional Sentiment Index. If we use the Dow Jones Industrial Average as a proxy for a mutual fund, we can calculate the compound annual gain during this period for two investment strategies: "buy and hold" and "switch." We terminated the

TABLE 15.1 Professional Sentiment Index
signals from August, 1979 to March, 1983

Date	Professional Sentiment Index	Dow Jones Industrial Average
8/31/79	Sell	885
11/02/79	Buy	815
1/25/80	Sell	875
5/02/80	Buy	810
10/03/80	Sell	965
12/19/80	Buy	947
4/16/81	Sell	1,006
4/02/82	Buy	839
11/05/82	Sell	1,052
1/07/83	Buy	1,076
3/25/83	Sell	1,140

Compound annual change		
Buy and hold	8%	
Switch	21%	

table on a "sell" signal to insure that any "buy and hold" investment would show a profit. (If we terminated the table on April 2, 1982, a "buy and hold" strategy would have shown a loss.) These figures assume an average dividend of 7%.

An investor who bought on August 31, 1979 and held until March 25, 1983 would have realized a compound annual rate of return of 8%. On the other hand, an investor who "switched"—buying on the buy signals and moving into a money market fund when a sell signal was given—would have achieved a compound annual rate of return of 21%! (This assumes receiving an average 8% interest from a money market fund.) The increased yield arises because switching plays both legs of the market cycle. During bullish up trends, the assets are in stocks, which increase in value as the market rises. During bearish downswings, money is on the sidelines while the price of stock falls; instead of experiencing a loss, the assets are earning 8% in a money market fund. When the market again starts to rise, the assets are switched back into stocks, and because prices are down, the investor is able to buy five shares for each four sold earlier. The greater the market loss, the more the gain, since a greater number of shares can be purchased for the same money.

Table 15.2 shows how switching compares to buy and hold in actual use. This table covers a 26-month period from December 19, 1980 until

TABLE 15.2 Value of $10,000 invested from December, 1980 to February, 1983[a]

Fund	Buy and hold[b]	Switch[b]
20th Century Select	14,505 (19%)	18,465 (33%)
Fidelity Magellan	12,922 (12%)	18,528 (33%)
44 Wall Street	8,672 (−6%)	17,269 (29%)
Value Line Leverage	14,701 (20%)	17,162 (28%)
Fidelity Equity-Income	13,530 (16%)	16,530 (26%)
Dreyfus No. 9	10,914 (4%)	14,596 (19%)
Dow Jones Industrial Average (947–1,121) (assuming 7% dividends)	(15%)	(24%)

[a]Professional Sentiment Index switch signals during this period: 12/19/80, buy; 4/16/81, sell; 4/02/82, buy; 11/05/82, sell; 1/07/83, buy.
[b]Figures in parentheses are annual *compound* rate of return.

March 1, 1983 for six high-quality mutual funds and shows the value of an initial $10,000 investment at the end of the period as well as the compound annual rate of return. In every case, switching increased the return, and in some cases (44 Wall Street, Dreyfus No. 9), the difference was striking. This table includes all dividends and distributions as well as the 3% "load" charge on the Fidelity Magellan Fund. But it does not take taxes into account, and since switching frequently generates short-term capital gains, the effect of taxes cannot be ignored.

The effect of taxes on the rates of return in Table 15.2 is shown in Table 15.3. We assumed a "worst case," a 50% tax bracket. The effect of taxes

TABLE 15.3 Effect of 50% taxes on total returns from December, 1980 to February, 1983

Fund	Compound annual rate of return (%)	
	Buy and hold	Switch
20th Century Select	15	18
Fidelity Magellan	9	18
44 Wall Street	−7	16
Value Line Leverage	11	14
Fidelity Equity-Income	10	14
Dreyfus No. 9	0	10
Dow Jones Industrial Average	10	12

varies among funds, since they have different mixes of dividends and long- and short-term capital gains. Taxes reduce the return from both the buy and hold and switch programs, but because of more short-term gains, the switch program is more seriously decreased. Despite the effect of taxes, in each case the return was greater with switching. A buy-and-hold philosophy will make money over the long haul but will not produce the aggressive returns that are possible in a switch program. We believe that investors should benefit from both rising and falling markets, and switching is the best way of accomplishing this.

PERSPECTIVE

Well, that's our current approach. We think it is a pretty good one; it has worked for us and for others we know. Financial independence takes some effort, but it should be obtainable by any professional. By applying the principles we have laid out, you should be able to construct a basic financial goal and develop a first-generation battle plan for attacking it. Since each of us is different, you will have to fine tune and individualize in many places. You will have some successes, and, undoubtedly, you will have some failures. The important thing is to remain flexible and learn from past mistakes so that you don't repeat them.

It is important to remember that you do not have to make all the decisions yourself; you should utilize outside advice. However, the final result and responsibility will be yours. You may delegate much of the responsibility for day-to-day operation to your advisors, but only you will be able to keep your eye on the final result. And in the end, it is only results that count. As long as an idea or an advisor is serving you well, go with it, but do not hesitate to change directions if things do not work out as planned. Remember that time is your most important ally. An individual mistake here or there won't sink your ship, but you will never reach your destination if you do not leave the dock.

APPENDIX A

FUTURE VALUE OF
$1.00 FACTOR
(COMPOUND INTEREST TABLE)

TABLE A.1 COMPOUND INTEREST TABLE: Future value of $1.00[a]

Interest rates

Period	5.0%	6.0%	7.0%	8.0%	9.0%	10.0%	11.0%	12.0%	13.0%	14.0%	15.0%	20.0%	25.0%
1	1.05	1.06	1.07	1.08	1.09	1.10	1.11	1.12	1.13	1.14	1.15	1.20	1.25
2	1.10	1.12	1.14	1.17	1.19	1.21	1.23	1.25	1.28	1.30	1.32	1.44	1.56
3	1.16	1.19	1.23	1.26	1.30	1.33	1.37	1.40	1.44	1.48	1.52	1.73	1.95
4	1.22	1.26	1.31	1.36	1.41	1.46	1.52	1.57	1.63	1.69	1.75	2.07	2.44
5	1.28	1.34	1.40	1.47	1.54	1.61	1.69	1.76	1.84	1.93	2.01	2.49	3.05
6	1.34	1.42	1.50	1.59	1.68	1.77	1.87	1.97	2.08	2.19	2.31	2.99	3.81
7	1.41	1.50	1.61	1.71	1.83	1.95	2.08	2.21	2.35	2.50	2.66	3.58	4.77
8	1.48	1.59	1.72	1.85	1.99	2.14	2.30	2.48	2.66	2.85	3.06	4.30	5.96
9	1.55	1.69	1.84	2.00	2.17	2.36	2.56	2.77	3.00	3.25	3.52	5.16	7.45
10	1.63	1.79	1.97	2.16	2.37	2.59	2.84	3.11	3.39	3.71	4.05	6.19	9.31
11	1.71	1.90	2.10	2.33	2.58	2.85	3.15	3.48	3.84	4.23	4.65	7.43	11.64
12	1.80	2.01	2.25	2.52	2.81	3.14	3.50	3.90	4.33	4.82	5.35	8.92	14.55
13	1.89	2.13	2.41	2.72	3.07	3.45	3.88	4.36	4.90	5.49	6.15	10.70	18.19
14	1.98	2.26	2.58	2.94	3.34	3.80	4.31	4.89	5.53	6.26	7.08	12.84	22.74
15	2.08	2.40	2.76	3.17	3.64	4.18	4.78	5.47	6.25	7.14	8.14	15.41	28.42
16	2.18	2.54	2.95	3.43	3.97	4.59	5.31	6.13	7.07	8.14	9.36	18.49	35.53
17	2.29	2.69	3.16	3.70	4.33	5.05	5.90	6.87	7.99	9.28	10.76	22.19	44.41
18	2.41	2.85	3.38	4.00	4.72	5.56	6.54	7.69	9.02	10.58	12.38	26.62	55.51
19	2.53	3.03	3.62	4.32	5.14	6.12	7.26	8.61	10.20	12.06	14.23	31.95	69.39
20	2.65	3.21	3.87	4.66	5.60	6.73	8.06	9.65	11.52	13.74	16.37	38.34	86.74
25	3.39	4.29	5.43	6.85	8.62	10.83	13.59	17.00	21.23	26.46	32.92	95.40	264.70
30	4.32	5.74	7.61	10.06	13.27	17.45	22.89	29.96	39.12	50.95	66.21	237.38	807.79
50	11.47	18.42	29.46	46.90	74.36	117.39	184.56	289.00	450.74	700.23	1,083.66	9,100.44	70,064.92

[a]The factors for various time intervals and rates of return are beginning of the year values (i.e., the amount present when the compounding period begins again) and are derived for the factor $(1 + i)^N$, where i is the interest rate or compound rate of return, and N is the time interval in years.

APPENDIX B

TIME VALUE OF ANNUITIES

PRESENT VALUE OF AN ANNUITY

An annuity is a series of periodic payments (or receipts), each equal in amount and paid at a regular time interval. Annuities have time value and we are often interested in the present value of an annuity—the amount of money we shall need to last a certain number of years if a fixed dollar amount is withdrawn at regular intervals. To find this, we use the time value of an annuity formula.

The number of dollars or present value of an annuity (PV_a) is obtained by knowing the amount of regular withdrawal payments (P_{out}) and the withdrawal annuity factor (A_{out}) associated with various rates of return from Table B.1 and substituting in the following formula:

$$PV_a = P_{out} \times A_{out}$$

EXAMPLE CALCULATING INSURANCE COVERAGE
Suppose you are concerned about the impact of your untimely departure on your spouse and newly arrived twins. You calculate that your family would need a minimum of 10 years of coverage at about three-fourths of your current family income, which works out to be $40,000 per year. You turn to your brother-in-law Izzy, the insurance agent, who suggests that you need $500,000 of term insurance to provide $40,000 for 10 years. Is he right? You decide to get the best second opinion you can—your own, aided by the time analysis of annuities discussed in this book and using the present value of an annuity formula. A quick call to the local Federal Reserve Bank reveals that you can get a 10% yield on treasury bonds, and so you decide to use 10% as the interest yield factor and begin your calculations:

$$PV_a = P_{out} \times A_{out}$$

179

TABLE B.1 Present annuity value of $1.00 ($A_{out}$)[a]

Period	Discount rates												
	5.0%	6.0%	7.0%	8.0%	9.0%	10.0%	11.0%	12.0%	13.0%	14.0%	15.0%	20.0%	25.0%
1	0.95	0.94	0.93	0.93	0.92	0.91	0.90	0.89	0.88	0.88	0.87	0.83	0.80
2	1.86	1.83	1.81	1.78	1.76	1.74	1.71	1.69	1.67	1.65	1.63	1.53	1.44
3	2.72	2.67	2.62	2.58	2.53	2.49	2.44	2.40	2.36	2.32	2.28	2.11	1.95
4	3.55	3.47	3.39	3.31	3.24	3.17	3.10	3.04	2.97	2.91	2.85	2.59	2.36
5	4.33	4.21	4.10	3.99	3.89	3.79	3.70	3.60	3.52	3.43	3.35	2.99	2.69
6	5.08	4.92	4.77	4.62	4.49	4.36	4.23	4.11	4.00	3.89	3.78	3.33	2.95
7	5.79	5.58	5.39	5.21	5.03	4.87	4.71	4.56	4.42	4.29	4.16	3.60	3.16
8	6.46	6.21	5.97	5.75	5.53	5.33	5.15	4.97	4.80	4.64	4.49	3.84	3.33
9	7.11	6.80	6.52	6.25	6.00	5.76	5.54	5.33	5.13	4.95	4.77	4.03	3.46
10	7.72	7.36	7.02	6.71	6.42	6.14	5.89	5.65	5.43	5.22	5.02	4.19	3.57
11	8.31	7.89	7.50	7.14	6.81	6.50	6.21	5.94	5.69	5.45	5.23	4.33	3.66
12	8.86	8.38	7.94	7.54	7.16	6.81	6.49	6.19	5.92	5.66	5.42	4.44	3.73
13	9.39	8.85	8.36	7.90	7.49	7.10	6.75	6.42	6.12	5.84	5.58	4.53	3.78
14	9.90	9.29	8.75	8.24	7.79	7.37	6.98	6.63	6.30	6.00	5.72	4.61	3.82
15	10.38	9.71	9.11	8.56	8.06	7.61	7.19	6.81	6.46	6.14	5.85	4.68	3.86
16	10.84	10.11	9.45	8.85	8.31	7.82	7.38	6.97	6.60	6.27	5.95	4.73	3.89
17	11.27	10.48	9.76	9.12	8.54	8.02	7.55	7.12	6.73	6.37	6.05	4.77	3.91
18	11.69	10.83	10.06	9.37	8.76	8.20	7.70	7.25	6.84	6.47	6.13	4.81	3.93
19	12.09	11.16	10.34	9.60	8.95	8.36	7.84	7.37	6.94	6.55	6.20	4.84	3.94
20	12.46	11.47	10.59	9.82	9.13	8.51	7.96	7.47	7.02	6.62	6.26	4.87	3.95
25	14.09	12.78	11.65	10.67	9.82	9.08	8.42	7.84	7.33	6.87	6.46	4.95	3.98
30	15.37	13.76	12.41	11.26	10.27	9.43	8.69	8.06	7.50	7.00	6.57	4.98	4.00
50	18.26	15.76	13.80	12.23	10.96	9.91	9.04	8.30	7.68	7.13	6.66	5.00	4.00

[a]The factors for various time intervals and rates of return are beginning of the year values (i.e., the amount present when the compounding period begins again) and are derived for the factor A_{out} for various interest rates or compound rates of return and yearly time intervals.

Substituting $40,000 per year for 10 years and an assumed 10% (from Table B.1, A_{out} = 6.14) yields

$$PV_a = \$40,000_{10} \times 6.14$$

$$PV_a = \$245,600$$

Well! Izzy had you covered, but you spot the overkill and take out a quarter instead of a half million in term insurance.

FUTURE VALUE OF AN ANNUITY

Another useful application of the time analysis of annuities occurs when we are interested in finding out the size of the monthly payment needed, if placed in an investment returning a certain compound interest rate, to produce a given sum of money. An example of such an annuity payment into an investment fund occurred in Chapter 5 in the form of the Monthly Financial Independence payment (MyFIP). We can find the future value of an annuity (FV_a) by using the future value of annuity factor table (Table B.2) and the following equation:

$$FV_a = P_{in} \times A_{in}$$

EXAMPLE   CALCULATING MONTHLY PAYMENTS TO COVER UNEXPECTED LOSSES

At age 35 you read *Financial Independence: The Doctor's Guide* and on the

TABLE B.2 Future annuity value of $1.00 ($A_{in}$)[a]

Period	5.0%	6.0%	7.0%	8.0%	9.0%	10.0%	11.0%	12.0%	13.0%	14.0%	15.0%	20.0%	25.0%
1	1.00	1.00	1.00	1.00	1.00	1.00	1.00	1.00	1.00	1.00	1.00	1.00	1.00
2	2.05	2.06	2.07	2.08	2.09	2.10	2.11	2.12	2.13	2.14	2.15	2.20	2.25
3	3.15	3.18	3.21	3.25	3.28	3.31	3.34	3.37	3.41	3.44	3.47	3.64	3.81
4	4.31	4.37	4.44	4.51	4.57	4.64	4.71	4.78	4.85	4.92	4.99	5.37	5.77
5	5.53	5.64	5.75	5.87	5.98	6.11	6.23	6.35	6.48	6.61	6.74	7.44	8.21
6	6.80	6.98	7.15	7.34	7.52	7.72	7.91	8.12	8.32	8.54	8.75	9.93	11.26
7	8.14	8.39	8.65	8.92	9.20	9.49	9.78	10.09	10.40	10.73	11.07	12.92	15.07
8	9.55	9.90	10.26	10.64	11.03	11.44	11.86	12.30	12.76	13.23	13.73	16.50	19.84
9	11.03	11.49	11.98	12.49	13.02	13.58	14.16	14.78	15.42	16.09	16.79	20.80	25.80
10	12.58	13.18	13.82	14.49	15.19	15.94	16.72	17.55	18.42	19.34	20.30	25.96	33.25
11	14.21	14.97	15.78	16.65	17.56	18.53	19.56	20.65	21.81	23.04	24.35	32.15	42.57
12	15.92	16.87	17.89	18.98	20.14	21.38	22.71	24.13	25.65	27.27	29.00	39.58	54.21
13	17.71	18.88	20.14	21.50	22.95	24.52	26.21	28.03	29.98	32.09	34.35	48.50	68.76
14	19.60	21.02	22.55	24.21	26.02	27.97	30.09	32.39	34.88	37.58	40.50	59.20	86.95
15	21.58	23.28	25.13	27.15	29.36	31.77	34.41	37.28	40.42	43.84	47.58	72.04	109.69
16	23.66	25.67	27.89	30.32	33.00	35.95	39.19	42.75	46.67	50.98	55.72	87.44	138.11
17	25.84	28.21	30.84	33.75	36.97	40.54	44.50	48.88	53.74	59.12	65.08	105.93	173.64
18	28.13	30.91	34.00	37.45	41.30	45.60	50.40	55.75	61.73	68.39	75.84	128.12	218.04
19	30.54	33.76	37.38	41.45	46.02	51.16	56.94	63.44	70.75	78.97	88.21	154.74	273.56
20	33.07	36.79	41.00	45.76	51.16	57.27	64.20	72.05	80.95	91.02	102.44	186.69	342.94
25	47.73	54.86	63.25	73.11	84.70	98.35	114.41	133.33	155.62	181.87	212.79	471.98	1,054.79
30	66.44	79.06	94.46	113.28	136.31	164.49	199.02	241.33	293.20	356.79	434.75	1,181.88	3,227.17
50	209.35	290.34	406.53	573.77	815.08	1,163.91	1,668.77	2,400.02	3,459.51	4,994.52	7,217.72	45,497.19	280,255.69

[a]The factors for various time intervals and rates of return are beginning of the year values (i.e., the amount present when the compounding period begins again) and are derived for the factor A_{in} for various interest rates or compound rates of return and yearly time intervals.

basis of the principles outlined, plotted your course for financial independence. At age 45, after working hard in the group practice and having become a full partner, you begin to have a little time and decide to check in and see how your net worth is doing. Unfortunately, you find out that the senior partner in the group—who had been handling the pension fund—had been doing some unsuccessful covered call writing and you are $100,000 below where you should be at this time. After the shock, you make two importance decisions. (1) You decide that for your financial independence program your senior partner's management is tantamount to rearranging the deck chairs on the Titanic, and you get direct control of your pension fund and start making your own decisions. (2) You set about the damage control program assuming that your best ally in this is the annuity equation and not your partner.

You are now 45 and wanted to be financially independent at age 55, so you have the time interval of 10 years fixed. However, during a seminar on the West Coast, you met an electrical engineer from Stanford who had been hired as a consultant for a high-tech Silicon Valley company. After a little checking, you decide that his estimate of 40% growth of the company for 15 years or more is realistic, but Diasonics and other things being what they are, you decide to settle for an estimated 20% growth for 10 years in your evaluation and begin substituting in the formula to find out what your yearly payments should be to recover the $100,000 loss in 10 years. From Table B.2 using a period of 10 years and 20% return, $A_{in} = 25.96$:

$$FV_a = P_{in} \times A_{in}$$

$$\$100,000 = P_{10\ yr} \times 25.96$$

$$P_{10\ yr} = \$3,852.08$$

In other words, if all of your assumptions are correct, you must commit around $4,000 per year to recover the shortfall in your account; $4,000 is exactly the amount the IRS will allow for yearly IRA contributions for you and your spouse, and so you open an account with a brokerage house and commit yourselves to contribute $4,000 to your IRA yearly for 10 years.

APPENDIX C

FUTURE ANNUITY VALUE OF $1,200 FACTOR

This annuity factor is to be used with the future annuity equation for calculating the future value of a regular contribution of $100 per month for a given period of years. This is not just a multiple of the future value of $1.00 factor because regular additional payments are made during the time period.

TABLE C.1 Future annuity value of $1,200[a]

Period	Interest rates												
	5.0%	6.0%	7.0%	8.0%	9.0%	10.0%	11.0%	12.0%	13.0%	14.0%	15.0%	20.0%	25.0%
1	1,200	1,200	1,200	1,200	1,200	1,200	1,200	1,200	1,200	1,200	1,200	1,200	1,200
2	2,460	2,472	2,484	2,496	2,508	2,520	2,532	2,544	2,556	2,568	2,580	2,640	2,700
3	3,783	3,820	3,858	3,896	3,934	3,972	4,011	4,049	4,088	4,128	4,167	4,368	4,575
4	5,172	5,250	5,328	5,407	5,488	5,569	5,652	5,735	5,820	5,905	5,992	6,442	6,919
5	6,631	6,765	6,901	7,040	7,182	7,326	7,473	7,623	7,776	7,932	8,091	8,930	9,848
6	8,162	8,370	8,584	8,803	9,028	9,259	9,495	9,738	9,987	10,243	10,504	11,916	13,511
7	9,770	10,073	10,385	10,707	11,041	11,385	11,740	12,107	12,486	12,877	13,280	15,499	18,088
8	11,459	11,877	12,312	12,764	13,234	13,723	14,231	14,760	15,309	15,879	16,472	19,799	23,810
9	13,232	13,790	14,374	14,985	15,625	16,295	16,997	17,731	18,499	19,302	20,143	24,959	30,963
10	15,093	15,817	16,580	17,384	18,232	19,125	20,066	21,058	22,104	23,205	24,364	31,150	39,903
11	17,048	17,966	18,940	19,975	21,072	22,237	23,474	24,785	26,177	27,653	29,219	38,581	51,079
12	19,101	20,244	21,466	22,773	24,169	25,661	27,256	28,960	30,780	32,725	34,802	47,497	65,049
13	21,256	22,659	24,169	25,794	27,544	29,427	31,454	33,635	35,982	38,506	41,222	58,196	82,511
14	23,518	25,218	27,061	29,058	31,233	33,570	36,114	38,871	41,859	45,097	48,606	71,035	104,339
15	25,894	27,931	30,155	32,583	35,233	38,127	41,286	44,736	48,501	52,611	57,096	86,442	131,624
16	28,389	30,807	33,466	36,389	39,604	43,140	47,028	51,304	56,006	61,176	66,861	104,931	165,730
17	31,008	33,855	37,008	40,500	44,368	48,654	53,401	58,660	64,487	70,941	78,090	127,117	208,363
18	33,759	37,087	40,799	44,940	49,562	54,719	60,475	66,900	74,070	82,073	91,004	153,740	261,654
19	36,647	40,512	44,855	49,736	55,222	61,391	68,327	76,128	84,899	94,763	105,854	185,688	328,267
20	39,679	44,143	49,195	54,914	61,392	68,730	77,043	86,463	97,136	109,230	122,932	224,026	411,534
25	57,273	65,837	75,899	87,727	101,641	118,016	137,296	160,001	186,743	218,245	255,352	566,377	1,265,749
30	79,727	94,870	113,353	135,940	163,569	197,393	238,825	289,599	351,839	428,144	521,694	1,418,258	3,872,609
50	251,218	348,403	487,835	688,524	978,100	1,396,690	2,002,525	2,880,022	4,151,409	5,993,426	8,661,260	54,596,629	336,306,831

[a]The factors for various time intervals and rates of return are beginning of the year values (i.e., the amount present when the compounding period begins again) and are derived for a standardized $1,200 payment into an investment program for various interest rates or compound rates of return and yearly time intervals.

APPENDIX D

USE OF THE COMPOUND INTEREST TABLE

THE BLUE MAX DIAMOND DEAL

American Diamond Investors Offshore is offering a limited partnership in Blue Max Diamonds for $10,000. To induce you to participate, they have produced their record of 15 previous partnerships in which the average limited partner investor received 100% profit at the end of the 7-year life of the partnership. Based on your $10,000 investment, this would mean that you would receive $20,000 in 7 years. You call up the local Federal Reserve Bank and find that for a 7-year treasury note you can receive 15% interest, and since this is a relatively safe investment, you decide that the minimal return you need in order to be induced to invest in this program is 15%. Going to our present value equation, we find as follows:

$$P = AF/[1 + i]^N$$

$$P = \$20,000/[1 + 0.15]^7$$

$$P = \$20,000/2.66$$

$$P = \$7,519$$

The present value figure ($7,519) is substantially below the amount we are being asked to invest, and thus, we politely reject the investment in the Blue Max and put our money into a 7-year treasury bond yielding a nearly risk-free 15%.

GEOSCARCE

One day you receive a phone call from your stockbroker announcing the fact that his brokerage firm is handling a new oil and gas drilling program that is sponsored by Geoscarce, one of the most reputable and successful drillers in the business. He tells you that in the long history of Geoscarce, no investor has ever received less than a 5-to-1, after-tax return in the limited partnerships available and that, lucky for you, the driller has a policy of capping successful wells and waiting for the price to go up before distribution and sales operations begin. The partnerships usually run 12 years, and at that time Geoscarce offers to buy all partners out at slightly over the market value for the reserves in the ground. The minimum partnership interest is $10,000, and your broker quickly calculates for you that at 5:1 you will get $50,000 back in 12 years and pauses for you to write your check. But you recall that in a relatively risk-free treasury bond you can currently get 14% and quickly set up the following formula:

$$P = \$50,000/[1 + 0.14]^{12}$$

$$P = \$50,000/4.82$$

$$P = \$11,682$$

Well, Geoscarce beats the Blue Max and is even profitable at the 14% level, but you again do yourself a favor, politely decline, and mail another $10,000 check for a 14% treasury bond. Why? The reason is risk. True, the investment is profitable at the 14% level, but obligations of the U.S. Treasury are as risk-free as you can get, and Geoscarce, as good as it is, is very risky and you should be paid more for risk—in this case a lot more—to compensate you for the risk inherent in drilling programs. Perhaps you should expect a return of twice the risk-free rate, i.e., 28%. In this case we must reject the offer. You should try to apply this type of analysis to all investments you make or currently have in order to gain experience and be prepared for the next series of investment suggestions offered to you from your advisors.

APPENDIX E

TRUST TERMINOLOGY*

Types of Trust	General Description
Accumulation	Retains all the income it earns as opposed to distributing it to an heir.
Charitable	A charity is the trust's beneficiary. It can be set up so that the property benefits an heir before passing to the charity.
Clifford	A trust lasting at least 10 years and a day.
Court	A testamentary trust (*see below*) that is subject to the jurisdiction of the probate court and thus is in the estate.
Discretionary (Sprinkling trust)	The trustee has the power to retain or pay out the income earned in whatever proportion he deems best, in other words, sprinkle assets around.

(continued)

---

*A single trust may have multiple characteristics, e.g., an "irrevocable, living, spendthrift, pour-over trust."

Types of Trust	*General Description*
Irrevocable	A living trust (*see below*) that may not be revoked, altered, or amended.
Life insurance	Receives the proceeds of life insurance.
Living	Established during trustor's lifetime.
Noncourt	A living trust that is not subject to probate court jurisdiction.
Pour-over	A living trust designed to receive property to be "poured over" from the trustor's will via his probate estate; thus, this trust enters probate.
Revocable	A living trust that may be revoked, altered, or amended at any time.
Spendthrift	Established so that the principal is protected from a beneficiary's creditors.
Support	Provides the funds necessary to support a beneficiary.
Testamentary	Established in the trustor's will and takes effect only after his/her death.

GLOSSARY

Arbitrage   Buying in one market and simultaneously selling the same or comparable instrument in another market, preferably at a profit. Securities, commodities, and foreign currencies sometimes sell for different prices in different markets, and arbitrage traders take advantage of the differences.

At the money   A put or call is at the money when the underlying stock sells at the same price as the exercise price of the option.

Balanced fund   A fund that seeks "balanced" performance through investment in preferred stock and bonds as well as common stock.

Bear market   A market in which prices are generally declining, accompanied by underlying pessimism.

Beta   A measure of the extent to which a stock's price moves in tandem with the market as a whole. Any issue that tends to rise and fall at the same rate as the market is assigned a beta of 1. A stock that moves up and down 50% more than the market has a 1.5 beta; it is said to be highly volatile. In bull markets, high betas pay off; on the way down, they magnify losses.

Bull market   A rising market, or a market in which further price increases are expected.

Call   An option that gives its owner, or holder the right to buy shares (usually 100) of the underlying stock at a specified price within a specified time period.

Capital appreciation   The increase in market value of securities.

Capital appreciation fund   A fund that tends to invest aggressively, occasionally selling short in the expectation of a decline in stock prices, and that trades in stock options.

Capital gains distribution   Payments, usually made annually, to mutual fund shareholders on gains realized from the sale of securities.

Class of options   A class of options consists of a group of puts or calls (i.e., one or the other) on the same security.

Closed-end fund   Also known as a "publicly traded" fund, an investment company that buys a set portfolio, such as a group of bonds, and limits its shares accordingly. Investors sell holdings through a broker just as they would ordinary stock. Supply and demand determine the price. Most mutual funds are "open-ended" funds, however.

Combination   An options trading strategy. Combinations involve buying or selling both a put and a call on the same stock.

Contrarian   A person who adheres to the theory that whenever a crowd forms or public investors become absolutely convinced that the market will move in one direction, it will move in the other. Investments are then made to take advantage of this situation.

Covered call writer   The writer of a call who owns the shares of stock on which he has written a call.

Covered put writer   The writer of a put who holds an identical put on the same class of stock, and one in which the exercise, or striking price, of the put held is equal to or greater than that of the written put. This is a fairly sophisticated option-trading technique.

Dual (leveraged) fund   A fund that offers the choice of investing either in shares providing income or those affording capital gains or both. In practice, investors can invest in either the dividends or capital appreciation of the portfolio.

Exercise price   Also the striking price. The price at which the holder of an option may purchase (in the case of call options) or sell (in the case of put options) an underlying stock.

Expiration date   The last date on which an option may be exercised at the striking or exercise price.

Fundamental analysis   The research technique under which investment prospects are sought according to their "value," based on price and reputation. In stocks, "fundamentalists" evaluate corporations by examining their earnings growth, cash position, assets, and profits.

Ginnie Mae, Fannie Mae, Sallie Mae   Three government-chartered agencies designated to buy up old mortgages from banks and similar lenders, who will then have the money they receive from the agencies to make new loans. Ginnie Mae, for example, provides a bank with new lendable dollars by buying up its old FHA (Federal Housing Authority) mortgages, which generally carry greater risk than a private firm can afford. The bank will then use the dollars it gets from Ginnie Mae to provide new mortgage money to new home buyers. Ginnie Mae resells the old mortgages to other investors, including pension funds and individuals.

Fannie Mae is the nickname for the Federal National Mortgage Association (FNMA), Ginnie Mae for the Government National Mortgage Association (GNMA), and Sallie Mae for the Student Loan Mortgage Association (SLMA).

Golden parachute   A contractual arrangement designed to protect key executives of a company in the event of a takeover by an unfriendly outsider causing the executives to leave. Typically, a golden parachute might provide for a long-term employment contract, including extensive benefits, but permit the executive to cancel the contract after a takeover and leave the company while retaining his salary and benefits.

Greenmail   A form of corporate blackmail whereby a target company is pressured to buy back a big block of its own shares at a substantial premium over the current selling price. One notorious example occurred in 1984 when Reliance Holdings Inc. forced Disney to buy back 11.1% of its stock for a total cost of $77.50 per share at a time when the stock was changing hands around $65 on the open market by threatening to do nasty things like take over the company, send Disney's management to look for unemployment checks, and sell off major Disney assets. The buy back cost Disney stockholders a big chunk of their owner equity.

Growth fund   A fund that invests principally in stocks with long-term growth potential.

Growth and income fund   A fund that looks to long-term growth but also seeks income from dividends.

In the money   In options trading, an option is in the money when it has intrinsic value. A call is in the money when the underlying stock's price is greater than the option's exercise price. A put is in the money when the underlying stock's price is lower than the option's exercise price.

Killer bees   Law firms, proxy solicitors, and public-relations firms employed to help a company management fight off an unfriendly takeover.

Leverage   The power to earn—or lose—disproportionately large sums on an investment as a result of borrowed funds or debt. Examples are commodity futures, for which you put up only a fraction of the contract price; options, which require a fraction of the stock price; or a margin account entitling you to buy shares on credit.

Limit order   An order in stock trading in which you ask your broker to buy or sell a certain amount of securities at a specified price. Sellers use limit orders in the hope that they can get more than the current price for their shares. Limit order buyers are seeking shares below the current price.

Liquidity   Easy convertibility to cash or easy access to your own money. The most liquid investments—money-market funds, for one—give you back your capital quickly and intact. Most stocks and many bonds can be sold easily but always at uncertain prices. Examples of illiquid investments include real estate and tax shelters. Risk is inversely related to liquidity.

Long   To own or be "long" in shares with the expectation that the price will rise. A bullish position in the market.

Market order   An order to buy or sell securities at the best price.

Margin call   A term generally referring to those unpleasant phone calls or letters from a broker asking his client to put up additional money in an existing account. Such margin calls occur because the client bought securities on credit—say, putting up only half of the cost of the stock and borrowing the rest from his broker. Now, if the securities have dropped in price to the point at which the broker is no longer willing (or legally permitted) to lend the client the outstanding amount, he is therefore asking for additional assets to back up the loan. Currently, you can expect a call if your account falls below the 30% margin requirement.

Mutual fund   A special corporation functioning as an investment pool of money. Mutual funds invest in nearly every type of security.

Net asset value per share   A fund's total assets on a given day—securities, cash, and accrued earnings—less any liabilities, divided by the number of shares outstanding. To obtain the current value of your investment, multiply the number of shares you have by the net asset value (NAV).

No-load fund   A mutual fund with no sales charge.

Odd lotter   An investor who buys or sells stocks in less than a round lot of 100 shares. You pay extra to be an odd lotter, and odd lotters are often on the wrong side of the market.

Option   The right to buy or sell certain property, such as common stock, at an agreed price within a specified time. A "put" option on a common stock gives the option holder the right to sell a certain number of shares at a set price at a certain time. A "call" option is the right to buy at a certain price and within a specific period.

Options-clearing corporation   The actual issuer of options. Moreover, in the event of an exercise, it is the corporation that becomes the source of securities for buyers of calls who exercise their options and the one to whom the put holder sells his shares.

Out of the money   An option with no intrinsic value. A call is out of the money when the exercise price is higher than the underlying stock's price. A put is out of the money when the exercise price is lower than the current market value of the stock.

P/E ratio   A fundamental measure of a stock's value. Often called the multiple, it is the price *(P)* of a share divided by the company's earnings per share *(E)*. The *P/E* in newspaper stock market listings reflects trailing earnings or earnings for the past four quarters.

Preferred stocks   Hybrids of debt and equity, preferred stocks pay more dependable, generally more generous dividends than a company's common shares but normally yield less than its ordinary bonds. The dividend usually is fixed, so you do not share in higher profits if the company prospers. The price of the stock responds mainly to changes in bond yields. With preferred shares, you are strictly interested in getting decent income from your investment. Since corporations get a tax break when they own preferred stock, and individuals do not, they are not particularly good investments for individual investors.

Premium   In options trading, the premium is the price paid by a buyer to the writer of an option. It is quoted on a per-share basis, and one contract covers 100 shares.

Put   An option that gives its owner, or holder, the right to sell shares (generally 100) at a specified price within a specified time period.

Ratio writing   A strategy used by option writers (i.e., sellers). It involves writing a covered call option as well as one or more uncovered call options. One of its objectives is to reduce some of the risk of writing uncovered call options, since the covered call does provide some degree of protection.

Red herring   The mandatory disclosure document (known formally as a preliminary prospectus) that companies provide before they issue new securities. It not only spells out how the proceeds will be used but also discusses candidly such sensitive matters as the strength of the competition and management's background.

Resistance level   If a stock trades at a price somewhat different than the price at which a good deal of buying and selling previously took place, the old level is said to represent "resistance." You can spot these areas by seeing where the long plateau areas are on the graph of the DJIA or individual stock graphs.

Shallow river running fast   Wall Street term referring to significant change in the price of securities, either up or down, for unknown reasons or in response to unsubstantiated rumors.

Shark repellents   A relatively recent slang term indicating various methods of protecting an entrenched management from outsiders who might want to take over the company. Typical shark repellents include amendments to the corporate charter requiring large majorities of 90% or more of the shareholders to approve certain kinds of takeovers; staggered boards, where only part of the board of directors is elected each year; and fair-price proposals, where investors buying some of the stock in order to obtain control must pay at least an equal price for the rest.

Short   Also called selling short. To "short" a stock is to sell borrowed shares one does not yet own in anticipation of a fall in the price of stocks, which then can be repurchased at a profit. The purchase of a put accomplishes somewhat the same purpose, although there are significant differences.

Spreads   An option trading strategy in which an investor or speculator buys one option and sells another on the same underlying stock but with a different expiration date and/or different strike price.

Stop order   Used by investors to protect against excessive losses. You tell your broker that you want to sell a security when it reaches a certain price below the current level. The order is given to a specialist and placed on his "book" for future execution. It can potentially protect you from a big loss and is a "stop loss" order.

Straddle   An options-trading strategy. A straddle involves writing (or selling) a put as well as a call on the same stock. Both options also carry the same striking price and the same expiration date.

Striking price   The exercise price, the price at which the holder may purchase (a call) or sell (a put) an underlying stock.

Technical analysis   Unlike fundamental analysis, which accounts for a corporation's financial position, technical analysis is the study of securities based principally on price trends, usually as represented on graphs of the stock's trading activity. Technicians also study trading volume and supply and demand. What's important in technical analysis is not so much what the company itself does but how its stock trading pattern behaves.

Tender offer   A request by one company to the shareholders of another to sell, or tender, their shares. The object is usually a takeover, often a hostile one.

10-K   A detailed financial statement that companies must file each year with the Securities and Exchange Commission. The 10-K is a font of data unavailable elsewhere on such pertinent matters as principal shareholders and earnings of subsidiaries. Companies must send this document to shareholders who request it. If you are not a shareholder, you can often get a copy from the company or from the SEC (Public Reference Room, Washington, DC 20549).

TIGRs, LIONs, CATS   Basically zero coupon bonds. They were first introduced in 1982, representing ownership of U.S. Treasury Bonds along with the interest payments due on them in future years. They are sold at a discount from their eventual cash-in value, pay no income at all during the period of time held, and then pay full cash-in value when due. Several brokerage houses came out with their own versions, all of which are in the cat family. TIGRs (Treasury Investment Growth Receipts) are Merrill Lynch's product. CATS (Certificates of Accrual on Treasury Securities) are offered by Prudential–Bache and Salomon, and LIONs (Lehman Investment Opportunity Notes) by Lehman Brothers.

Time spread   The purchase and sale of options with the same exercise price on the same stock but with different expiration dates. Also known as calendar and horizontal spreads.

Time value   Or time premium, the portion of the premium that reflects the remaining life of an option. The amount over the option's intrinsic value.

Underlying security   The security underlying an option. It would be purchased or sold were the option exercised.

Warrants   Warrants are like calls except that they are issued directly by the company. As an added inducement to buy new issues of stocks or bonds, companies thus sometimes attach warrants to them. It gives owners the right to buy more shares at a fixed priced until an expiration date, usually several years away. The prices of warrants move with the value of the underlying shares. If the stock goes up, the warrants are likely to rise much faster, and vice versa.

White knight   A company that is taking over another company on a friendly basis and thus saving it from an unfriendly takeover. If a company is threatened by a takeover from outsiders who are considered unfriendly (outsiders who might fire all of the current management, for example), and it feels it cannot fight off the attacker on its own, it may look for a friendly savior. The idea is that if one must be taken over, it's better to have an amicable acquirer.

Writer   In option trading parlance, the person or organization that sells an option is called the writer of the option. Covered call writing, for example, is when a call is written on stock owned by the writer.

BIBLIOGRAPHY

FINANCIAL PLANNING PERIODICALS FOR FURTHER READING

Where to Get Help

Barron's, Dow Jones & Co., 200 Burnett Road, Chicopee, Massachusetts 01021.

> *Barron's* is a weekly financial news publication with many in-depth articles and data relating to the previous week's economic and market activities. This publication frequently has in-depth reviews of performance records, such as the last 10 years of mutual fund performance, and so forth. It is available on most newsstands

Mansfield Stock Chart Service, 2973 Kennedy Blvd., Jersey City, New Jersey 07306.

> *The Mansfield Stock Chart Service* offers a series of charts covering both general market activity and individual stock and bond activity relating to the New York, American, and Over-The-Counter stock exchanges. The publication can be ordered at various intervals, and any one of the three exchanges can be selected.

DB INVESTOR, P.O. Box 4824, Stanford, California 94305.

> *DB INVESTOR* provides investment services for individuals, businesses, and trusts based on the principles outlined in this book. Investors may subscribe to *DB INVESTOR* for timely advice and background material. *DB INVESTOR* identifies periods of risk or safety based on the Pareto principles outlined in

Chapter 15. The parent corporation, the Professional Financial Security Corporation, also provides account management.

The Value Line Investment Survey, Value Line, Inc., 711 Third Avenue, New York, New York 10017.

The Value Line Investment Survey offers extensive fundamental information on selected stocks on the New York, American, and Over-The-Counter exchanges. It is published weekly with a complete list of latest prices, a Value Line timeliness and safety ranking, beta, estimated earnings, and dividends. Specific features are included in a section titled *Ratings and Reports*. The Value Line rating system has consistently outperformed a random selection of stocks over the years.

The Wall Street Journal, Dow Jones & Company, 200 Burnett Road, Chicopee, Massachusetts 01021.

The Wall Street Journal is published daily with the exception of weekends and holidays and provides an up-to-the-minute statistical review of market activity as well as brief reviews of business, finance, and worldwide news. The articles are usually not in-depth features as in *Barron's*; however, many useful background features on industry and individual companies are regularly published.

FINANCIAL PLANNING BOOKS FOR FURTHER READING

Credit and Insurance

Walker, Glen. *Credit Where Credit is Due*. New York: Holt, Reinhart & Winston, 1979.

Well written and to the point.

Cobleigh, Ira U. *What Everyone Should Know About Credit Before Buying or Borrowing Again*. Washington, D.C.: U.S. News and World Report Books, 1978.

A basic primer on borrowing. Good as a reference.

How to Buy Insurance and Save Money. 4th ed. Washington, D.C.: U.S. News and World Report, 1978.

Covers all types of insurance and has many, usually overlooked, suggestions.

Tobias, Andrew. *The Invisible Bankers: Everything the Insurance Industry Never Wanted You to Know*. New York: Simon & Schuster, 1982.

An excellent book dealing mainly with life insurance. Written in the usual, humorous Tobias style.

General

VanCaspel, Venita. *The Power of Money Dynamics*. Reston, Va.: Reston Publishing, 1982.

Simple and complete. Assumes no prior knowledge and covers all aspects of financial planning.

Hallman, G. Victor, and Rosenbloom, Jerry S. *Personal Financial Planning*. 3d ed. New York: McGraw-Hill, 1983.

Very well written and fairly technical.

Tobias, Andrew. *The Only Investment Guide You'll Ever Need*. Rev. ed. New York: Bantam, 1983.

Written for a time of high inflation; however, the book is still delightful.

Investment

Graham, Benjamin, et al. *Security Analysis*. 4th ed. New York: McGraw-Hill, 1962.

The classic of all time. Everyone should read this book.

Darst, David. *The Complete Bond Book: A Guide to All Types of Fixed-Income Securities*. New York: McGraw-Hill, 1975.

Offers a thorough treatment of fixed income investing.

Christy, George A., and Clendenin, John C. *Introduction to Investments*. 8th ed. New York: McGraw-Hill, 1982.

Readable and very basic information.

Harper, Victor L. *Handbook of Investment Products and Services*. Rev. ed. Englewood Cliffs, N.J.: Prentice-Hall, 1977.

Basically reference material.

Tracy, John A. *How to Read a Financial Report: Wringing Cash Flow and Other Vital Signs Out of the Numbers*. 2d ed. New York: John Wiley & Sons, 1983.

Only necessary for those interested in searching out their own companies.

Real Estate

Harrison, Henry S., and Leonard, Margery B. *Home Buying: The Complete Illustrated Guide*. Chicago: Realtors National Marketing Institute, 1980.

Creedy, Judith, and Wall, Norbert. *Real Estate Investment by Objective*. New York: McGraw-Hill, 1979.

Koch, James H. *Profits from Country Property: How to Select, Buy, Improve and Maintain Country Property.* New York: Van Nostrand Reinhold, 1982.

Retirement

Weitzen, Hyman G. *The Retirement Daybook.* Radnor, Pa.: Chilton, 1978.

> Financial and other matters in retirement.

Selected Topics

Randle, Paul A., and Swensen, Philip R. *Personal Financial Planning for Executives.* Atlanta: Life-Long Learning Library, 1981.

> More material on the time value of money. Excellent.

Januz, Lauren R., and Jones, Susan K. *Time Management for Executives.* New York: Scribner, 1982.

> Must reading. Lists, techniques, pitfalls.

Taxes

> The books in this section should be used as reference in conjunction with your tax advisor; especially recommended is the book by Strassels and Wool.

Brosterman, Robert. *The Complete Estate Planning Guide For Business and Professional Men and Women and Their Advisors.* Rev. ed. New York: New American Library, 1981.

Strassels, Paul N., and Wool, Robert. *All You Need To Know About the IRS: A Taxpayer's Guide, 1981 Edition.* New York: Random House, 1981.

> All taxpayers should read this.

Tannenhauser, Robert, and Tannenhauser, Carol. *Tax Shelters, A Complete Guide.* New York: New American Library, 1980.

Widowhood

Kirsch, Charlotte. *A Survivor's Manual to Wills, Trusts, Maintaining Emotional Stability.* Garden City, N.Y.: Doubleday, 1981.

> Written from a women's point of view, but applicable for anyone with little knowledge of the family financial operation.

Newman, Joseph. *Teach Your Wife to be a Widow.* New York: Simon & Schuster, 1974.

> Information useful for both husband and wife.

Wills

Ashley, Paul P. *You and Your Will: The Planning and Management of Your Estate.* New York: New American Library, 1977.

Will help in working with lawyers in setting up your will.

SUBJECT INDEX